THE POWER
OF PERSUASION

THE POWER
OF PERSUASION

How We're Bought and Sold

Robert Levine, Ph.D.

WILEY

John Wiley & Sons, Inc.

Published by John Wiley & Sons, Inc., Hoboken, New Jersey
Published simultaneously in Canada

For general information about our other products and services, please contact our
Customer Care Department within the United States at (800) 762-2974, outside the
United States at (317) 572-3993 or fax (317) 572-4002.

Wiley also publishes its books in a variety of electronic formats. Some content that
appears in print may not be available in electronic books. For more information
about Wiley products, visit our web site at www.wiley.com.

Library of Congress Cataloging-in-Publication Data:

Levine, Robert V.
    The power of persuasion : how we're bought and sold / Robert V. Levine.
        p. cm.
Includes bibliographical references and index.
    ISBN-13 978-0-471-26634-1 (cloth)
    ISBN-10 0-471-26634-5 (cloth)
    ISBN-13 978-0-471-76317-8 (paper)
    ISBN-10 0-471-76317-9 (paper)
1. Persuasion (Psychology)   I. Title.
    BF637.P4 L48 2003
    153.8'52—dc21

                                                        2002009952

Printed in the United States of America

10 9 8 7 6 5 4 3 2 1

To my mother, Esther Levine,
the leader of the band

CONTENTS

ACKNOWLEDGMENTS

I would like to single out a few of the many people who have contributed to this book. Thank you to my colleagues Roberta Asahina, Heinz Kusel, Harrison Madden, Richard Nordstrum, Karl Oswald, Richard Pinkerton, Paul Price, Aroldo Rodrigues, Criss Wilhite, and Lynnette Zelezny, and to my former and present students Christopher Boudreau, Robin Buck, Michelle Massey, Lori Pollard, and Karen West for their invaluable input and assistance. To the many students at California State University, Fresno, who have taken my Psychology of Mind Control class over the past eighteen years for their personal research, insights, and ceaseless prodding. To Jerry Burger, Michael Cohen, Fiona Jack, Stephen Jones, Dan Kahan, Michael Langone, Esther Levine, Craig Maxim, Annan Paterson, Cass Sunstein, David Thom, and Gabriel Weimann for generously granting interviews and answering my many questions. To Robert Cialdini for his groundbreaking approach to field research, which was the model for this project.

Very special thanks to my students Karla Burgos, Nathanael Fast, Joseph Gerber, Kennard Nears, and Albert Rodriguez for so ably guiding and carrying out our research. To Michael Gasio for introducing me to the world of car sales. To Deborah Layton for helping me understand how normal people get caught up in pathological situations. To Thomas Breen for his support and focus. To Constance Jones for her continuous, invaluable feedback. To Nancy Woods for allowing me into her living room. To Trudi, Andy, and, of course, Zach for keeping me sane, sort of.

Thank you to my agent, Kris Dahl of International Creative Management, for sticking with this project, and to my editor, Stephen Power, for being pitch perfect.

INTRODUCTION

When I was growing up in Brooklyn we had a standard put-down for intellectuals: "Good school smarts, no street smarts." I suspect most of us who make our way up the academic ladder are prone to the shortcoming. After all, in the majority of our disciplines we're trained to conduct research and write manuscripts, to give lectures and exams, not to live by our wits. But in my own field—social psychology—the affliction can be particularly onerous. If you're studying nuclear physics, it doesn't really matter what you know about real life. You don't need a lot of social skills to run a linear particle accelerator or a spectrophotometer. Social psychologists, however, are in the business of people. Who cares if we master technical jargon and sophisticated research methodology if it doesn't add to our understanding of real people in real settings?

Which means that to research this book properly, I had to leave the academy and journey into that tangled netherland social scientists call "the field" and everyone else calls "the real world." So, along with a number of adventurous students, I threw myself directly into the path of persuasion professionals, those whose lives depend not on theories but on actual results, in order to observe their methods firsthand and discover their secrets. I would quickly learn that we persuasion professors have much more to learn from them than they have to learn from us.

We began with the salespeople. We listened to hucksters selling everything from Tupperware and cosmetics to health and religion. We listened to pitches for time-shares and kitchenware. One of us watched a woman in a neighbor's home—a "good friend from Florida" who happened to be visiting—sell a roomful of friends a "one-size-fits-all magnetic Model 52 shoe insole, proven in scientific research to change your body's energy field—only $70 plus tax." We put ourselves at the mercy of the purest of the trade's artists: automobile salespeople. I observed those who use their skills to control others' lives—the heavyweights—such as politicians, psychotherapists, and religious and cult leaders.

I also spoke to many people who have been on the receiving end of the process. These range from consumers who were induced to make purchases they didn't need to former Moonies and Jonestown survivors. They vary from individuals who are convinced they've been saved to those who believe they were ruined by psychobabbling control freaks.

Finally, I've tried to learn firsthand. I went to seminars and training sessions that teach the tricks of the trade. I studied magicians, mentalists, and assorted flimflam men. Most educational of all, I took jobs selling cars and hawking cutlery door-to-door.

To be sure, this book also draws heavily on my school smarts, be what they may. As a professor and researcher in the field, I've studied many of the numerous systematic investigations—of which, for better and for worse, there are thousands—that have been conducted on the psychology of persuasion and its many applications. These scientific findings permeate this book. But I've tried to be selective about which studies I report. One of the accusations sometimes leveled at social science research—a variant of the "no street smarts" problem—is how often our findings fall into the category of "*Bubbe* psychology": using academic jargon to describe something your grandmother could have told you. I've done my best to extract findings that are at best surprising and at the very least useful.

For instance, the direct, verbal approach—where I try to win you over to my way of thinking—has been studied extensively, most notably in a classic series of experiments by psychologist Carl Hovland and his colleagues at Yale University. They and other researchers would consider such questions as whether it's more effective to present one or both sides of an argument (answer: one-sided appeals are most effective when the audience is already sympathetic to your position; two-sided appeals work better when the audience is already considering a conflicting argument), and whether you should present a carefully reasoned argument or one that appeals to emotions (answer: it depends on the audience—less-educated people are generally more susceptible to emotional appeals; better-educated audiences are more responsive to rational appeals).[1]

But the actual content of the message is just one part of the persuasion process. Over and over I learned that what is said is often less important than how it is said, when and where it is said, and who says it. It's the setup, the context, the nondirect, nonverbal features of the process that persuasion artists know how to exploit. These subtle, silent features of the process are the focus of this book.

My research had led me to three broad conclusions. First, we're more susceptible to persuasion than we think. People tend to have a curious illusion of personal invulnerability to manipulation—a belief that we're not as vulnerable as others around us. In part, this illusion derives from the subtlety of clever operators who make it hard to see that you're being manipulated. In part, it feeds off another "normal" illusion—that we're more capable and, so, better defended than other people. The illusion of invulnerability is a comforting notion for moving forward in an unpredictable and dangerous world. Unfortunately, however, the more immune we feel, the less likely we are to take precautions and, as a result, the more susceptible than ever we become.

Second, the most effective persuaders are the least obvious. Almost everyone is savvy enough to put his or her guard up against the fast-talkers—pushy salespeople, aggressive con artists, and egotistical leaders. The people who often get through to us, however, are more subtle. They seem likable, honest, and trustworthy. As Abraham Lincoln once observed, "There's nothing stronger than gentleness." And they move gradually—so gradually, in fact, that we may not realize what we've gotten ourselves into until it's too late. The most successful salesmen, as we'll see, don't appear to be salesmen at all. In the 1950s, Vance Packard wrote a best-selling book, *The Hidden Persuaders,* in which he claimed to reveal how Madison Avenue was using extraordinary, devious techniques based on the powers of psychoanalysis, most famously in the form of subliminal messages, to sell us products with astonishing rates of success. Subsequent research offers virtually no support for Packard's hypotheses—neither that subliminal techniques were often used nor that they had any success when they were. But the term *hidden persuader* is a good one: the most effective persuasion often takes place when we don't recognize we're being persuaded. It borders on the invisible.

Third, the rules of persuasion aren't all that different no matter who is the source. Whether people are selling Tupperware or eternity, it seems that most are reading from the same manual, and often the same page. I've come to agree with the words of advertising commentator Sid Bernstein: "Of course you sell candidates for political office the same way you sell soap or sealing wax or whatever; because, when you get right down to it, that's the only way anything is sold."[2] The effectiveness of virtually all these experts' strategies can be explained by a finite number of principles. The content of the come-on may differ dramatically, but not the form. I don't mean to make persuasion sound overly mechanical. There's a great deal of artistry involved—watching the professionals makes it clear it's as much an art as it is a science— and it's often the creativity and artistry that make it so fascinating to watch. But the persuasion artist is only effective to the degree he or she follows certain rules of psychology. I've tried in this book to highlight the psychological techniques you're most likely to come across in the world of persuasion. They vary around a few common themes. But we best be prepared for their swift intensity.

It's important to recognize, however, that persuasion isn't an inherently exploitive force. It's not so much a crystallized weapon as it is a process; no less, in fact, than the process underlying virtually all meaningful social communication. After all, doesn't communication boil down to either requesting information that may in some way change us or dispensing messages that we hope will change others? Persuasion covers considerably more than the conniving tricks of bullies and con artists. Teaching, parenting, and friendship rest on skills of persuasion, as do self-change and discipline. "Mastery of others is strength; mastery of yourself is true power," Lao-tzu once wrote. If we accept that humans are social animals, then the psychology of persuasion—knowing both how to use it and how to resist it—should be viewed as an essential life skill. Questions of the morality of persuasion are best reserved for how and for what purposes the process is used, not whether it's used. (I'll have more to say about ethics in the last chapter.)

I use the term *persuasion* in its broadest sense in this book. By it, I refer to the psychological dynamics that cause people to be changed in ways they wouldn't have if left alone. The term serves as an umbrella that encompasses a number of related concepts in psychology: basic processes such as influence, control, attitude change, and compliance; and more ominous-sounding extremes like mind control and brainwashing.

My ultimate interest is how people are manipulated to do things they never thought they'd do and are later sorry they did. The following chapters contain tales of human imperfection and the psychology behind them. They're offered in the spirit of some old advice from Eleanor Roosevelt: "Learn from the mistakes of others. You can't live long enough to make them all yourself."

ONE

The Illusion of Invulnerability

Or, How Can Everyone Be Less Gullible Than Everyone Else?

They couldn't hit an elephant at this dist . . .
—General John B. Sedgwick (Union army Civil War officer's last words, uttered during the Battle of Spotsylvania, 1864)

It was January 1984 and I was on the lookout for Big Brother. Being a social psychologist—one who researches mind control, no less—I'd been pumping up for George Orwell's banner year for some time. In a few weeks, I would be offering a special course called "The Social Psychology of 1984." That morning, I'd been preparing my outline.

I wanted my students to become familiar with the despots. How might unwitting victims defend against tyrants like O'Brien, the party spokesperson in *1984*, who tells us, "You are imagining that there is something called human nature which will be outraged by what we do and will turn against us. But we create human nature. Men are infinitely malleable"? Grr!

We would hunt down Big Brothers. I reread the opening page of Orwell's novel:

It was a bright cold day in April, and the clocks were striking thirteen. Winston Smith . . . , who was thirty-nine, and had a varicose ulcer above his right ankle, went slowly, resting several times on the way. On each landing, opposite the lift shaft, the poster with the enormous face gazed from the wall. It was one of those pictures which are so contrived that the eyes follow you about when you move. BIG BROTHER IS WATCHING YOU, the caption beneath it ran.[1]

I'd begin with the obvious totalitarian monsters. There were Hitler, Stalin, Mussolini. I was moving my way down the list when the doorbell rang. Damn. No doubt it was the pushy, scam-artist salesman I'd heard so much about from my neighbors. I walked to the door. Big Brother's image (as I recalled it from an old magazine illustration, at least) was in my mind's eye and the music from the shower scene in *Psycho* was playing in my ears. I put on my best natural-born-killer stare and ripped open the door. But, alas, it was Mario, a sweet young gentleman who—I'd completely forgotten—had an appointment to clean my chimney. Mario jumped back, frightened, and courteously asked if he had come at a bad time. I apologized for my rudeness and invited him in.

This was the first time Mario had worked for me. We'd met just a few days earlier at a children's soccer game. I liked Mario at once. He was soft-spoken, un-self-centered, and had a clever sense of humor—just the sort of person I find easy to talk with. It turned out we had quite a bit in common. Both of us were recent fathers. We'd traveled to many of the same places. We knew some of the same people. To cap off my attraction, when I revealed my occupation and that I sometimes wrote for popular magazines, Mario excitedly recalled reading one of my articles a little while back. In fact, he still talked to friends about it. When I learned that Mario worked as a chimney sweep—I knew that my fireplace was long overdue for maintenance—I hired him on the spot.

After recovering from my nasty greeting at the door, I left Mario to his task and returned to working on my Big Brother list. Let's see, we should certainly study Mao Tse-tsung, or should I call him Mao Zedong? Then, after these hall of fame dictators, we'll move on to recent clones—maybe Idi Amin, Mu'ammar Gadhafi, Saddam Hussein. An hour later, I was getting around to the Svengali-like cult leaders. I could start with Charles Manson, then Jim Jones, and . . .

Mario called out to announce he was finished. After I inspected his work, Mario handed me the bill. It was a few dollars less than our agreed-upon amount. "The job was easier than I expected," he proudly explained. Was this a good man or what?

"But," he added, "I had a problem requiring action. There was damage on several bricks that posed a serious fire hazard." Apparently only one known chemical, something known informally in the trade as brikono, would correct the problem. Unfortunately, brikono was very expensive. It had just jumped in price, and was now listing for a "criminal" $200 a quart. Even worse, it was very hard to find at any price. But he made me promise I'd call around for at least two quarts before lighting the fireplace. I thanked Mario. We said good-bye. He got into his truck.

A few moments later he was back at my door with a big smile on his face. "I found two quarts of brikono in the back of my truck," he said. "They're the last of my old batch. You can have them for the old price—$125 apiece." I inquired about his fee for the work. "How about I just put it on for free and you can owe me one?" he answered. I wrote out a check on the spot. The job took all of twenty minutes.

Two days later I was again hard at work on my Big Brother hit list. At the moment I was considering whether to add a category for terrorist psychopaths. We could study the Boston Strangler and then the Hillside Strangler and . . .

Suddenly I thought of Mario, and—as EST guru Werner Erhard, yet another master of manipulation, would say—*I got it.* I phoned the chimney-sweep company. They'd never heard of Mario. I tried the soccer league commissioner. Same answer. I called my bank. Sorry, my check had been cashed. Two hundred fifty dollars' worth of brikono?

Suckered again.

Looking back, I suppose my $250 were well spent. One of the most successful means for building resistance to mind control is early, controlled exposure to the tricks we're likely to encounter. Two hundred fifty dollars may not have been the cheapest of inoculations, but who knows how much the next Mario would have cost me. My dose was hardly a permanent cure—I'm forever surprised by my gullibility—but it has led me to sound the danger alarm that much sooner on many warranted occasions.

More important, Mario expanded my vision of mind control. "The Social Psychology of 1984," it became clear, needed to become much more than a hunt for Big Brothers. In today's world they are the least of our problems because we usually recognize them. We know who and what we're dealing with. It's the people we're unprepared for who present the greatest threat. The fast-talking salesman puts us on alert. But the nice guys, the friendly thieves who sell beneath the threshold of our awareness, put us at their mercy.

The psychology of persuasion emanates from three directions: the characteristics of the source, the mind-set of the target person, and the psychological context within which the communication takes place.

Think of it as them, you, and—as Martin Buber called it—the between. Any or all of the three can tilt the power balance either toward or against you. If the latter occurs, you're vulnerable.

Mario had me going on all three fronts. First, I was seduced by his appeal as a person—his nonthreatening, trustworthy, family-man come-on. Second, his patient, careful arrangement of the context made the unreasonable appear reasonable. The context, this matter of the between, is a complicated one. How it impacts people encompasses much of the domain of my field of social psychology, and of this book. If Mario hadn't built up slowly to his brikono pitch—if he'd come on a "cold call," as it's known in the trade; or, if I'd met Mario in another context (Sing Sing would have been nice)—his pitch might have been laughable. But, as my grandmother used to say, if I had four wheels I'd be a bus. Finally, Mario had the good fortune to walk in when my mind-set—watching for ominous Big Brothers—had me ridiculously disarmed for his amiable assault.

Psychological disarmament is what often sets the stage for persuasion. One of life's crueler ironies is that we're most vulnerable at those very moments when we feel in least danger. Unfortunately, the illusion of invulnerability pretty well defines our resting state. Even when there is no manipulative outsider pulling our strings, most of us have a tendency to view our futures with unrealistic optimism. Studies have shown that people generally approach the threats of life with the philosophy that bad things are more likely to happen to other people than to themselves. With uncanny faulty logic, most people will tell you they're less prone to become victims than everyone around them.

Our perception of immunity casts a wide net. Studies have found, for example, that people will tell you they're considerably less at risk than other people when it comes to disease, death, divorce, unwanted pregnancy, work and jobs, and natural disasters.

Disease. Most people believe they're less likely than others to be stricken by diseases—everything ranging from pneumonia and lung cancer to senility and tooth decay.[2] The ratio of individuals who believe they're less at risk than the average person to those who say they're more at risk is 2 to 1 for lung cancer, 3 to 1 for influenza, 5 to 1 for pneumonia, 7 to 1 for food poisoning, and 9 to 1 for asthma. In some cases, there may be some sensibility to this perceived immunity. When people say (as almost everyone does) that they are less likely to develop lung cancer, for example, perhaps they're actually taking precautions to prevent this disease. In many cases, however, the people who are most at risk are the ones most convinced of their immunity. In an Australian study, for example, an overwhelming number of smokers said their own risk of developing heart disease, lung cancer, and other smoking-related diseases is significantly less than that of other smokers. Another study, this one in the United States, followed smokers who went through a smoking-cessation clinic. Those who relapsed midway through the program actually gave lower estimates of their smoking risks than they'd given at the beginning of the program. In yet another U.S. survey, it was found that only a small minority of smokers (17 percent) believed the tar level of their cigarette brand was higher than average.[3]

Death. Most people are convinced they have a better chance of living past eighty than the next person. In one study, college students (the maestros of perceived invulnerability—take it from a professor), after being informed the average age of death in the United States is seventy-five, went on to estimate their own age of death at, on average, eighty-four years.[4]

Divorce. The current divorce rate in the United States hovers around 50 percent. But if you ask single or currently married people, it seems the next victim is always going to be someone else. In one large survey, people who had recently applied for marriage licenses estimated, with impressive accuracy, that about half of all marriages made in the United States today will end in divorce. But when asked about the probability of their own marriage dissolving, the median estimate was exactly 0 percent.[5]

Should the impossible happen, and their marriages don't work out, respondents were just as unreasonably optimistic about how they'd be affected. More than 40 percent of men expected to get primary custody of the children if they divorced, even though the same men estimated that children live primarily with their divorced fathers only 20 percent of the time. Women, on average, estimated that 80 percent of divorced mothers have primary custody of their children, but more than 95 percent of them expected this to be the case if they divorced. Women estimated (very optimistically) that 40 percent of divorcing women are awarded alimony, but 81 percent of them were confident they would get it if they asked. And those deadbeat fathers we read about? Not in any of these homes. Women estimated (fairly accurately) that some 40 percent of parents who are awarded child support actually receive all their payments. But, if they were the ones awarded support, 98 percent of the women were sure their spouse would pay up faithfully.

Unwanted pregnancy. Sexually active women college students, asked to compare themselves to peers, said they were 34 percent as likely to get pregnant as other coeds, 21 percent as likely as other women their age, and 20 percent as likely as average American women of childbearing age.[6]

Work and jobs. College students say their colleagues are over 42 percent more likely to end up with lower starting salaries than they are, 44 percent less likely to end up owning their own home, and 50 percent less likely to be satisfied with their postgraduation job. People in general believe they're 32 percent less likely to get fired from their jobs than are other people.[7]

Natural disasters. In a survey of people living in California's high-risk earthquake areas, respondents underestimated the likelihood of a major quake occurring in the next two decades by 27 percent.[8] In another survey, people who had experienced the devastating 7.1 earthquake that struck northern California in 1989 were asked to estimate the likelihood that they and other people would be seriously hurt by a natural disaster, such as an earthquake, in the future. Three days after experiencing the quake, the obviously shaken survivors had turned pessimistic: they said they were more likely to be seriously hurt by a future disaster than were other people. But when questioned again three months later, the same survivors had returned to their old illusions of invulnerability: they believed the likelihood they'd be hurt in the future was significantly less than that of either the average student or the average person living in their area.[9]

And the list goes on. Studies show we underestimate our own chances of being victimized by everything from being sued to getting mugged to tripping and breaking a bone to becoming sterile. "All men think all men are mortal but themselves," as poet Edward Young wrote.[10]

I'm not saying our illusion of invulnerability is cast in stone. Hardly. Studies show, for example, that when someone close to us is victimized, we often flip 180 degrees, now becoming unrealistically pessimistic about what may happen to us. This is especially true when the victim seems at all similar to ourselves. If someone your age drops dead of a heart attack, and you hear that person lived the same lifestyle and ate the same diet you do, I challenge you *not* to consider your own vulnerability.

There are also vast individual differences in the voracity of our beliefs. Some individuals are obviously as chronically pessimistic about the future as others are optimistic. ("How do you know the sky has fallen?" asked Henny Penny. "I saw it with my eyes," said Chicken Little. "I heard it with my ears. And a piece of it fell on my poor little head.") It's notable that the most severe pessimists often grasp their vulnerability most clearly. In one study, for example, clinically depressed and psychologically normal people were asked to surmise what others thought about them. The depressed group, it turned out, more accurately judged the impression they made than did the normals. People in the normal group tended to have inflated images of themselves.[11] Depressives, it seems, must forgo the comfort of self-enhancing, selective blindness.

Nor does the illusion of personal invulnerability seem to be hardwired at birth. It's telling that there are cultural differences. Downplaying one's vulnerability doesn't sit very well, for example, in group-focused cultures like those throughout much of Asia, where your personal well-being is less important than the prosperity of the larger collective. For example, studies in Japan—arguably the crown jewel of group-oriented cultures—have found that people there rate their own likelihood of encountering serious future problems—disease, divorce, academic failure, and the like—as about the same as for their compatriots.[12] In many ways, in fact, the Japanese go out of their way to avoid overoptimism about their own futures. In a national public opinion poll taken in 1990 by the Japanese Cabinet Public Information Office, only a small minority (23.4 percent) of people in Japan said they expected to be better off in the future than they are now. And this was before the subsequent downturn in the Japanese economy.[13]

In the West, however, the illusion of invulnerability is the prevailing norm. A 1998 Gallup Poll found Americans' expectations about the quality of their future "at all-time highs, well above any ratings previously recorded by Gallup" over the past thirty-four years. The survey reported that 72 percent of Americans expected to be having "the best possible life" for themselves, or close to it, five years from now; however, only 26 percent said their lives had been nearly that good five years earlier.[14]

The illusion is remarkably resilient. Two weeks after the September 11 terrorist attacks on the World Trade Center and the Pentagon, 53 percent of Americans said they were somewhat or very worried that they or a family member would be the victim of a future attack. By January, the figure had shrunk to 38 percent.[15] A poll taken six months after the attacks was even more revealing: 52 percent of American believed it was somewhat or very likely that there would be new terrorist attacks in the United States over the coming several weeks, but only 12 percent said there would likely be attacks in their own community.[16]

If we can convince ourselves we're immune to natural events like disease and earthquakes, it should be no surprise we also believe ourselves capable of controlling mere psychological forces like social influence and persuasion. In fact, when it comes to social behavior, we carry an added illusion about ourselves: that our very personalities render us better armed than our neighbors to resist manipulation. Research unequivocally shows that people—once again, particularly westerners—typically believe they're stronger and more capable than their peers. We rate ourselves as above average on a long and diverse list of desirable characteristics, ranging from intelligence and personal competence to leadership and social skills.[17]

My students Nathanael Fast and Joseph Gerber and I studied how the better-than-average illusion applies to persuasion.[18] We began by asking subjects to rate how strongly various personality characteristics were related to vulnerability to psychological manipulation. The highest-rated characteristics were then presented to 268 university and community college students, who were asked to compare themselves to other students their age and gender on each.[19] The better-than-average effect appeared in almost every case:

- Fifty percent of students said they're less naive than the average student their age and gender; only 22 percent said they're more naive than average.
- Forty-three percent said they're less gullible than average; only 25 percent believed they're more gullible than average.
- Forty-six percent rated themselves less conforming than average; only 16 percent said they're more conforming than average.
- Seventy-four percent described themselves as more independent than average; less than a tenth as many (7 percent) rated themselves less independent.
- Sixty-three percent said they're above average in self-confidence; only a fifth as many (13 percent) said they're less self-confident.

- Fifty-five percent said they're more assertive than their average peer; only 15 percent said they're less assertive.

People also told us they possess special knowledge and skills that protect them from unwanted persuasion:

- Seventy-seven percent said they're more aware than average of how groups manipulate people; only 3 percent said they're below average.
- Sixty-one percent said they're more knowledgeable about methods of deception than their average peer, compared to 11 percent who said they're below average.
- Sixty-six percent believe they have above-average critical-thinking skills, compared to 5 percent who said they're below average.

In the world of perception, we're a lot like the citizens of Garrison Keillor's Lake Wobegon, a place "where all the women are strong, all the men are good-looking, and all the children are above average." And so, of course, bad things are not going to happen to us.

There are, of course, vast individual differences in the better-than-average effect. Some people have the opposite problem—a tendency to focus on their shortcomings and deny their strengths. The effect may also vary depending on the situation. But what's most remarkable is how generalized the bias is: it's the norm—as in "normal"—in our culture to think we're more capable than the next person of fending off undesirable persuasion.

How do otherwise intelligent people convince themselves, in defiance of all odds, that they're more competent than everyone else? Social psychologists call the process the fundamental attribution error. When asked to explain *other* people's problems, we have an uncanny tendency to assign blame to inner qualities: to their personality traits, emotional states, and the like. If I hear you've been suckered by a salesman, I conclude it's because you're easily deceived. When it comes to ourselves, however, we usually blame it on features of the situation. If I get suckered, it's because the salesman rushed me or conned me or I was just in the wrong place at the wrong time.

In part, the fundamental attribution error results from the information we have to work with. I know I don't usually let myself get taken advantage of, so it must be something unique to the situation that made a difference. But the error is driven by more than just rational information processing. It's a self-deluding, psychological comfort blanket that helps us forget how vulnerable we are. Few of us want to dwell on the true randomness with which perilous events so often strike. By attributing people's misfortunes to something unique about them, we deceive ourselves into believing the same fate can't befall us.

Fortunately, once burned, many of us are more reticent the next time around. Others, however, get taken in again and again. Why don't they learn from their mistakes?

There's a self-sustaining element to the better-than-average illusion. Research has found that the least competent among us are often the most overconfident of their abilities. In a recent series of experiments, cognitive psychologists David Dunning and Justin Kruger gave Cornell University college students tests reflecting a variety of skills: English grammar, logical reasoning, and humor. In each area, those scoring in the lowest quartile turned out to be the most likely to grossly overestimate how well they'd performed. In English grammar, for example, subjects who scored in the tenth percentile guessed that their scores were in the sixty-first percentile and that their actual ability was in the sixty-seventh percentile. On the logical reasoning test, subjects who scored in the twelfth percentile estimated, on average, that they'd scored in the sixty-second percentile, and they placed their overall skill level in the sixty-eighth percentile.[20]

Why don't the incompetent learn from their failures? One reason, Dunning and Kruger believe, is that the skills required to succeed at a task are often the very same ones necessary to recognize failure at the same task. If you're weak at logic you're also probably less capable of evaluating the logic of your argument. The skills required to construct a grammatical sentence are the same as those needed to recognize if a sentence is grammatically correct. "The same knowledge that underlies the ability to produce correct judgment is also the knowledge that underlies the ability to recognize correct judgment," Kruger and Dunning found. "To lack the former is to be deficient in the latter."

We see this defect in many domains. In tennis, it has been shown, novices are less accurate than masters at judging whether they hit a successful shot. Beginning chess players are poorer than experts at estimating how many times they need to look at the board before memorizing a position. Amateur physicists are worse than experts at gauging the difficulty of physics problems.[21] In effect, not only do the less competent perform poorly and make poor choices, but their incompetence robs them of the ability to recognize their deficiencies. This isn't necessarily the case for all skills. Less-competent people are, for example, more likely to grasp reality in situations where they get direct and unambiguous feedback. When a golfer hits a shot into the woods, for example, he knows he's done something wrong.

In the domain of persuasion, however, conditions are ripe for self-sustaining incompetence. For one thing, the feedback we get in social encounters is usually unclear and, so, is wide open to self-serving perceptions. When an outsider is trying to manipulate us, the problem gets even worse. The clever manipulator feeds our illusion that we're above being manipulated. The salesman who just sold you last year's leftover will go out of his way to let you know what a fine choice you've made. Gullibility begets gullibility.

There exists an unusual neurological disease known as anosognosia. The condition, which is caused by certain types of damage to the right hemisphere of the brain, leads to paralysis on the left side of the body. But more remarkable, the patient is unable to acknowledge his own disease. "Imagine a victim of a major stroke," observes neurology professor Antonio Damasio, "entirely paralyzed in the left side of the body, unable to move hand and arm, leg and foot, face half immobile, unable to stand or walk. And now imagine that same person oblivious to the entire problem, reporting that nothing is possibly the matter, answering the question, 'How do you feel?' with a sincere, 'Fine.'"[22]

As dramatic as the denial of his condition is the anosognosic's complete lack of emotion or concern about its gravity. The news that he's suffered a major stroke, that there's a high risk of further brain and heart damage, in some cases that he's suffering from a cancer that has invaded his brain, is met with blasé, detached equanimity, never with sadness, tears, despair, or anger.[23] When asked to look at his paralyzed limb, the patient has no difficulty acknowledging it's his and there's something wrong with it. But he's unable to make an internal connection between the condition of *that* arm or leg and *his* physical condition. As a result, no matter how many times he's asked, "How do you feel," the answer is, "Fine."

Gullibility can be thought of as a social psychological analog of anosognosia. The chronic patsy refuses to acknowledge his weakness.

His denial is nourishing to his self-esteem. "Ignorance more frequently begets confidence than does knowledge," Charles Darwin observed.[24] But it also prevents you from avoiding the same mistake next time.

The illusion of invulnerability is a comforting notion. And, as many health psychologists will tell you, optimism is sometimes an important ingredient of psychological adjustment. But *over*optimism can exact a stiff price. It leaves us psychologically disarmed. It's often said that laughter is the best medicine. Perhaps, but a little realism may keep you out of the hospital in the first place. Research shows, for example, that:

- People who feel at risk for health problems are more likely to gather disease prevention information.
- Smokers who minimize their own risk of disease are less likely to try quitting.
- Sexually active women who deny their chances of becoming pregnant are less likely to use effective methods of birth control.
- People in high earthquake risk areas who downplay their danger are more likely to live in poor structures.[25]

Oftentimes, in fact, how you face your vulnerability can be more important than the vulnerability itself. It's well established, for example, that individuals born with fair skin are considerably more susceptible to skin cancer later in life. With proper education, however, light-skinned people are more likely to take precautions that minimize their risks—for example, wearing sunscreen and avoiding direct sunlight. Paradoxically, then, the very people who are genetically disposed to skin cancer may be the least likely to end up with it in the end—that is, if they're willing to confront their vulnerability before it's too late. As the geneticist David Searls observed, "The tendency for an event to occur varies inversely with one's preparation for it."

It's natural to have an image of the "type" of person you are. It's comforting to think there is considerable predictability in how we behave—that, based on our past, we can identify our frailties and our strengths and that within these boundaries we're in safe territory. Often we're right. But frequently not. There's no such animal as the type of person who can't be manipulated to act out of character. Worst of all, these errors often occur just when we have the most to lose.

Certainly, some of us truly are more resistant. There are people who tend to be less gullible, or less susceptible to conformity, or cooler under pressure. These individual differences are what psychologists call traits. Add the traits together and you get what we call our personality. For many years, the guiding mission of the field of psychology was to "describe, explain, and predict" people's behavior. But after dedicating almost a century[26] of research to developing personality assessment instruments—it is estimated that there are more than twenty-five hundred commercially published psychological tests now on the market—psychometricians have learned in no uncertain terms that traits are nothing more than probability statements. In any given place and time it's only *somewhat* more likely you'll be stronger or weaker or smarter or more foolish than the fellow sitting next to you, no matter what score you got on some personality test. In fact, the demands of the situation—the particulars of the time, the place, and the social context—are often better predictors of how people will act than is the *type* of person they are.[27]

The power of the situation is the driving force in effective persuasion. We'll see in the coming pages how social psychological forces often cause a person to do things he never would have predicted— sometimes for the better, too often not—no matter who he is or how he has acted in the past. Several years ago, an Everest climb leader was asked whether an old veteran climber had a chance at the summit. "He may," the leader responded. "But in the end it's the mountain that will decide who will climb it." Similarly, whether you're persuaded may simply depend on who and what you're matched against.

The psychology of persuasion may be a subtle process. But its effects, once in motion, are anything but. When the elements of the situation are arranged so they exploit your inner needs—perhaps your craving to be accepted or appreciated, to be seen as a good person, or simply to feel safe—it can feel like being struck by a laser. At these moments you are no more able to be your "usual" self than if you'd been locked in chains. A friend of mine named Debbie describes it well. Usually, Debbie says, she thinks of herself as a person willing to speak her mind. But there are certain situations—most notably, when it involves bucking the consensus of her friends—in which speaking out is so difficult that it seems physically restrained. "When I try to talk," Debbie says, "I feel verbally paralyzed. I literally can't say the words. It's as if my vocal cords have been anesthetized. I'm no more able to rise above my inhibitions—even when I know I should—than it must be for a person with muscular dystrophy to walk normally."

Perhaps, you say, you really are less vulnerable than most. You say you know what these influence experts are up to, and you're too savvy to be taken in by their nonsense. If you believe this, you're in good company. It's perfectly normal. Unfortunately, most of you are wrong.

Consider advertising, perhaps the most straightforward domain of persuasion. The rules of this game are right on the table: you get to watch the show or read the magazine; companies get time or space to try to persuade you to buy what they're selling. Does advertising work? Barely at all, say most consumers in surveys, of which there have been many. Advertising, people maintain, is such an obvious form of manipulation that it's ridiculous to think it has the intended effect on us. It doesn't, eh? "Almost everyone holds the misguided belief that advertisements don't affect *them*, don't shape their attitudes, don't help define their dreams," observed advertising critic Jean Kilbourne. "What I hear more than anything else, as I lecture throughout the country, is 'I don't pay attention to ads . . . I just tune them out . . . they have no effect on me.' Of course, I hear this most often from young men wearing Budweiser caps."[28]

If you believe you're immune, I have a few questions for you. What comes to mind when you hear the words "Golden Arches"? When you hear the phrase "Just do it"? Who's Tony the Tiger? What kind of person smokes Marlboros? What tastes great, but is less filling? You can ask these questions of practically anyone, anywhere, in the United States (and many other countries) and get the same answers.

And why shouldn't this be? Advertising accounts for 40 percent of the average American's mail and 70 percent of our newspaper space. American companies spend more than $200 billion a year on advertising.[29] It costs, on average, $250,000 to produce a national television commercial and another $250,000 to put it on the air. For premier events, costs skyrocket higher. The NFL charged $2.4 million for a thirty-second ad spot for the 2005 Super Bowl. Why would Anheuser-Busch purchase ten of them?[30] Because they had figures to show the ads would more than pay for themselves in alcohol consumption.

They might even hit the jackpot. During the 1999 Super Bowl, when Victoria's Secret ran a thirty-second spot featuring a parade of models decked out in panties and bras, more than a million fans left their television sets to log onto the company's web site.[31] And lest you think it's just rabid men who are prey to ads, consider why companies would spend a million dollars for a thirty-second spot during the Academy Awards.[32] Probably because advertisers know the show, which Madison Avenue calls "the Super Bowl for women," will have over 60 percent of the females in the nation in front of their sets. The *Chicago Tribune* painted the picture all too accurately in an ad it placed in *Advertising Age*. The ad shows several people arranged in boxes according to income level under the slogan "The people you want, we've got all wrapped up for you."[33]

Prescription drug companies, which have only recently begun direct, mass consumer advertising, would certainly agree. An October 2004 study conducted by the nonprofit Henry Kaiser Family Foundation found that retail spending on prescription drugs is perhaps the fastest growing item in the nation's health care budget; it has increased at double-digit rates in each of the past eight years, more than quadrupling in a recent twelve-year period.[34]

The twenty-five most heavily advertised drugs the previous year, in fact, totaled more than 40 percent of the rise in retail drug spending. For example, consumer advertising for the cholesterol-lowering drug Lipitor, a product of Warner-Lambert, rose from $7.8 million in 1998 to $55.4 million in 1999; sales increased 56 percent (to $2.6 billion) over the same period. AstraZeneca invested $79.4 million advertising Prilosec, an ulcer medication, in 1999; sales increased 24 percent, to $3.6 billion. Bristol-Myers Squibb spent $43 million in consumer advertising for the oral diabetes drug Glucophage in 1999; sales increased 50 percent, to $1.2 billion. Even if advertising only accounts for a portion of these sales figures, the investments were obviously extremely profitable. As another indicator of the effects of direct consumer advertising, the study points to increased visits to doctors' offices for the most heavily advertised illnesses. Between 1990 and 1998, for example, visits for allergy symptoms were relatively stable at 13 million to 14 million patients per year. In 1999, however, advertising for allergy drugs increased markedly—Schering-Plough spent $137 million on Claritin alone, the most spent on any drug—and visits for allergy symptoms jumped to 18 million.[35]

The most accurate technique so far developed for isolating the effectiveness of advertising is the "split-cable" method. In these studies, advertisers hire cable companies to intercept the cable signal before it reaches households. They then send different advertising to different people in the same market. Members of each household are given ID cards that they show every time they make a purchase. Variables such as past brand and category purchases and special promotions for particular products are statistically controlled.

Split-cable tests verify the effectiveness of good advertising. They typically find that more than half of all advertising campaigns significantly increase short-term (within six months) sales, a remarkable figure when one considers the variability in advertising quality. Success rates are highest for new products, where advertising leads to increased profits in 60 percent of all tests; moreover, for campaigns that are successful, the increase in sales averages a whopping 21 percent. These, however, are just the short-term effects. In follow-up tests, studies found that groups that received more advertising were still buying an average of 17 percent more of the product one year after the advertising ended and 6 percent more two years later. In one major study, the increase in sales volume actually widened over a two-year follow-up period for 40 percent of the products that were previously advertised heavily. Good advertising easily pays for itself.[36]

Children are particularly vulnerable. Almost all major advertising agencies have children's divisions. These often have cute names: Kid2Kid, Just Kids, Inc., Small Talk, Kid Connection. There are major industry publications like *Youth Market Alert*, *Selling to Kids*, and *Marketing to Kids Report* that chronicle the latest market research.[37]

For food alone, the average American child sees over ten thousand commercials each year; 95 percent of these promote candy, soft drinks, sugarcoated cereals, or fast foods.[38] Studies show that children who watch more television are more likely to ask their parents for foods they see in commercials, to eat more of these foods, and to go to frequently advertised fast-food restaurants.[39] Two decades ago, children drank twice as much milk as soda. Thanks to advertising, the ratio is now reversed. A survey conducted by the Center for Science in the Public Interest found that eight- to twelve-year-old students could name more brands of beer than they could presidents of the United States.[40] Another survey found almost every six-year-old in America could identify Joe Camel, as many as could identify Mickey Mouse.[41]

A frequent aim of children's advertising is getting them to nag their parents. Marketers use terms like the "pester factor" and "nudge power."[42] Perhaps the leading authority on marketing to children, James McNeal, has conducted systematic analyses of children's "requesting" styles. In his book *Kids as Customers: A Handbook of Marketing to Children*, McNeal shows there are seven main styles of nags: *pleading* ("Mom, Mom, Mom"; "please, please, please"), *persistent* (ongoing requests), *forceful* ("Well, then, I'll go and ask Dad"), *demonstrative* (tantrums in public places, holding their breath), *sugarcoated* ("you're the best Dad in the world"), *threatening* (pledges of running away from home or hating you forever if the request isn't met), and *pity* ("All the kids will make fun of me if I don't have one").[43]

Advertisers apply information like this, often with all-too-impressive results. One study found that on 65 percent of the occasions parents denied their child a product for which the child had just seen an ad, the denial ended in their having an argument. In another study, children saw a program either without commercials or with two commercials for a toy. They were then shown pictures of a father and son and told the father had just rejected the boy's request for the toy. Sixty percent of the children who hadn't seen the commercials thought the boy in the picture would still want to play with his father; less than 40 percent of the children who saw the commercials thought he would. Still worse, when asked whether they'd prefer to play with the toy or another child, twice as many children who'd seen the commercials opted for the toy. Worse yet, when asked whether they'd prefer to play with a "nice boy" without the toy or a "not so nice boy" with the toy, 70 percent of the children who hadn't seen the commercials chose the nice boy; only 35 percent of the children who'd been exposed to the commercials chose him.[44] Advertising delivers.

And most people do concede that advertising works. Just not on them. My students Joseph Gerber, Karla Burgos, Albert Rodriguez, and Michelle Massey and I recently conducted a study in which we showed people various magazine ads. Knowing the illusion of invulnerability, it didn't surprise us that people usually said they were unpersuaded by any of the ads. It didn't matter what the content of the ad or how it was phrased—whether the ad appeared technically sound, credible, or well-researched—people told us none of the ads affected them. But then we asked how other people would react to the same ads. Now it was a different story: subjects said others would be more persuaded and more likely to buy the products in almost all the ads we showed them. Finally, we posed two questions aimed point-blank at this self-serving bias. First,

"How affected are you by advertising?" And second, "How affected do you think most people are by advertising?" Overwhelmingly, we were told others are much more influenced by advertising than they are.[45] Welcome to Lake Wobegon.

Advertisers know all about your skepticism. If you put yourself in the category of the immune, then you should know there are specialists whose very job is getting through to people like you. They look for ways to slip under your radar.

One approach is to camouflage the ads as background. Web surfers, for example, are known to be tough sells. Research shows that conventional advertising on web sites is increasingly being ignored. One way some advertisers have tried to get around this is by sponsoring "advergames" that display their products. Procter & Gamble sponsors an online game called Mission Refresh in which players help the hero destroy dandruff creatures with bubbles and bottles of Head & Shoulders shampoo. Dodge Speedway lets you race a car that's plastered with the company's logo; ads for Dodge cars appear on every billboard along the track's walls. Major companies like Toyota, Ford, General Motors, Radio Shack, and Sony Entertainment have developed games featuring their products.

Advertisers can covertly monitor these games to get information about the styles and preferences of the players, to be used for future marketing. The games can usually be spread virally, meaning they can be sent to friends via e-mail. Often the games are pieces of larger television campaigns in which television viewers are encouraged to visit the web site and web site users are urged to watch the television program. There is accumulating evidence for the advergames' effectiveness. Before Toyota's Adrenaline racing game appeared on Microsoft's MSN Gaming Zone site in 2000, for example, a survey of Gaming Zone users found Toyota's brand awareness ranked number six among major car companies. Three months after the game went online, Toyota's brand awareness leaped to number two.[46]

The motion picture industry has for many years been selling so-called product placement, whereby they charge companies to display their products in films. When a movie close-up shows an actor wearing a particular brand of sneakers or a character talks about a certain brand of potato chip, there's a good chance it's the result of a paid endorsement. James Bond's BMW roadster, the Ray-Ban sunglasses worn by the stars of *Men in Black*, and all of Forrest Gump's Dr Pepper drinking

("One of the best things about meeting the president was you could drink all the Dr Pepper you wanted," Forrest declares) all appeared courtesy of company sponsorships.[47] The tobacco industry has been notably active in this practice. Cigarette advertising is banned on television, but it has been permissible for tobacco companies to pay to have movie characters smoke their brands or otherwise display their logos. In the movie *Superman II*, for example, Philip Morris paid $42,000 to have Superman destroy a Marlboro (one of their brands) truck. When the movie, with scene intact, was later shown on television, the company had to a considerable degree managed to circumvent television's ban on tobacco advertising.[48]

It's been argued that product placement is deceptive advertising. Opponents of the practice have petitioned the Federal Trade Commission to require that sponsors be listed in the movie credits. (Some even want the word *advertising* flashed on-screen whenever a product appears.) The FTC has declined these petitions, concluding that product placement presents no obvious pattern of deception.[49]

Embedded product placement reached something of a new level in the summer of 2001 when Fay Weldon, the popular British novelist, accepted an "undisclosed sum" from the Italian jeweler Bulgari to mention its brand at least a dozen times in her new book. It was shock enough to hear that a well-known writer had sold billboard space in her book—appropriately titled *The Bulgari Connection*—to an advertiser. Equally notable, however, was the depth of the product placement: the novel includes a character obsessed by the aesthetics of Bulgaris, vivid descriptions of Bulgari pieces, and a plot involving the sale of a painting that contains a Bulgari necklace.[50]

Not only does Madison Avenue have ways to sidestep your mistrust; it has created an entire school of advertising that thrives on it. Like jujitsu masters, the advertisers align with your mistrust and then turn it against you to promote what they're selling. They flatter your hipness, your cleverness, "conceding" that they know you're far too astute to be manipulated by advertising. One way is to dress the ad up as an anti-image message. For example:

- An ad for Scotch whiskey tells us: "This is a glass of Cutty Sark. If you need to see a picture of a guy in an Armani suit sitting between two fashion models drinking it before you know it's right for you, it probably isn't."

- A shoe company tells us: "If you feel the need to be smarter and more articulate, read the complete works of Shakespeare. If you like who you are, here are your shoes."
- A Sprite ad shows teenagers on a beach drinking a brand named Jooky. As the camera pulls back, we realize it's actually a television commercial. Two teenagers are watching the commercial. They open their own cans of Jooky and are clearly disappointed. The logo for Sprite then comes on with the slogan "Image is nothing. Thirst is everything."
- A sneaker ad says: "Shoe buying rule number one: The image wears off after the first six miles." Another sneaker advertises: "Marketing is just hype."
- The U.K. division of French Connection ran a series of double-page advertising spreads using the slogan "fcuk advertising."[51]
- In 1987, ABC Television advertised its new season of shows with self-deprecating humor that sounded like put-downs you might hear from an intelligent, witty friend sitting in the chair next to you. One spot, for example, showed a viewer sprawled in front of a TV under the headline "Don't worry, you've got billions of brain cells." Another ran the headline "If it's so bad for you, why is there one in every hospital room?" Good question.

Advertising critic Leslie Savan refers to the sort of person these ads target as "winkers." The winker condescendingly rolls his eyes at the idiocy on television, convinced that his detachment puts him in control of what he's seeing rather than the other way around. The advertiser poses as his understanding consort in this nonsense. The message: if you want to be the type of person who's too clever to be taken in by condescending advertising, you're one of us. But, as Savan observes in her classic book *The Sponsored Life*,

> as a defense against the power of advertising, irony is a leaky condom—in fact, it's the same old condom that advertising brings over every night. A lot of ads have learned that to break through to the all-important boomer and Xer markets they have to be as cool, hip, and ironic as the target audience like to think of itself as being. That requires at least the pose of opposition to commercial values. The cool commercials—I'm thinking of Nike spots, some Reebooks, most 501s, certainly all MTV promos—flatter us by saying we're too cool to fall for commercial values, and therefore cool enough to want their product.[52]

In other words, you above-it-all winkers, Madison Avenue has your number, too. They know the best way to reach people wary of propaganda is to disguise it to look like anything but. It's all in fun, just entertainment. While you're laughing, maybe rolling your eyes, the commercial does its work.

But perhaps you're still not convinced of your vulnerability. The balance of power, you say, is changing. The professionals have overplayed their hands and today's educated consumers have caught on to their game. You might argue that our culture has become so media savvy, informed, and cynical, our lives so inundated with salesmen and hucksters, that most of us are unaffected by all but the most extraordinary acts of influence. Whether today's consumers are less gullible is open to question. What's clear, however, is that the other camp, the experts with something to sell, have more effective tools in their arsenal than ever before.

Consider, for example, the burgeoning field of consumer anthropology, a professional discipline that has become a staple research tool of applied psychologists in areas ranging from sales and marketing to politics and religion. Not long ago, new anthropology Ph.D.s' might have chosen between studying a primitive culture in the South Pacific or the social order of orangutans in Sumatra. Now they're as likely to be paid to watch shoppers move through Safeway or Bloomingdale's. Or, if they want something more ethnic, they can get a job with a major sneaker company to hang around inner-city streets to learn what language and images to use to package the latest shoe—name, color, logo, advertising models—so it will sell in the ghetto. Toyota has had social scientists following a group of young people around the last three years to get ideas for designing cars that appeal to youth.[53] Other anthropologists are now hired to spend time in consumers' homes, looking through their closets and bathroom cabinets and listening in on their conversations. Every potential market is fair game.[54]

Consumer anthropologists have devised an arsenal of sophisticated techniques to help their clients sell more. They conduct "beeper studies," "fixed-camera analyses," "shadowing," "visual stories," "brainstorming sessions," and—the holy grail of the industry—"focus groups."[55] Children are big targets. Consumer researchers stage slumber parties where children are interviewed throughout the night. They conduct focus groups for children as young as two and three. Children are surveyed outside toy stores, fast-food restaurants, and anyplace else they're likely to be found. Companies spend fortunes learning about consumers. Look-Look, an international research company specializing in youth culture, employs more than ten thousand children they've identified as trend-setters to report on what they and their friends are doing and talking about.[56] The research unit of Nintendo U.S. interviews over six thousand children each month.[57]

If I were trying to help my client decide at which location to set up a new fast-food restaurant, for example, I might pay local pedestrians to carry around a palmtop computer for a few days and "beep" them at regular intervals. At each beep the pedestrian would pull out the computer and answer questions ranging from where they are to whether they're hungry to what sort of mood they're in and how adventurous they feel. In a few days we'd know which location would capture the most customers.

Or if I were advising my supermarket client how to arrange his products on the shelves, I might set up video cameras to monitor the most minuscule movements of shoppers hunting and gathering their way through the store. Some organizations put tiny cameras inside the frozen-food cases. I'd look, for example, at the "capture rate"—how much of what's on the shelves is actually seen by shoppers as they move through the market. In supermarkets, the rate turns out to be about 20 percent. Then I'd determine the "reliable zone"—the shelf placements that are seen by most shoppers. In most markets this goes from about knee level to just above eye level. Next I'd target the "conversion rate"—the proportion of browsers who see the product and decide to buy it. I'd interview the owner about his product line.

Grocery industry studies show that about two-thirds of consumers' purchases are unplanned. So I'd make sure the items less likely to be on customers' shopping lists—maybe a new breakfast cereal—were squarely in the reliable zone. (The vast majority of women carry lists into supermarkets, but only about a quarter of men do—yet another observation of consumer anthropologists.) Necessities that we know will be hunted down—milk, for example—could afford to occupy less-visible space. The owner might also tilt the bottom shelves up a bit and, when push comes to shove, keep smaller items (the sponge scrubbers, say) in the reliable zone and concede larger items (laundry detergent, perhaps) to space in the hinterlands.[58]

Specialists in a new subfield known as retail anthropology will tell you all this about your shopping habits and considerably more. Paco

Underhill, for example, author of the book *Why We Buy: The Science of Shopping*, works as a consultant to many of the largest retail stores. His discerning cameras have charted people's movements through stores with disturbing precision.

Underhill and his research team have learned, for example, that shoppers entering a new store need a few moments, about five to fifteen paces, to settle down and get their bearings. They need to slow down from walking speed to shopping speed, particularly if they've just rushed in from a parking lot or a busy street. As a result, they take little notice of anything placed squarely at the entrance—an area Underhill calls the "decompression" or "transition" zone. Underhill advises his clients not to attempt anything important in this zone and to take steps to keep the zone as small as possible. "I guarantee it," he observes. "Put a pile of fliers or a stack of shopping baskets just inside the door: Shoppers will barely see them, and will almost never pick them up. Move them ten feet in and the fliers and baskets will disappear. It's a law of nature—shoppers need a landing strip."[59]

Shoppers also have an uncanny tendency to drift toward the right. (In England and Australia, where people drive on the other side of the road, it's to the left.) Because of this, the most valuable real estate in a store is the front right just beyond the decompression zone. This is where the make-or-break merchandise that requires maximum exposure should be placed. Shoppers also have a strong tendency to reach to the right (including in England and Australia), meaning the best way to get a product into the hands of customers is to place it slightly to the right of where they're likely to be standing. "If you're stocking cookies, for instance, the most popular brand goes dead center—at the bull's eye—and the brand you're trying to build goes just to the right of it," Underhill has found.[60]

He's also tackled the problem of getting shoppers to explore the furthest reaches of the store, to keep them from going halfway down an aisle and reversing field. He studies which products and displays pull customers to the rear displays. These usually turn out to be basic staples that people buy a lot of and know the store carries. Gap stores, for example, have learned to place denim on the back wall.

This just scratches the surface. Shopping scientists can tell you everything from how much time you'll spend in a store (in one national housewares chain, for example, it's an average of 8 minutes, 15 seconds for a woman shopping with another woman; 7 minutes, 19 seconds for a woman with children; 5 minutes, 2 seconds for women alone; and 4 minutes, 41 seconds for a woman shopping with a man) to how long you'll stare at a label before making a purchase (women spend an average of 5 seconds reading the label of shower gels, 16 seconds for moisturizers).[61] In other words, consumer anthropologists know more about your habits than you do. They can bounce you through a store like a billiard ball.

Consumer anthropology isn't inherently malevolent or even anti-consumer. As Underhill sees it, his research ultimately causes sellers to meet the desires of shoppers rather than the other way around. "Build and operate a retail environment that fits the highly particular needs of shoppers and you've created a successful store," Underhill observes. "Just as [anthropologist] Holly Whyte's labors improved urban parks and plazas, the science of shopping creates better retail environments—ultimately, we're providing a form of consumer advocacy that benefits our clients as well."[62]

There's some truth to Underhill's argument. Nonetheless, there's no avoiding that the increasing sophistication of this new breed of applied social science leaves us more susceptible to their message. Consumers may be getting wiser, but the professionals are, too. It's like an evolving war between bacteria and antibiotics—stronger antibiotics are countered by more resistant bacteria, which leads to the development of new antibiotics, and so on. The problem is that because it's a full-time job for the professionals, they're like the bacteria—always a step ahead of you.

This book is intended as consumer anthropology, too, but from the opposite perspective. I've spent the last several years watching the experts, trying my hand at sales, and attending seminars, sales events, and the like to observe people's vulnerabilities—how, when, and where we're prone to manipulation. The chapters that follow draw on a wide range of research and disciplines, all under the assumption that the more we understand about the psychology of the persuasion process—what we're liable to encounter and how most people will react—the better we shift the balance of control to our side.

TWO

Whom Do We Trust? Experts, Honesty, and Likability

Or, the Supersalesmen Don't Look Like Salesmen at All

> Pay no attention to that man behind the curtain.
> —*The Wizard of Oz*

If there's one common denominator to the most effective salespeople I've encountered in my research, it's that they almost never look like "real" salespeople. The ones to watch out for hold the uncanny ability to first set you at ease about their motives. Then they sell.

I discovered an impressive example of this at a sales presentation called a "Pampered Chef" party. The event was based on the Tupperware "recruit the next hostess" approach, in this case selling various products for cooking and serving food. The woman (I'll call her Betty) whose party I attended had a reputation as the local queen of Pampered Chef hostesses. This party, in fact, was advertised as her seven hundredth show. I soon saw why.

Betty was attractive, sweet, charming, and bubbling with knowledge and enthusiasm for her products. She also overflowed with family values, an approach that appeared to impeccably fit her audience—virtually all (about seventy-five) of whom seemed to be mothers themselves. (The only obvious exceptions were myself and a Japanese man who was obviously dragged there by his wife. The man kept digging his shoe into the dirt below his seat as if he was trying to burrow an escape under Betty's backyard.) Betty's young children

29

greeted us at the door, made our name tags, and conducted the draw-ings for door prizes. They seemed to love helping out as much as Betty loved demonstrating the products. Her presentation was laced with mentions of her husband, children, dog, going to church, and shopping at the Bible store. A half-dozen volunteers cheerfully and visibly worked away at various tasks, including preparing food and desserts (using Pampered Chef products, of course) for the guests. Betty let us know her helpers had been working all day to make our party a success.

Betty blurred the line between the seemingly contradictory objec-tives of monetary profit and neighborly caring. She even found ways to frame the two so they enhanced one another. For example, she empha-sized a charity tie-in and how proud she was that a percentage of prof-its from her sales were donated to a community food bank. This generated something of a communitarian, Rotary Club feeling—a non-profit spin to the profiteering. But Betty's finest creation, I thought, was a scrapbook she passed around, entitled "The Pampered Chef—My Story Can Be Your Story." The purpose of the book was to encour-age new hostesses who would work as "downlines" for Betty. It contained company-prepared flyers and descriptions of the products. Mixed in with this glossy information, however, were Betty's personal touches. She'd added photos of her children playing baseball, the fam-ily on a camping trip, vacationing at Disneyland. She'd also pasted in photocopies of her substantial commission checks. Best of all, Betty wrote comments throughout these pages, almost all of which equated her profit motive with nothing more than good family values:

> My boys enjoy baseball. 4 boys in little league is expensive. My com-mission checks sure come in handy.
> I love being able to work when I choose. I chose not to work this weekend and took my kids to the country fair at their school. It's great to have a very flexible schedule.
> My husband and I have made this a family business. He bonds with the kids the nights I choose to work.

If you want a prototype for a supersalesperson, I suggest you for-get about aggressive used-car dealers. It's people like Betty who have you at their mercy. She's a good, honest person who cares more about people than money. What's not to trust in a woman like this? Not much, apparently. At the end of the party, guests were lined up ten deep to place orders.

Betty's secret? Research shows that three characteristics are related to persuasiveness: perceived authority, honesty, and likability. When someone has any or all of these characteristics, we're not only more willing to agree to that person's request, willing to do so without carefully considering the facts. We assume we're on safe ground and are happy to shortcut the tedious process of informed decision making. As a result, we're more susceptible to messages and requests, no matter their particular content. Betty worked this triad of trustworthiness elegantly.

Expertise

From earliest childhood, we learn to rely on authority figures for sound decision making because their authority signifies status and power, as well as expertise. These two facets often work together. Authorities such as parents and teachers are not only our primary sources of wisdom while we grow up, but they control us and our access to the things we want. In addition, we've been taught to believe—mostly from these same parents and teachers—that respect for authority is a moral virtue. As adults, it's natural to transfer this respect to society's designated authorities, such as judges, doctors, bosses, and religious leaders. We assume their positions give them special access to information and power. Usually we're correct, so that our willingness to defer to authorities becomes a convenient shortcut to sound decision making.

It's so effective, in fact, that we often embrace the further shortcut of assuming that people who simply display *symbols* of authority should be listened to. Studies show that Americans are particularly susceptible to three types of authority symbols: titles, clothing, and luxury cars.[1] Most of the time these symbols offer good approximations of the information we need: people with "Dr." before their name usually are, in fact, experts in their field; the man in the tailored business suit is often a well-connected businessperson; and the driver in the Lexus generally has elements of success in his or her background.

Consider the title "doctor." Condom makers spent many years peddling the virtues of their product—it offered birth control, disease prevention, and reasonable tactile pleasure—but had little success increasing sales. Then, in 1987, C. Everett Koop, the surgeon general of the United States, recommended that people, even teenagers, should use condoms and sales went through the roof. A simple okay from Koop was exponentially more effective than any marketing campaign the good folks from Trojan could have paid for.

In Koop's case, the public response was logical; after all, whom should we trust for medical advice if not the bearer of the ultimate title of medical and public health authority?[2] But we can be equally deferential to symbols of authority that signify nothing. Oftentimes, in fact, the mere appearance of authority works as well as the real thing, even when everyone knows it's just a facade. When the television show *M*A*S*H* was popular, the actor Alan Alda, who played a physician on the show, was often asked to speak to groups of doctors. One year, for example, he gave the keynote address to the graduating class at Columbia University Medical School. Now that they'd learned to be doctors, Alda told the audience, he wanted to teach them how to act like ones. None of the real-life doctors seemed concerned that Alda's most intimate experience in the art of doctoring was having worn surgeons' scrubs on a television stage. Not long after, Jack Klugman (a.k.a. Quincy, ace medical examiner) was sharing his wisdom about the medical profession at the Mount Sinai Medical School graduation across town.

If real doctors are so receptive to a fake doctor, is it any wonder the public is, too? Consider, for example, the ads for Sanka (decaffeinated) coffee that featured the actor Robert Young warning us about the dangers of caffeine. Young sold so much Sanka that he was hired to do several versions of the ad over a period of several years. His singular qualification to give medical advice was that he'd played the role of wise old Marcus Welby, M.D., on the enormously popular, long-running television series. Other television doctors have followed in Young's lucrative footsteps. Not long ago, for example, Bill Cosby was successfully peddling Jell-O Pudding, because it's "good for you." People know, of course, that Cosby, unlike C. Everett Koop, has no legitimate qualifications as a health expert. But, like Alan Alda and Robert Young, he appeared to be a medical doctor—on television, anyway. And, besides, kids would probably get spooked if you made them look at a close-up of C. Everett Koop. As a Madison Avenue maxim goes, "If you have nothing to say, have a celebrity say it."

I'm a great admirer of the documentary filmmaker Errol Morris, particularly for his facility for getting people to reveal things they hadn't come to the interview intending to reveal. In his quirky classic *The*

Thin Blue Line, Morris got a man to confess on camera to the murder of a policeman, a crime the authorities had already declared closed with an innocent man sitting on death row. The key to eliciting self-disclosure, Morris observes, is for the interviewer to appear engrossed in the interviewee's story. It's not necessary to actually be engrossed, mind you—just to look like you are. In fact, Morris advises, it can be counterproductive to actually get too interested in the story because this can distract you from looking interested. The same goes for authority: looking like the real thing may have more impact than actually being it.

People are perceived as more credible when they make eye contact and speak with confidence, no matter what they have to say. In a mock jury study, researcher Bonnie Erickson and her colleagues had people listen to a witness answer questions about a supposed accident—for example, "Approximately how long did you stay there before the ambulance arrived?" Some jurors heard the witness respond straightforwardly: "Twenty minutes. Long enough to help get Mrs. David straightened out." Others listened to the witness hem and haw: "Oh, it seems like it was about, uh, twenty minutes. Just long enough to help my friend Mrs. David, you know, get straightened out." What the witnesses said turned out to be less important than how they said it: the straightforward, confident witnesses were rated significantly more credible and competent.[3]

Other studies show that decisive, swift talkers are actually no more sure of their facts than are their more hesitant counterparts. But, more important, they create the impression of confidence and, as a result, are perceived to be more expert, intelligent, and knowledgeable.[4] It's noteworthy that observers rate decisive speaking styles as more masculine; softer, hesitant, qualified deliveries are perceived as more feminine.

False confidence is the reason many courtrooms prohibit hypnotically refreshed testimony. Studies show that hypnosis is no more effective than other methods at conjuring up forgotten memories. What hypnosis does produce, however, is greater confidence that what you're remembering is in fact the truth. As a result, these witnesses can be dangerously persuasive. Some legal scholars refer to it as "unfair influence."[5]

The inclusion of statistics, even when they're meaningless, can signal expertise. My students and I found evidence for this in our study of advertising effectiveness.[6] We showed one group of subjects a series of real magazine ads that featured statistical information arguing for their product. One ad, for example, was for a breakfast cereal that contained "60% of the minimum daily requirement of calcium, 90% iron and 100% folic acid." We showed other subjects the same ads, except this time we airbrushed out the statistics. When we asked subjects about their own impressions of the advertised products, it didn't much matter which version of the ad they'd seen—neither version of the ad, they said, persuaded *them*. Given the illusion of invulnerability, this was no surprise. More revealing was what subjects said about how other people would be affected. Those exposed to the ads with statistics, they believed, would be much more likely to buy the product. This supports what advertisers have been saying for years: "The more facts you tell, the more you sell."[7]

Technical jargon can be similarly persuasive. Everyone claims to hate unnecessary jargon. Why must that airplane pilot have to announce that "there is a probability of an episode of significant precipitation" instead of just saying "it's going to rain"? But the truth is, if you're out to give the impression of special expertise, jargon often works. In a mock jury trial conducted by researchers Joel Cooper, Elizabeth Bennett, and Holly Sukel, subjects were asked to evaluate a plaintiff's claim that the company he'd worked for exposed him to a dangerous chemical that caused his cancer. Some jurors listened to the supposed expert witness, Dr. Thomas Fallon, a professor of biochemistry, explain in simple terms that the chemical in question causes the type of liver cancer the plaintiff had been stricken with. Fallon described, for example, how previous studies found that the chemical "caused not only liver disease but also cancer of the liver and . . . diseases of the immune system as well." Other subjects heard Dr. Fallon go off on the dangers of the chemical in complicated, often incomprehensible language. He explained how the chemical led to "tumor induction as well as hepatomegaly, hepatomegalocytosis, and lymphoid atrophy in both spleen and thymus." The results of the study showed that when Dr. Fallon was presented as a man of outstanding credentials, the jury was almost twice as likely to be convinced if he spoke in obscure jargon than if he presented in simple and straightforward language. The researchers concluded that when the witness spoke simply the jurors could evaluate his argument on its merits. But when he was unintelligible, they had to resort to the mental shortcut of accepting his title and reputation in lieu of comprehensible facts. And so, another paradox: experts are sometimes most convincing when we don't understand what they're talking about.

As long as they have credentials, that is. In another experimental condition, Dr. Fallon was introduced with shakier credentials. When this was the case, people were less convinced when he spoke in jargon than in straightforward language. In other words, if people think you're a bullshitter to begin with, better not lay it on too thick.[8]

Then again, *shaky* is a relative term. A study by a team of doctors and nurses from several midwestern hospitals showed what can happen when authority is trusted uncritically. In this experiment, one of the investigators made a phone call to the nursing stations on twenty-two separate wards. Calls were made at an evening hour when the staff nurse would be there alone. The caller, a complete stranger to the nurse, said he was the hospital physician for a specific ward patient. He instructed the nurse to administer a massive dose (twenty milligrams) of a potent drug (Astroten) to his patient. "I'll be up within ten minutes," he continued, "and I'll sign the order then, but I'd like the drug to have started taking effect."

Think about this. An unfamiliar voice, someone you've never seen in person, whose only evidence of authority is that he claims to be a doctor, orders you to administer a powerful drug you're unfamiliar with. When the researchers asked a separate group of nursing students what they'd do in this situation, none of them—0 percent—predicted they would give the medication as ordered.[9] The illusion of invulnerability strikes again. Here's an excerpt from a transcript of what turned out to be a typical nurse's response:

> *Caller*: Will you please check the medicine cabinet and see if you have some Astroten.
> *Nurse*: Some what?
> *Caller*: Astroten. That's A-S-T-R-O-T-E-N.
> *Nurse*: I'm pretty sure we don't.
> *Caller*: Would you take a look, please?
> *Nurse*: Yes, I'll take a look. But I'm pretty sure we don't.
>   —(45 seconds pause)—
> *Nurse*: Hello.
> *Caller*: Well?
> *Nurse*: Yes.

Caller: You have Astroten?
Nurse: Yes.
Caller: O.K. Now, will you give Mr. Carson a stat dose of 20 mil-
    ligrams—that's four capsules—of Astroten.
Nurse: Twenty cap . . . Oh, I mean 20 milligrams.
Caller: Yes, that's right.
Nurse: Four capsules. O.K.
Caller: Thank you.
Nurse: Surely.

In fact, nearly every nurse in the experiment was as mindlessly sub-missive as this one. Overall, 95 percent went straight to the medicine cabinet for the Astroten and were on their way to administer it to the patient before being stopped by one of the experimenters, who explained it was just an experiment.[10]

Michael Cohen, who is founder and president of the watchdog agency called the Institute for Safe Medication Practices, observed to me that "the people who give the medicines to patients often feel inse-cure in their knowledge level. Even when they recognize what might be a serious problem they feel they're not in a position to challenge a board-certified subspecialist doctor. The person can be intimidating, or maybe we're in awe of them because they have a reputation as an expert in their field. It's especially a problem for an inexperienced phar-macist or nurse. They assume the doctors must know what they're doing and back down. It's mindless respect for authority. Too often it's at the expense of patients."

Cohen and his colleague Neil Davis describe one unfortunate patient who was administered a radioactive chemical into his eye. "Those eye drops you're giving me," the patient reported to his physi-cian the next day, "they really hurt." No wonder. It turns out the physi-cian had written the initials O.J. on the man's prescription, which was intended to mean that the drug should be taken orally with orange juice. But the doctor's sloppy handwriting was interpreted as O.D., or right eye. The patient got the radioactive chemical inserted in his eye on two different shifts. Then there was the case of the rectal eardrops. A doctor had prescribed drops to be administered in a patient's right ear but, unfortunately, had abbreviated his order with the instructions "place in R ear." The duty nurse read "R ear" as one word and promptly inserted the eardrops into the patient's rectum. After reviewing many drug prescription errors like these, Davis and Cohen concluded, "The nurse must trust to a point, but never let her knowledge or experience be overshadowed by her trust."[11] Any arguments?

These are examples of how uncritical trust can go wrong even when the orders come from a legitimate, well-intentioned authority. When unscrupulous manipulators come into the picture, the range of errors multiplies. For one thing, who's to know whether authority is legitimate? It's not very hard to fake a college degree or professional credentials or to buy an official-looking badge or uniform. And even when the symbols are legitimate, there's no assurance the person behind them is a font of wise counsel. The world is full of people who got As on their exams but haven't the faintest idea how life outside the classroom operates. Finally, we have a ridiculous tendency to confuse expertise in one domain with expertise in general. To assume there's credibility when a successful actor promotes a cold remedy, or when a psychology professor offers his views about politics, is—to borrow a current buzz phrase in education—bad critical thinking.

The Mentalists

Which leads us to the most absurd but no less successful extreme of fabricated authority: people who use psychological tricks to imply they possess special knowledge or powers. I learned some of the most impressive of these tricks by studying people who pass themselves off as "mentalists": individuals who are supposedly blessed with paranormal abilities to read minds, conduct psychokinesis, predict the future, and the like. I didn't find much in the way of psychic skills in these performances. What I did see, however, were extremely effective packages of self-presentation, salespersonship, and social psychology. Here's how it's done.

First, no matter what you say or do, give yourself plenty of wiggle room. To begin with, stick to vague language. This is particularly true when you're doing a "cold reading." The venerated psychic Edgar Cayce liked to qualify his predictions with phrases like "I feel that . . ." and "Perhaps . . ." Most psychics like to phrase their statements as a cross between suggestions and questions. When the psychic says, "I sense a tall man here," he's really inviting a response. The psychic looks for a reaction, perhaps a subtle nod or some other confirmation, before deciding if and how to follow up. Detailed information—such as the man's actual height or name—is always provided by the subject, not the reader. For a typical example, consider the famous psychic James Van Praagh. An analysis of a reading by Van Praagh for the TV program *48 Hours* revealed that he'd asked 260 questions while making only 2 actual statements over the almost sixty-minute period. When a subject responds with specific information, Van Praagh acts as if his question was actually a statement because he knew the answer all along. For example:

> Van Praagh: "Did your husband linger on in the hospital, or did he pass quickly?"
> Subject: "Oh, he died almost immediately."
> Van Praagh: "Yes, because he's saying to me, 'I didn't suffer. I was spared any pain.'"[12]

Another famous psychic, Peter Hurkos, likes to offer the impression he's being specific by tossing around actual numbers. But his numbers are fluid. For example:

> Hurkos: "I see four people. Maybe five."
> Subject: "No, there are only three of us in the house."
> Hurkos: "No, there are four I see . . ."
> Subject: "Oh, my brother. He hasn't been with us for a long time now. There are only three of us now."
> Hurkos: "But there *is* your brother. Yes, it is your brother."[13]

An often-effective approach during the initial stages of a reading, when you're still fishing around, is to phrase questions as double negatives. If your target looks like a university student, for example, you might ask: "You're not a student at [name of the local] University, are you?" If they are, give a knowing nod. Otherwise, move on to the next prediction. Heads, you win; tails, they lose.

This brings me to a common theme in the tricks used by mentalists: ignore the misses and take credit for the hits. This is sometimes called the Jeane Dixon effect, after the self-described psychic. It's terrible science but effective performance. At a "psychic institute" I visited, a staff member walked up to me, apologized for intruding, and excitedly told me she was struck by all the music she saw in my aura. "Is it possible you play an instrument or perform or something like that?" she asked me. I told her I didn't; in fact, that I've always been disappointed about how pitifully little musical ability I have. Without missing a beat, she then asked if I enjoy listening to music. I did, I told her. (Well, duh!) "Yes, that's what I'm seeing," she proudly announced.

Mentalists, like good poker players, know when to hold them and when to fold them. At the same psychic institute, I paid to have my past lives read. The psychic kept telling me she saw "some kind of loneliness" in these past lives. (She saw me, first, as a bachelor shopkeeper during the Civil War and, second, as a Hawaiian living by myself next to a volcano in the 1880s—how odd, I thought, considering my ancestors were living in shtetls in Poland during the same time periods.) "Do you live alone or are you lonely?" the psychic asked me. "No and no," I answered honestly. She immediately dropped the past lives. "Do you have siblings?" she asked. "Yes," I said. "Do any of them live out of town?" she asked. "Yes," I said. "What I'm seeing is you sometimes miss them. Am I correct?" "Yes, of course," I said. "That's it. That's the loneliness I was seeing," she concluded.

If he's good, the mentalist will pick up cues as the reading goes on, eventually enabling him to make predictions that, when one connects, appear startling. If, for example, he sees out of the corner of his eye that the subject has been exchanging cold looks with her apparent date in the next seat, the psychic might offer a vaguely worded comment about how he senses she's in the process of making an important decision in her love life right now. If that gets the hoped-for reaction, he might add that he senses her decision centers on someone currently in her proximity. If the mentalist has had an assistant eavesdropping on the couple's conversation in the lobby, who heard them discussing divorce, he might get more specific yet: "For some reason, I see someone in a courtroom. Could he be some type of lawyer?" The stage mentalist always ends a performance after a difficult "hit" so everything before that appears to be just a warm-up.

The really slick operators can spin success from failure. In an experiment conducted during the *Apollo 14* spaceflight several decades ago, the popular psychic Olof Jonsson was one of three people (the two others were never named) who received brain wave transmissions from the astronaut Edgar Mitchell. In a subsequent test of his receptor ability, Olof failed miserably. Undaunted, he bragged that the odds against his performance were three thousand to one. True, but what Olaf didn't mention was that the odds were three thousand to one against doing as *badly* as he had. His performance was lauded by supporters as a spectacular demonstration of what they called "psi-missing."[14] As the philosopher-theologian Alan Watts once observed, "To be considered a guru, simply take credit for whatever coincidence occurs."[15]

Perhaps you'd like to prove you have a gift for reading people's personalities. Stare into your subject's eyes. Ask the person a few general questions. If you have time, maybe give him or her a short personality test or consult your tarot cards or astrological charts. Then say this:

> People close to you have been taking advantage of you. Your basic honesty has been getting in your way. Many opportunities that you have had offered to you in the past have had to be surrendered because you refuse to take advantage of others. You like to read books and articles that improve your mind. In fact, if you're not already in some sort of personal service business, you should be. You have an infinite capacity for understanding people's problems and you can sympathize with them. But you are firm when confronted with obstinacy or outright stupidity. Law enforcement would be another field you understand. Your sense of justice is quite strong.[16]

Most subjects will not only confirm the validity of your insights but will probably be amazed how you uncovered corners of their character very few people have seen. In point of fact, I took this reading verbatim from one given in Las Vegas by Sydney Omarr, one of the best-known and best-paid astrologers in the United States. Omarr based the reading on a thorough astrological interview with his subject. The subject was stunned by the accuracy of the reading. The thing is, though, when you give people the same reading based on no astrological information they're usually just as impressed. Psychologists call this willingness to embrace vague, flattering descriptions the P. T. Barnum effect—named after the nineteenth-century businessman and circus impresario who was said to have coined the phrase "There's a sucker born every minute."

You'll want to adjust your statements to fit your audience, of course. A reading that rings true for a room full of social workers, for example, probably won't score high hit rates with a group of marines. Specifics aside, however, the trick is to tell people what they want to hear without being blatantly ingratiating. Try to strike on an idealized image your subjects have of themselves, perhaps one they've never quite articulated. Sprinkle in a few seemingly negative characteristics that are really virtues ("Your incessant honesty has been getting in your way"). Include a lot of verbiage so that your reading has the appearance of complexity, even though you may actually be using many terms that say basically the same thing. Most important of all, you need to find the right balance between vagueness and specificity: be sufficiently vague that you can slip out of your misses but specific enough that, when you do score a hit, it looks like you've discovered something special or unique about your subjects. For some good templates, study astrological readings. "The best way to predict the future," observes magician Gregory Wilson, "is to influence it."[17]

My favorite mentalist trick takes advantage of what might be called the multiple option ploy. There are many variations of this technique. Here's one I learned from the illusionist-educator Bob Fellows and adapted as a lecture demonstration.[18]

I begin by telling the audience that, through years of psychological training, I've developed the ability to mentally transport psychic energy. I can, for example, influence people's actions by staring into their eyes. Most people who make claims like this—those folks you see at state fairs or on cable television—are phonies, I explain. I've studied those charlatans and can tell you the tricks they use. My skill, on the other hand, is based on scientific experiments and requires intensive doctoral-level training. (Almost every mentalist begins by telling the audience there are lots of flimflam men out there claiming special powers. Since most of the audience is skeptical of psychic powers to begin with, this is a good way to defuse their resistance. The performers then regain the offensive by offering some reason why they, themselves, are different. You'll want to prepare your own explanation.)

I ask for a volunteer. Three different objects are placed on a table in front of the volunteer—perhaps two paper clips, two rubber bands, and two quarters. (Instead of quarters, I sometimes use two old Chinese coins and say I learned the skill from Chinese mystics.) I then reach into my pocket and draw my hand out in a fist, which, I inform the subject, contains an identical match to one of the three objects. I tell the subject to hold my wrist in one hand to prove I won't use sleight of hand to switch objects. This distracts the subject from the sleight of mouth I'm getting ready to pull off on him or her. I now stare into the subject's eyes, perhaps adding some mumbo jumbo about how he or she seems to be resisting my messages or how someone in the audience is emitting interfering vibrations.

I instruct the subject to remove two of the objects from the table. Say I'm holding a paper clip in my hand. If the subject leaves the paper clip on the table, I announce, "If I'm not a psychic, then explain to me how I could possibly have known you were going to choose the paper clip," and open my hand to reveal the clip in my hand. Am I the man or what?

But what if the subject leaves one of the other objects on the table? Not to worry. I immediately turn to the two objects in the subject's hand. I nonchalantly push the object on the table off to the side and resume staring into the subject's eyes. The subject is now instructed to place one of the two objects he or she is holding on the table in front of him or her. If the clip is placed on the table, I bring my fist next to the clip, open my fingers to reveal my own clip, and announce, "If I'm not a psychic, then explain to me how I could possibly have known you were going to choose the paper clip." Or, if the subject puts the remaining object on the table, I bring my hand up to the subject's, reveal my clip, and announce, "If I'm not a psychic, then explain to me how I could possibly have known you were going to choose the paper clip."

What I find most remarkable about this trick is how few people catch on. A small percentage—almost always those who have previously seen some variation on the multiple option technique—typically get it right away. The vast majority, however, are convinced I either pulled off a sleight-of-hand exchange or just don't know what to think. Some become convinced I really do have special powers. What I really gave them, of course, was a lesson in basic salesmanship. If a customer shows a preference for a blue Chevy, the smart salesman compliments the choice; if the customer leans toward a green Oldsmobile, the salesman finds reasons to applaud that one. As long as the customer keeps making choices, the salesman will eventually be right. To the extent the customer likes reassurance, he'll embrace the salesman's advice and, by extension, affirm the salesman's expertise. With the customer's trust in hand, the sale becomes that much easier.

Forthcoming magicians or mentalists will tell you their displays of power require the collaboration of the audience. It's not the reality of the demonstration but the audience's perception of that reality that's being sold. The mentalist knows how to feed and manipulate these perceptions. He plays on your ignorance of subtle clues and methods. He employs the basic principle of magic: disguising the false move to look like the real move. In the end, however, you're the one who must fool yourself. *"Homo vult decipi; decipiatur"* ("Man wishes to be deceived; deceive him").

In other words, you'd be well advised to question authority (Timothy Leary got that one right) and situations in which you unexpectedly find yourself in subordinate power relationships. Look critically at symbols of authority—titles, uniforms, claims to special powers. Monitor your willingness to obey people of higher status, especially when they encourage you to believe they're too harmless to be worth your worry. I like a recent malapropism from Kim Anderson, the mayor of Naples, Florida, who commented to a reporter: "I think we're on the road to coming up with answers that I don't think any of us in total feel we have answers to."[19] Now there's an authority I could learn to trust.

Honesty

Authority generates respect, but another type of trustworthiness is even more compelling: that resulting from character.

The honesty, integrity, and morality of a persuasion professional are particularly important when objective issues are vague. In political campaigns in the United States, for example, candidates tend to avoid clear stands on potentially divisive issues, seeking instead a middle ground. It is often difficult to firmly grasp what a candidate stands for. As a result, most of the attention in U.S. elections concerns character issues. Is the candidate a person who abuses power? A liar? Did he con his way out of the draft? Cheat on his wife? Inhale? Candidates aren't packaged according to their views, but as people "who care" or "you can depend on."

We tend to assess morality in other people on a digital scale. A person can be trusted or can't, with perhaps one or two "I'm not too sure about that guy" gradations in between. This is very different from expertise and authority, which we gauge in small increments—the president carries more weight than the vice president who counts more than his aide; a general is above a colonel is above a sergeant; and so on.

Also, when it comes to gauging the trustworthiness of other people we envision morality as a stable and consistent personality predisposition, one that varies little across time or situations. In fact, honesty and trustworthiness, like all personality traits, are highly dependent on the situation. As early as 1928, for example, researchers demonstrated that whether a child cheated in one situation was a poor predictor of whether he'd cheat in an even slightly different one. Some cheated on multiple choice tests but not on essays; others were just the opposite.[20]

Nonetheless, because moral trustworthiness is perceived as relatively unwavering, a little of it goes a long way. Once a reputation is established, it grows legs of its own. This is particularly true for negative reputations. If you're labeled as untrustworthy, good luck in reversing the appraisal. Almost anything you do, no matter how well-meaning, will be read as dishonest manipulation or shameless ingratiation.

To some extent, a parallel process works to sustain positive reputations. We usually want to believe that the person we've labeled as trustworthy will continue to meet our expectations. Life is easier that way. And so, once the halo is attached, we do our best to ignore and explain away indiscretions that might compromise our impression. However, a good reputation is less durable than a bad one. Studies show that it requires many more good behaviors to alter a bad image than it does bad behaviors to alter a good image. Then again, studies also show that it takes fewer bad behaviors to establish a bad reputation in the first place. In other words, good reputations are difficult to acquire but easy to lose. Bad reputations are easy to acquire and difficult to lose.[21]

It's no surprise that persuasion experts dedicate exorbitant resources to developing and maintaining an image of trustworthiness. A trusted brand or store name is priceless. The name itself becomes a mental shortcut for consumers, and even the most compulsive data gatherers among us need shortcuts. It's estimated that some fifty thousand new products come out each year. Forrester Research, a marketing research company, calculates that children have seen almost six million ads by the age of sixteen.[22] An established brand name helps us cut through this volume of information. It signals we're in safe territory. No need to bother with details.

"The real suggestion to convey," advertising leader Theodore MacManus observed in 1910, "is that the man manufacturing the product is an honest man, and the product is an honest product, to be preferred above all others."[23] One of MacManus's competitors, the equally legendary adman Raymond Rubicam, cashed in on this wisdom when he devised one of the most successful of early advertising slogans, for his client Squibb: "The priceless ingredient of every product is the honor and integrity of its maker." Rubicam's slogan was rated one of the three greatest of the first half of the twentieth century in a poll conducted by the industry magazine *Printers' Ink*.[24] A contemporary advertiser, Roy Spence of the GSD&M Agency, puts it even more squarely: "What you stand for as a brand is as important as what you sell, because everybody's selling the same thing."[25]

But the very people who have the most to gain by conveying trust often have the toughest time at it. A 2004 Gallup poll asked people to rate the honesty and ethical standards of people from various occupational groups on a five-point scale from "very high" to "very low." The following table shows the percentage of respondents who rated each group as "high" or "very high" on honesty.

Occupation	Honest
Nurses	79%
Druggists, pharmacists	72%
Military officers	72%
Medical doctors	67%
Police officers	60%
Clergy	56%
Judges	53%
Day care providers	49%
Bankers	36%
Auto mechanics	26%
Local officeholders	26%
Nursing home operators	24%
State officeholders	24%
TV reporters	23%
Newspaper reporters	21%
Business executives	20%
Lawyers	18%
Congressmen	10%
Advertising practitioners	10%
Car salesmen	9%

Source: Gallup Poll, November 19–21, 2004

If you're a nurse or a pharmacist, persuasion comes easily. Most people are primed to believe that you have their best interests at heart and will accept your message relatively uncritically. As the actor Spencer Tracy once said, "Just know your lines and don't bump into the furniture." But if you're in sales or advertising or another profession low on the list, creating a context of trust is a challenge. You're up against an inherent contradiction. How do you convince someone you're honest and unbiased while at the same time trying to sell them something for your profit?

The following are a few strategies those seeking your trust might use.

Testimonials and Endorsements

In the testimonial, a satisfied customer testifies about how terrific the product or person is. The technique goes back to the earliest days of advertising, when satisfied customers might be shown describing how some patent medicine cured their lifelong battle with "nerves" or how Dr. Scott's Electric Hair Brush healed their baldness ("My hair [was] falling out and I was rapidly becoming bald, but since using the brush a thick growth of hair has made its appearance, quite equal to that I had before previous to its falling out," reported a satisfied customer in an 1884 ad for the product).

An effective testimonial not only loads the context with credibility but also applies the principle of social proof. In the absence of further information, we look to how others behave to decide what's correct. It's the power of conformity. If other people parked their cars on this street, it must mean it's allowed. Everyone is whispering, so I will, too. All things being equal, we follow the crowd. Clothes, habits, tastes—nearly every human social behavior—are susceptible to the principle. Social proof is especially effective when it comes from people we identify with or want to emulate. If "nine out of ten screen stars care for their skin with Lux toilet soap,"[26] as the company used to advertise, who are we peons to argue?

Nowadays, the testimonial has evolved into its own cottage industry: the omnipresent business of product endorsements. The most effective endorsements come from an established, trustworthy source who clearly has no personal stake in the product. The reason C. Everett Koop was taken so seriously when he promoted condom use not only reflected his reputation as a medical authority but also his objectivity. After all, Koop was an openly evangelical Christian. It didn't take a genius to figure out that recommending birth control paraphernalia wouldn't score Koop many points with his religious colleagues. In fact, Koop was quickly and fiercely attacked by the religious right for his stance. But what he lost in the way of support from these groups was countered by how greatly his reputation as a man of honor was enhanced in other circles. If this wasn't an apolitical and incorruptible scientist, then who was?

In the publishing business, it's become a given that nothing sells more books than a recommendation from Oprah Winfrey. Oprah is effective both because she's extremely well connected and the people she connects to trust her. Publishers would gladly invest huge sums to obtain Oprah's seal. But the catch is that the seal loses its value as soon as it can be bought.

Few companies, however, are as fortunate to find squeaky-clean spokespeople like Koop and Oprah, so they're forced to find other ways to convey integrity. A simple solution is to just go out and pay for an endorser with a trustworthy reputation and an honest face. But the moment money gets involved, there's that contradiction: Why should people trust that a person getting paid to say something really believes what she or he is saying?

One clever resolution to this predicament is seen in what some still consider the greatest of all testimonial campaigns. In 1924, the advertisers for Pond's Cold Cream convinced Mrs. O. H. P. Belmont, the established matron of New York society and a prominent feminist to boot, to vouch for their product in exchange for a donation to her favorite charity. The company built on the Belmont ad by obtaining other "great lady" endorsements, women from around the world who were "Distinguished in the society of five nations," according to one company headline. "They trust their beauty to the same sure care." An ad in the *Ladies' Home Journal* with the queen of Romania attracted 9,435 coupon replies; another with Mrs. Reginald Vanderbilt pulled in 10,325 responses; and the duchess de Richelieu went over the top with 19,126.[27]

In a variation on this approach, the product and endorser are linked to a common nonprofit cause. In a successful 1980s campaign, for example, the Ogilvy & Mather advertising company set out to alter the faceless image of International Paper Company. Rather than promoting the company's product directly, the agency published a series of op-ed style essays by different established authors under the title "The Power of the Printed Word." One column, for example, was a two-page essay by Kurt Vonnegut titled "How to Write with Style." Vonnegut advised writers to "find a subject you care about," "sound like yourself," and "say what you mean to say." It sounded like a sermon on honesty and integrity. The net results: Kurt Vonnegut didn't compromise his reputation for artistic purity, International Paper built an image of trustworthiness and good citizenship, Vonnegut got paid, and International Paper sold more paper.

Business consultant Camille Lavington advises her clients to involve themselves with philanthropic organizations, not just as donors but as active participants. It not only generates a virtuous image, as Lavington learned through personal experience; it can also lead to other, unexpected good fortune:

> The opportunities that can come from participating in a philanthropic organization are astonishing. One unlikely example is the time I met the Dalai Lama as a direct result of my involvement with an international charity. The people you meet through charity work tend to invite you to take advantage of their personal and business association. If they're off to meet the Dalai Lama, you might be granted an audience. If tonight's dinner guest is the CEO of a company you long to work for, you might get the informal interview of a lifetime.[28]

Even when a product spokesperson has obvious commercial motives, there are ways to solicit trust. Michael Jordan's agent goes to considerable expense to make it known his client only endorses products he sincerely believes in. (Research shows, in fact, that a celebrity's reputation of trustworthiness is negatively related to the number of products he endorses.)[29] Jordan, it is claimed, would never endorse just for the money. With this established, who better to advise us gym rats that Gatorade really works? And Wheaties. And you mean I can have a body like Mike's and still eat at McDonald's? Ball Park hot dogs, too? If you want to be like Mike badly enough, you buy in.

There is also a rather disingenuous version of the celebrity endorsement in which celebrities promote a product without revealing that they're being paid to do so. Prescription drug companies, in particular, have been accused of this disturbingly popular practice. In a typical recent case, the actress Lauren Bacall gave a rare interview on the NBC *Today* program during which she told the audience about a friend who'd recently gone blind from an eye disease called macular degeneration. "It's just—it's frightening because it—it can happen very suddenly," she observed in the March 2002 interview. Fortunately, Bacall told the audience, there is a new drug on the market, Visudyne, that can treat the disease. Neither Bacall nor NBC mentioned that Novartis, the maker of Visudyne, was paying Bacall to tell her story. Over the past year, dozens of celebrities have been paid similarly high fees by drug companies to appear on talk shows and morning news programs to reveal intimate details about the ailments they or their friends have suffered. The celebrity then plugs a brand-name drug without usually revealing his or her financial ties to the drug's manufacturer.[30]

Celebrity endorsements are a frequent feature in commercials aimed at children. The practice has aroused considerable ethical concern, and research shows that the concern is every bit warranted. In a 1984 study funded by the Federal Trade Commission, over four hundred children aged eight to fourteen were shown one of various commercials for a model racing set. Some of the commercials featured an endorsement from a famous race car driver, some included real racing footage, and others included neither. Children who watched the celebrity endorser not only preferred the toy cars more but were convinced the endorser was an expert about the toys. This held true for children of all ages. In addition, they believed the toy race cars were bigger, faster, and more complex than real race cars they saw on film. They were also less likely to believe the commercial was staged.[31]

Sometimes implicit endorsements are commandeered from trusted dead people. The law prohibits anyone from using the unauthorized image of a living person for commercial reasons. The deceased, however, are pretty much fair game. The Apple Computer company capitalized heavily on this legal loophole in its extremely successful "Think Different" campaign. We saw ads showing icons of integrity and purity—people like Albert Einstein, Pablo Picasso, Jackie Robinson, and Mahatma Gandhi—under the "Think Different" tag line. Gandhi used a Mac? Apple never said so. They simply pictured him on the same page, thus implying he shared Apple's philosophy. As we heard in a voice-over for one television spot, "Here's to the crazy ones, the misfits, the rebels, the troublemakers, the round pegs in the square holes . . . because the people who are crazy enough to think they can change the world are the ones who do." Implying, of course, that Steve Jobs and the rest of the Apple crew are made of the same stuff as Einstein, Gandhi, and the rest of the gang. The campaign, which was developed as the company was entering bankruptcy, was an acrobatic display of spin control: "We're not going broke because of an inadequate product," they implied, "but because we won't sell out to convention."

The "Think Different" campaign was also an interesting solution to another Herculean advertising contradiction: blatantly telling people what to do ("Buy Apple") while at the same time urging them to think for themselves. It reminds me of the scene in Monty Python's movie *The Life of Brian*, when the mistaken messiah pleads to his crowd of misguided followers, "Don't follow me! Don't follow anyone! Think for yourselves! . . . You are all individuals," and the crowd replies in unison: "We are all individuals!"[32]

Presenting Propaganda as Education

Another route to believability is to disguise propaganda as objective information. This is also tricky if the customer knows the salesman's livelihood depends on making the sale. One straightforward solution is the "An educated consumer is our best customer" routine. (This is the actual motto of Syms discount clothing stores, the pioneers of the "brand names for less" chains.) The salesman conveys the impression that he's not trying to sell you something you don't want but merely wants to educate you about your options. An implicit message here is that being informed is in everyone's best interest—a win-win, as they say in pop psychology—because they're confident that when all the cards are on the table more than enough consumers will conclude theirs is the best choice. Since confidence signifies expertise, using this approach conveys authority and integrity, too.

The majority of retail salespeople are a far cry from the slick stereotype. They're mostly young, inexperienced walk-ons, working on a fixed salary, with no personal stake in whether you do or don't make a purchase. Management sometimes exploits this situation by making it appear that the salesperson is an ally of the customer—that the salesperson and, by extension, the store, is your friend. The training manual given to new sales representatives by the retail giant United Colors of Benetton, for example, teaches this: "Selling is actually a way of serving others. By helping your customers find what they want and need, you are creating solutions to existing problems."[33] One doubts that the stockholders for Benetton share this altruistic vision of their organization. Ironically, however, the salesmen's very naïveté and inexperience may make it seem their message really is delivered in the spirit of education.

Sophisticated sales professionals, particularly those who work on commission, face an uphill battle to gain the customer's trust. But even they may try the "salesman as educator" strategy. When I sold cars, for example, one agency instructed us to introduce ourselves as "automotive specialists." Another agency said to introduce ourselves as "product consultants." The sales manual for another company instructed us: "If [the] customer tells you they do not want to be bothered by a salesperson, your response is 'I'm not a salesperson, I'm a product consultant. I don't give prices or negotiate with you. I'm simply here to show you our inventory and help you find a vehicle that will fit your needs.'" Needless to say, we never mentioned that our salaries were almost completely based on commission.

Presenting Propaganda as News

The line between education and propaganda has become especially blurry in one of cable television's more surreal cultural contributions— the peculiarly named infomercial. Long-form commercials were banned back in the 1960s when the FCC was trying to limit television advertising time. But deregulation under the Reagan administration, coupled with the boom in cable TV access, changed all that, paving the way for today's multibillion-dollar infomercial market. The aim of a good infomercial is to blend with the surroundings, to make it look more like a news show or a documentary or a home movie than a contrived commercial. Sometimes the presentation uses a talk show format in which we watch the company spokesperson being interviewed by the show's "host." There are audiences, often dressed in T-shirts sporting the company logo, who applaud enthusiastically when the product operates with distinction—when the latest golf club outperforms the Big Bertha or the Aura car wax is still shining even after the hood of the Rolls-Royce is set on fire. We see testimonials, celebrity drop-ins, "scientific" research. Perhaps the most disorienting blurring of reality occurs in infomercials that pause for commercial breaks, during which we're usually told how to order the product. "We'll be back," the narrator promises us, deadpan.[34]

Children, as the FTC study showed, are particularly prone to confuse staged performance with reality. In a study of "host selling," seven- to eight-year-old children viewed either a Fruity Pebbles Flintstone or a Smurfberry Crunch cereal commercial. For half the Flintstone group, the commercial was inserted into an actual Flintstone program; the other half saw it embedded in a Smurfs cartoon. Likewise, the Smurfs group had their commercial inserted into either a Flintstones or Smurfs cartoon. Results showed that children were more impressed by the product when the character from the same show appeared in the commercial. It also produced more difficulty distinguishing between the commercial and the regular program.[35]

These findings underscore the potency and danger of the increasingly common practice of having familiar entertainment characters double up as product pitchmen in children's advertisements. Children don't understand what it means when Fred Flintstone has sold out. Even PBS has gotten into the act. McDonald's and Burger King not only underwrite the popular toddler-oriented *Teletubbies* show, but McDonald's recently distributed stuffed-toy versions of the four Teletubby characters in Happy Meals. *Sesame Street* characters are splashed on boxes of Count Chocula cereal.[36] To Children, it's all a big, confusing infomercial.[37]

Coloring the Choices

Many studies show that communicators who present both sides of an argument—both for and against their agenda—are perceived as less partial and more trustworthy. It's especially effective to give the impression they're arguing against your own self-interest. But how to do this and at the same time sell their product is another thorn in the advertiser's inherent contradiction.

Henry Kissinger, when he was secretary of state, believed he could make better policy decisions than his boss, Richard Nixon. But Kissinger's prescribed role was supposedly confined to gathering information and carrying out his boss's orders. Making significant decisions by himself would be perceived as insubordination by the notoriously insecure president. Kissinger liked to say that his solution was to always present three or four choices to Nixon, but to "color the choices" and frame them so his own preference always stood out as the best. "The absence of alternatives clears the mind," Kissinger observed.

The Kissinger approach is common among professors writing letters of recommendation. When there's a preferred candidate, you want to emphasize everything about the person that makes them special. But reference letter readers are well aware that no one's perfect, so focusing solely on the applicant's positive qualities can make your assessment appear nonobjective and even manipulative. On the other hand, applicants usually face a very competitive market, so any unflattering information about your candidate can spell doom. To resolve this dilemma, effective letter writers often include negative information about the candidate that is either trivial (e.g., "Mr. DeNiro had difficulty concentrating on studies his first semester in junior college, probably because he'd just returned from his highly decorated mission in the Gulf War, but he has straight As since then") or is really a compliment disguised as a shortcoming ("The only criticism I have about Mr. Alger is he often tries too hard" or "I sometimes wish Mr. Gehrig weren't so modest about his accomplishments").

The Norman Mailer Technique

A related strategy is one perfected by Norman Mailer. Some of Mailer's most poignant writings emphasize his personal flaws—how he is self-centered, arrogant, egotistical—with such perceptive, naked acumen that the reader is left marveling over this courageous man's self-insight and honesty. In the process, we conveniently forget how self-centered, arrogant, and egotistical Mailer is.

A variation on the Mailer technique is becoming increasingly popular among political candidates with embarrassing secrets from their past—drug use and extramarital sexual encounters are the most common bombshells. Many are now choosing to reveal their youthful mistakes before their adversaries do. These self-revelations steal potential thunder from the opposition and, if the confessions are executed skillfully, the most enduring image we're left with is that the candidate is honest and forthcoming and—think Hugh Grant here—that he's a regular, vulnerable person, just like the rest of us.

The best way to overcome objections is to address them before they occur. When someone says, "You're not going to believe this," he's trying to defuse your disbelief in what he's about to say. If someone says, "This may sound silly," it establishes license to say something silly. This is the power of prepersuasion.[38]

Presentation Style

The style of presentation can be critical. People who speak confidently, as we've seen, are perceived as more credible. Nonverbal cues are also important. Studies show that trial witnesses who stare their questioner straight in the eye instead of looking away are not only perceived to be more authoritative, but also more honest.[39] Even nonvoluntary responses can convey meaning: No worthy marketer will forget how much Richard Nixon's sweaty brow and heavy beard cost him in his television debates with John Kennedy.

The Peer

Imagine you read an ad that claims a new restaurant has the best food in your city. Now imagine a friend tells you this new restaurant has the best food in the city. Whom are you more likely to believe?

Surveys show we turn to people around us for many decisions. A 1995 poll found that 70 percent of Americans rely on personal advice when selecting a new doctor. The same poll found that 53 percent of moviegoers are influenced by the recommendation of a person they know.[40] In another survey, 91 percent said they're likely to use another person's recommendation when making a major purchase.[41]

Persuasion professionals are, of course, well aware of data like these. They're usually, in fact, the ones paying for the surveys. As a result, they may try to disguise their message as word of mouth from your peers. For example, Cornerstone Promotion, a leading marketing firm that advertises itself as under-the-radar marketing specialists, might hire children to log into chat rooms and pretend to be fans of one of their clients, or pay students to throw parties where they subtly ciculate marketing material among their classmates.[42]

Advertisers apply a more subtle approach. A recent ad for a new Apple laptop computer, for example, began with the headline "The best advertising is word of mouth." The ad then listed statements from journalists and other apparently neutral sources claiming how much they loved the new computer. You half expected to see the ad signed by the "Citizens for Apple Computers Committee."

In 1992, the Saturn automobile company sponsored a two-day "customer enthusiasm" event—the "Saturn Homecoming"—at its plant in Spring Hill, Tennessee. The event drew more than thirty thousand supporters from all over the country. Out of this, the company created a series of ads showing the enthusiasts milling around the factory, socializing with workers, touring the facilities, and giving the appearance that they and the company were one big, happy family. Some subsequent Saturn commercials added old-fashioned product testimonials. But, unlike the usual glitzy car ads that show testimonials from race car drivers or famous and gorgeous people, the Saturn testimonials were from customers. "And not just any customers," observed

John Yost, one of the executives who developed the ads, "but customers that actually acted and behaved like real people."[43]

Another series of Saturn ads showed company employees seeming to converse informally with the viewer, mostly to tell us they felt as much a part of the Saturn "family" as anyone. In one typical spot we see a smiling worker named Aldon Smith saying, "Here we don't have management and we don't have labor. We have teams. And we have what you call consensus. Everything's a group decision." Cousin Aldon later lets us know that money is the least of the reasons he's building Saturns. "You work through breaks and you work through lunch," he says. "You're here all hours and even sometimes Saturdays. And you don't mind. Because no one's making you do it. It's just that here you can build cars the way they were meant to be built."[44] It all sounds so much like a family business that you almost forget Aldon gets paid by General Motors. The Saturn campaign, crafted by Hal Riney & Partners, was named one of the top twenty ad campaigns from 1980 to 2000 by *Adweek*.[45]

The Maven

More persuasive yet, however, is to involve peers face-to-face. Rather than overinvesting in formal advertising, businesses may plant seeds at the grassroots level, hoping that consumers themselves will then spread the word to each other. The seeding process begins by identifying so-called information hubs—individuals the marketers believe can and will reach the most other people.

The seeds may be planted with established opinion leaders. Software companies, for example, give advance copies of new computer programs to professors they hope will recommend it to students and colleagues. Pharmaceutical companies regularly provide travel expenses and speaking fees to researchers willing to lecture to health professionals about the virtues of their drugs. Hotels give travel agents free weekends at their resorts in the hope that they'll later recommend them to clients seeking advice.

The most influential information hubs, however, often connect on an informal, word-of-mouth level. There's a Yiddish word, *maven*, that refers to a person who's an expert or a connoisseur, as in a friend who knows where to get the best price on a sofa or the coworker you can turn to for advice about where to buy a computer. This is the type of person who "likes to initiate discussions with consumers and respond to requests," observes marketing professor Linda Price, a pioneer in the burgeoning field of maven research. "They like to be helpers in the marketplace. They distribute coupons. They take you shopping. They go shopping for you. . . . They distribute about four times as many coupons as other people. This is the person who connects people to the marketplace and has the inside scoop on the marketplace. They know where the bathroom is in retail stores. That's the kind of knowledge they have."[46]

Mavens are marketer's dreams. "Reach the right bird and the whole flock will follow," *Barron's* tells its advertisers. Mavens are these birds. They (1) know a lot of people; (2) communicate a great deal with people; (3) are more likely than others to be asked for their opinions; and (4) enjoy spreading the word about what they know and think.[47] Most important of all, they're trusted. Mavens aren't professional salespeople. They're more like altruists who genuinely want to help their fellow consumers—people like Betty, with her Pampered Chef party.

Likability

If we know that celebrities like Michael Jordan and Bill Cosby aren't really experts, and that they're being paid to say what they're saying, why do their endorsements sell so many products? Ultimately, it's because we like them. And, more than any single quality, we trust people we like. Roger Ailes, a public relations adviser to Presidents Reagan and the elder Bush, observed: "If you could master one element of personal communication that is more powerful than anything . . . it is the quality of being likeable. I call it the magic bullet, because if your audience likes you, they'll forgive just about everything else you do wrong. If they don't like you, you can hit every rule right on target and it doesn't matter."

Likability drives persuasion from many directions. To begin with, we strive to identify with these people. This is much of the appeal of celebrities. We're also more likely to respect and trust people we like. These are also the people whose approval we value most, so we do our best to please them—by conforming to their expectations and obeying their requests. Finally, it's convenient to be susceptible to people we like. When we need advice or a reality check, they're the ones it's often easiest for us to approach.

Figuring what makes a communicator likable is, of course, a complex matter. It's why image consultants like Roger Ailes are paid so much. But there are some basic rules. For example, we clearly prefer people who are physically attractive. In fact, we prefer them to a disturbing extent: various studies have shown we perceive attractive people as smarter, kinder, stronger, more successful, more socially skilled, better poised, better adjusted, more exciting, more nurturing, and, most important, of higher moral character—all this based on no other information than their physical appearance.[48]

We're more prone to like and trust people we know personally. In a 1999 *New York Times*/CBS News poll, 63 percent of those interviewed said you "can't be too careful" in dealing with "most people" and 37 percent said "most people would try to take advantage of you if they got a chance." But in the same survey, respondents said they would expect 85 percent of the people they "know personally" to try to be fair.[49] Trusting one's friends, of course, makes perfect sense. But we sometimes infer personal connections based on rather incidental similarities. Experiments by Jerry Burger and his colleagues have found we're more likely to comply with a request from a person who shares our first name, has similar fingerprints, or even has the same birthdate as our own.[50] Salespeople, of course, are well aware of the power of establishing personal connections. Why do you think they so often turn out to have a friend from your hometown, or children the age of yours, or are sure they've met you before?

Even big companies want you to be their pal. This is nicely articulated in confidential documents from the recent "My McDonald's" advertising campaign created by the giant fast-food chain. McDonald's was facing a number of marketing problems, most notably a flight of customers to competitors like Burger King and Wendy's that was cutting into its profit margins. "More customers are telling us that McDonald's is a big company that just wants to sell . . . sell as much as it can," one executive wrote in a confidential memo. To counter this perception, McDonald's called for ads directed at making customers feel the company "cares about me" and "knows about me," to make customers believe McDonald's is their "trusted friend." A corporate memo introducing the campaign explained: "[Our goal is to make] customers believe McDonald's is their 'Trusted Friend.' Note: this should be done without using the words 'Trusted Friend.'" Theoretically, of course, there's something admirable about a huge company holding out its hand in fraternal trust. The sincerity of the gesture, however, is compromised by a message in bold red letters on the first page of the memo proclaiming: "ANY UNAUTHORIZED USE OR COPYING OF THIS MATERIAL MAY LEAD TO CIVIL OR CRIMINAL PROSECUTION."[51]

My Career Selling Cutco Knives

A salesperson who conveys the triad of trust can be difficult to resist. There are companies whose very structures, in fact, seem created to take advantage of the principle. One of the cleverest—and most exploitive—systems I've observed is practiced by the Cutco Cutlery Company. Cutco describes itself as the largest manufacturer and marketer of high-quality kitchen cutlery and accessories in the United States. There seems little reason to question this assertion. But it's their sales process that's worth examining. I'd heard so much about this system, in fact, that I decided to look in on them firsthand by training to be one of their salesmen.[52]

Cutco uses no formal advertising. It operates solely through door-to-door salespeople. Most are short-term recruits lured by come-ons like "earn easy extra cash," "flexible hours," and "no experience necessary." You may have seen their ads on public bulletin boards, telephone poles, or as chronic fixtures in the employment classifieds. When I called for an interview, I was told the job involved absolutely no telemarketing (a stretch of the truth), no door-to-door sales (a bigger stretch), and wasn't based on commissions (a lie).

On the surface, the Cutco technique seems little different from that of the classic door-to-door salesperson of the past, perhaps best epitomized by the Fuller Brush Man. But what distinguishes the Cutco salesperson is that unlike his predecessors, he never makes a cold call. (*Cold call* is a sales term for a solicitation in which the salesperson has no introduction to the prospect and/or where the prospect has no known need for the product.) Every contact is grounded in a trusted referral.

The referral process is activated from the beginning. Our first homework assignment during sales training—what our teacher touted as "the most important assignment you'll ever do"—was to draw up a list of at least two hundred people we know. "If you put your mind to it, you'll be surprised at how many names you can come up with," he told us. "Use your address book, yearbooks, club rosters, church lists." For added motivation, the assignment was made into a contest. (I learned over the course of training that this wasn't particularly special. Cutco turned every sales task into a contest.) The next morning we compared lists. My cotrainee Amanda, who came up with 339 names, was declared the winner. She got a free potato peeler and the right to sit in a cushy leather chair the rest of the day. None of us, however, came close to what our instructor said was the all-time Cutco record— 3,042 names—set just two weeks before.

Next we were asked to put marks next to the people on our list who were homeowners (H), aged thirty to forty-five (A), and married (M). This process is what's known in sales as "qualifying" the customer. We then circled the ten "HAMs" we thought would be our best customers and wrote them into our "First People to See List." These would be our initial "practice" appointments. As you'd expect, many recruits felt awkward about selling to friends and family. The instructors and sales managers know this and were prepared to ease our discomfort. Christopher Boudreau, who worked several months for Cutco, recalls the explanation he received.

"Don't you believe these knives are a quality product?" his supervisor asked.

"Yes," Boudreau answered.

"Wouldn't you be doing your family and friends a favor by showing them these products, especially if there's no sales pressure?" the supervisor pointed out.

"Um . . ."

When a costudent in my training group expressed reluctance, our instructor asked, "If you started working in a restaurant, wouldn't you want to tell people you like about it, if it's a good product?" The instructor then reasoned, "If they buy, it's a good deal. If not, they get a good education. They'll see a salesman from Cutco eventually. It's better for both of you to mess up with a person you know."

We were given a script for phoning for appointments. Selling knives was to be downplayed. "The reason I'm calling," our script read, "is I need your help. I just started a new job and as part of my training I need to put on some training appointments and get your opinion on something. I'm doing it for training so you don't have to spend any money or buy anything. I need to have (x number of) appointments by (specify date)." We were told to "avoid words such as 'marketing,' 'selling,' 'knives,' 'demonstration,' 'presentation.'" If the customer asked, "How long will it take?" we were told to answer: "It doesn't take long at all. I'll be in and out before you know it."

This pretense continued when we went to the customer's house. "I'm here to get experience and to improve my communication skills," we were told to say. But before showing the knives, our manual instructed, we were supposed to add: "As I mentioned on the telephone, this is a training appointment and you don't have to get anything. However, I am allowed to let you get something if you really like it. When you see some things you like, let me know." None of this was deception, it was explained to us. After all, "It's not really practice unless the customer could buy if they wanted to," our manual stated.

Cutco hopes these first presentations to your inner circle will generate sales. More important, however, it activates the referral process. Before leaving, we were required to get the customer to refer ten to fifteen of *his* or *her* family and friends. And when these new individuals were called upon, we were instructed to have them, too, list ten to fifteen people.

Cutco explained the importance of referrals in the training manual:

> Names are very important to your business. If you follow this simple program, you will always have a fresh, abundant supply of people to see. Getting names starts with your very first presentation. You must develop an attitude and understanding that names are money! Every time you get just one additional name, you have automatically increased your income. It is a proven sociological fact that the average American knows hundreds of people by name. We are looking for 3% to 5% of those.

We also received scripts for eliciting referrals. Another former Cutco salesperson, psychology student Joseph Gerber, explained his approach.[53] At the end of his sales presentation, Gerber would say: "I appreciate your taking the time to let me come by, [Dr. Levine], but the last part is where you can really help me. You've been so nice that I figured you'd be willing to help just a little bit more and your good friend [naming whoever referred me] said you would. The fact is that I only get credit if I show the product to people I've been personally referred to and, as you know, [Dr. Levine], I can only win the college scholarship [or the contest for a big bonus or a special vacation or whatever] if you decide to be nice enough and write down fifteen of your closest friends and relatives. In addition to helping me, I can submit your name into our monthly $1,000 shopping spree." For every five names the customer came up with, they were given an extra chance to win the shopping spree. If they hesitated, Gerber would point out, "Remember, these people don't have to buy anything. I'm just asking them to be nice enough to listen, like you have." He'd persist like this until they got out their address book and began writing down names. "Eventually, I get your fifteen names and phone numbers," he observed.

The salesperson sometimes turbocharges the process by asking the customer to phone ahead to the referral and tell them the salesperson will be contacting them. Sometimes the customer is even asked to qualify his or her referrals. "I'll ask you if the people on your list are married, wealthy, homeowners, live in the area, are over the age of thirty, and which household member is most likely to use Cutco products," Gerber says. "Believe it or not, most people would tell me everything about their friends and family. This only makes it easier for me to get them to buy something."

When we introduced ourselves to our friends' referrals, naturally, we were to present ourselves as friends of friends. Our manual gave us the following script:

> Hi, (name of customer). This is (name of salesperson). I don't think we've met, but I was visiting over with (name of referral source) the other day. Did she/he get a chance to tell you I was going to call? Well, (name of referral source) and I were talking and your name came up. He/she thought you might be nice enough to help me out.

We'd then go on to give the usual explanation of how we'd just started this job and were trying to improve our social skills and get some good experience. We'd been given an assignment to show people a product, and if we got enough people it would qualify us for some prize or trip or scholarship.

Once a Cutco salesman gets into your house, the odds of a sale are in his favor. Cutco statistics show that on average, half of all referrals result in appointments and 60 percent of appointments result in a sale. For every ten names he gets, in other words, the average rep will make three sales. "Leads equal presentations, presentations equal sales, and sales equal income," we were lectured during training.

I hear a lot of concern about so-called multilevel marketing (MLM) organizations in which friends sell products directly to their friends or recruit them as distributors. In Amway, for example, distributors are arranged by level such that "uplines" profit from the sales made by the "downlines" they "sponsor" (i.e., recruit). The more people you bring into the organization, and the more people the new ones bring in, the more money you earn.[54]

Multilevel marketing derives from the same geometry exploited by pyramid or Ponzi schemes. In a traditional Ponzi scheme, each investor recruits several new investors, each of whom in turn recruit several more investors. The organizer promises large profits to contributors by investing their money but actually uses their investments to pay off previous contributors. Since the number of investors increases exponentially at each level (if I recruit ten customers, who then each recruit ten customers, who then each recruit ten more, we're up to one thousand people in just three generations), those at the earliest levels stand to make huge profits. They entice new investors with their success stories, who entice a new round of investors with their success stories—until the well runs dry. The idea is named after Charles Ponzi, an Italian immigrant with a flair for geometry who, in 1920, used a scheme like this to bilk thirty thousand investors out of almost $10 million in seven months.[55]

The spread of reputations follows a similar process. Like monetary Ponzi schemes, they might begin on shaky grounds but, once established, grow exponentially through repetition. It is even true in the animal world. Mating season among the sage grouse, for example, is a competitive affair. The males gather in large groups, called leks, where they dance, strut, and puff up their inflatable chests, hoping to be chosen to inseminate the females. Most of them could just as well have stayed home, because it's usually one or two males holding court in the center of the lek who get most of the action. On average, 90 percent of the matings are performed by 10 percent of the males. Experiments with dummy females show that the reason so many females choose the same male is simply that other females are surrounding that male. They're copycats. Breaking from fashion can be costly. If a female picks an unpopular male, she increases the probability her sons will inherit their father's unpopularity. It creates a cascade effect in which the momentum builds with each occurrence: the more often a male is chosen, the more likely he'll be chosen by the next female.[56]

Humans aren't very different. Say you discover a leak under your sink and need to call a plumber. You look in the yellow pages, where you discover pages of listings for plumbers. How do you choose? You could select the most compelling ad. You're well aware, however, of the pitfalls in this approach. Or, you could call the local plumber's union or the Better Business Bureau. But you probably won't muster up the motivation to do that, either.

Instead, if you're like most people, you'll probably phone a friend for advice. The last time I needed a plumber I phoned my friend Lenny. Lenny told me he hadn't used a plumber lately, but his neighbor had just hired Plumber X and Lenny hadn't heard any complaints from his neighbor. For all I know, the neighbor hired Plumber X on the basis of a similarly vague recommendation from another friend. But Lenny's tip was all I needed or wanted to know. I called Plumber X, who charged a lot of money but fixed my sink. Now when someone calls me about plumbers, I tell them I just used Plumber X, who was recommended by a friend, and X wasn't cheap but he fixed my sink. If they call Lenny, he tells them he knows two people who've used Plumber X and hasn't heard complaints from either of them. Neither Lenny nor I have any idea how Plumber X compares to the competition. Nevertheless, Plumber X is currently a fixture (no pun intended) in our neighborhood with the reputation of being expensive but worth the cost. And Lenny builds points as a maven. It's what communication specialists call a self-perpetuating information feedback loop.

I certainly don't want to downplay the considerable dangers of MLMs and other monetary pyramids. But the consequences of organizations, like Cutco, that parlay trust and personal reputations are potentially even vaster. I assume the salesman is legitimate because my friend invited him into his house. And I'm even more confident when I learn my friend heard about the salesman from another friend. And so it goes. Has anyone checked the salesman's background? The company's? It's highly unlikely. And as each additional reference accumulates in the salesman's dossier, it becomes less likely anyone will. The salesman becomes accepted through familiarity, like a trusted brand name. Social proof begets social proof; and the process multiplies exponentially. Cutco says it's simply "selling by word of mouth." Maybe so, but there's a lot of ventriloquism manipulating those mouths.

The social pyramid process has proven extremely profitable for Cutco. Their sales force numbers as many as forty thousand people over the course of a year with an annual revenue, according to a 2005 report, of $182 million.[57] Their logo is built around the slogan "Building Relationships for 50 Years . . . One Family at a Time." As Charles Ponzi would tell you, those single families can add up quickly.

THREE

Killing You with Kindness

Or, Beware of Strangers Bearing Unexpected Gifts

Tada yori takai mono wa nai
[Nothing is more costly than something given free of charge].
—Popular Japanese saying

It often seems that people are the greediest of animals, that we're happiest when we get as much as we can while giving up as little as possible. It's not so. Research shows that most of us are usually driven by a sense of equity and fairness. When someone does something for us or gives us something, we feel obligated to do something for that person in return. The favor may create any of several feelings: gratitude, a sense of decency and social responsibility, or simple feelings of guilt. No matter which, it activates one of the most powerful of social norms, the reciprocity rule, whereby we feel compelled to repay, in equitable value, what another person has given to us.

Alan Gouldner, in his seminal study of the reciprocity rule, found that it appears in every culture.[1] "There is no duty more indispensable than that of returning a kindness," wrote Cicero. "All men distrust one forgetful of a benefit." For example, when Columbus first set foot in America he encountered people who'd been devoid of any cultural contact with Europeans or their ancestors for many tens of thousands of years, probably going back to the Mesolithic era. No one at those early meetings, however, needed to be instructed about the reciprocity rules. One of the very first activities Columbus and the Indians began was giving each other gifts. In colonial America the term *Indian gift* came to mean a gift for which you expected an equivalent one in return.[2]

Columbus's experience has been repeated in endless cross-cultural encounters.

Reciprocity is one of the oldest and most fundamental guides for human social interaction. It lays the basis for virtually every type of social relationship, from the legalities of business arrangements to the subtle exchanges within a romance. Without it, there can be no assuredness that if I give to you this time you'll give back the next time. And if there's no trust, there can be no trade. Given the evolutionary value of trade—between individuals, businesses, and governments—it's no wonder the law of reciprocity has become so strongly ingrained. It's been called the moral memory of humankind.

The reciprocity effect was first experimentally demonstrated in a classic study by social psychologist Dennis Regan. Regan had subjects work in pairs on a bogus task supposedly measuring art appreciation. One of the subjects, let's call him Andy, was actually a paid actor working as Regan's assistant. During a short rest period in the middle of the experiment, Andy left for a couple of minutes. For half the subjects (the gift group), Andy returned with two Cokes, handing one to the subject and keeping one for himself, explaining, "I asked him [the experimenter] if I could go get myself a Coke, and he said it was OK, so I brought one for you, too." For the other half (the control group), Andy returned without a gift. In both conditions, Andy later asked the subject to do him a favor. Andy said that he was selling raffle tickets for his high school back home and that he'd get a prize if he sold the most tickets. Would the subject be willing to buy one or more tickets? In clear support of the reciprocity theory, Andy sold almost twice as many tickets to people he'd given a free Coke earlier.

Most surprising, however, was the power of the effect. In another part of the study, Regan varied the likability of the actor. Here, the receptionist left on an errand just as the subject and Andy were waiting for the "experiment" to begin. The phone rang shortly later and, after several rings, Andy picked it up. In half the cases (the pleasant condition), Andy answered the call appropriately and politely. For the other half (the unpleasant condition), he acted obnoxiously, responding: "Nah, there's no secretary here. . . . Look, I don't work here, lady, for chrissake. . . . Just call later . . ." Andy hung up, clearly in midconversation, without saying good-bye.

It's well established, as we've seen, that people are more willing to do favors for people they like. It comes as no surprise then that Andy sold more tickets when he acted pleasantly. Here's what was remarkable, however: the importance of Andy's likableness paled in comparison to whether he'd given the subject an unsolicited gift. Whereas the free Coke almost doubled raffle sales, acting obnoxiously (compared to acting pleasantly) reduced sales by only about 20 percent. More telling yet, the free Coke had as much of an effect on ticket sales when Andy was an obnoxious person as when he was polite. In other words, when the need for reciprocity was aroused, it didn't matter whether they liked him or not. They "owed," and so they paid. Reciprocity can be a dictatorial force, and it can come in many shapes and sizes.[3]

Giri: Reciprocity, Japanese-Style

In some cultures, the reciprocity principle is even more influential. I stumbled headfirst into this realization a few years ago. I'd been making plans to spend several months as a visiting researcher at a university in Sapporo, Japan. The work arrangements had fallen nicely into place but questions about day-to-day living had me frightened. After all, I was a gaijin (the Japanese term for foreigner or, literally, outside person) heading into the abyss of not only an alien country, but a ridiculously expensive alien country. Complicating the pressures even more, I was traveling with my wife and young son. How would we survive without knowing the language and without going bankrupt?

But my hosts-to-be, in an astonishing display of Japanese-style graciousness and efficiency, came to the rescue. First they found us a university-owned apartment for our stay—for free, no less. Then they passed the hat among their friends and rounded up more than enough furniture and household paraphernalia to get us by. Our only cost was a cleaning crew (which was exorbitantly expensive but, boy, was that apartment clean). Mind you, these gifts were from people we'd never met before.

Soon after our arrival in Sapporo, we went shopping for a thank-you gift for my department chairman's wife, the woman who more than anyone was responsible for our very generous arrangements. Everything we considered, however, was shockingly expensive. One friend had suggested that being from California, we might consider giving our hosts a gift melon, a popular cantaloupe-type fruit that is frequently given as presents. The decent ones, however, turned out to start at close to $100 each, with the premium specimens selling for upwards of $500. After a few hours of discouraging shopping like this, we settled on flowers—a bottom-of-the-line, very simple bouquet of flowers.

I looked up the Japanese words for "It's not much, but please accept this small token," and, that evening, we presented our humble offering. Our hostess looked confused and, when she realized we were giving her a gift, shocked.

"Please wait," she pleaded, and ran back to find her husband. From the other room, we heard a hysterical conversation in Japanese. Obviously, we'd done something very wrong. But what?

"Cheapskate," my wife whispered to me. "I told you we should have popped for the roses."

After a few minutes, the couple calmed down and seemed to have arrived at a solution. They led us into the dining room and apologized profusely because what they were about to give us was *way* inferior to our bouquet of flowers. They then sliced each of us a fat helping of a really nice-looking melon. We were terribly embarrassed and began apologizing equally profusely for our flowers. After a couple of minutes of this competitive apologizing, we all shut up and ate our melons.

My wife and I left assuming the crisis was over. But we were way out of our league. Early the next morning, there was a knock on our door. Our hostess, now looking completely in command, proudly handed us three gift-wrapped boxes. She apologized, naturally, for the meager offerings she was insulting us with. The first box contained a set of books for my son, the second was a vase (no, it couldn't be that $150 piece we saw while shopping, could it?), and the third held the biggest bouquet of flowers I'd seen since my cousin Tessa's bat mitzvah. She then insisted we join her for lunch at a nice restaurant.

Think about this. A woman we barely knew—and not a particularly wealthy one, from what I could tell—had just given us well over a hundred dollars in gifts. I would have liked to believe it was because we were such a lovable family. But, it now seemed clear, this was a question of culture.

I phoned a bicultural friend, a former New Yorker named Howard, who'd been living in Japan for many years. Howard understood the situation right away. I'd apparently walked into one of the most powerful yet subtly defined of Japanese cultural norms: the principle of *giri*, or obligation. The group-oriented Japanese culture, my friend explained, is driven by rules about duty—duty to one's family, company, and country, and even culturally illiterate outsiders like me. These rules are written nowhere, but you won't find a Japanese person with a morsel of maturity who doesn't understand them. Faltering on one's *giri* is a serious offense that carries the stiffest of Japanese penalties: shame and rejection.

The particular *giri* I had created in my hosts carried a double whammy. To begin with, because I was a foreign guest—in fact, a guest at their university—they had an obligation to treat me with first-rate Japanese hospitality, which is, in fact, an enormous standard. (To my everlasting gratitude, our hosts and their colleagues met this obligation in spades, over and again, during our months in Japan.)

But the trickier problem my gift had created was connected to status—that most explosive of Japanese minefields for the gaijin to maneuver. Howard explained that because my host was also my department chair, protocol dictated that he and his wife make a public display of giving more to us than we gave to them. Always. To call this "protocol" would be a severe understatement. In Japan, protocol is not a delicate suggestion. If it had a voice in Japanese, it would probably sound less like Emily Post than Tony Soprano banging at your door. In Japan, protocol *demands* obedience.

Any favors my hosts received, uninvited or not, were expected to be repaid several times over. Our little bouquet, which was intended as a casual offering of goodwill, became their burden. It is revealing that the Japanese word for obligation, *on*, also means "a debt."[4] (These debts are so frequent and compelling in Japanese society that there are secondhand gift stores to recycle the presents that are passed around.)

We were one sorry group of guests. First we put our hosts through outrageous trouble to set us up in an apartment. Then, as our way of saying thank you, we toss them a hot potato that would cost them more to get out of their hands than they could probably afford. No wonder their predecessors closed Japan to water buffalo foreigners like my family for centuries.[5]

"Now," Howard explained, "you have two choices. You can offer an old-fashioned American humble pie—bow down low and say 'I'm not worthy' a few times. They'll bow lower. If you don't move, it will end your exchange right there. Or . . ."—Howard broke into a big smile—"you could play dumb, generous gaijin—which you are, anyway—and up the ante with a few more rounds of gifts. In a few days, you could be millionaires."

Howard was, of course, kidding with his last suggestion. (Weren't you, Howard?) But, culturally speaking, he was absolutely correct. I'd set the stage for what could have been the biggest sale of my life. I controlled my hosts like marionettes on strings. Pull this cord and they'd relax. Tug on that one and they're out the door buying me gifts. And the irony was that I—a guy who usually can't control a dog—had worked this scheme without a hint of insight into what I was doing. Such is the insidious potential of the reciprocity rule.

The Free Lunch

Because the rules of reciprocity are unwritten, we may be unaware when the game is in operation. And any time people are unaware, we're subject to manipulation. Naturally, reciprocity has become a favorite tool of persuasion professionals.

One of the most common manipulations is to get the consumer to accept an unsolicited free gift. Consider the case of one of America's most curious business success stories, the International Society for Krishna Consciousness (ISKCON), better known as the Hare Krishnas. The Krishna movement had a relatively low-profile, 450-year tradition in India. That changed in 1965, however, when it was brought to the United States by Swami Prabhupada, a seventy-year-old devotee who had spent most of his life until then as A. C. Bhaktivedanta, the manager of a successful Indian pharmaceutical company. Although he arrived in the United States with neither money nor a following, Prabhupada used his skills to rapidly accumulate both. Two years after starting his first temple, on the Lower East Side of New York City, Prabhupada opened a second one in San Francisco. By 1970, there were 21 Krishna Centers in the United States and the movement had spread to Japan, Germany, Canada, England, and Australia. In 1982, at their peak, the number of centers had grown to 50 in the United States and over 175 worldwide, along with a string of farms, vegetarian restaurants, and other businesses.[6]

The Krishnas are, of course, in the business of religion. But what made their financial success so unique was that it mostly derived from small contributions from nonbelievers—donations for their book, an elaborate edition of the Bhagavad Gita, and magazine, *Back to Godhead*, or simply gifts of spare change. The Krishnas hit up passersby for these donations on the street, in shopping malls, on college campuses, and—their most infamous setting—at airports.

More noteworthy, still, was how they solicited these contributions. Even in the colorful sixties, the Krishnas were easy to spot. They dressed in bright saffron robes, leg wrappings, holy bells, and beads. Most of the males had their heads shaved (this was pre–Michael Jordan, when shaved heads were mostly limited to medical conditions). The Krishnas did the majority of their fund-raising in groups, all dancing and chanting the same mantra—"*Hare Krsna, Hare Krsna, Krsna Krsna, Hare Hare . . .*"—during which they appeared to be in a state of heavenly ecstasy, for hours on end. The Krishnas broke nearly every rule of persuasion. They lacked credibility and trustworthiness. They were clearly soliciting in their own self-interest. And, worst of all, they were low in attractiveness and likability; most passersby with money in their pockets found the Krishnas anywhere from noisy and strange to downright repulsive. They were so unpopular at first that many towns passed laws, many of which were later overturned, prohibiting their soliciting in certain areas.

With fund-raising initially a complete failure, the leadership called in professional sales consultants. A technique was devised: before asking passersby for money, the solicitor would hand them a free flower or, more often, go right up and pin one on their jackets. It was a graceful sixties act that turned out to be a stroke of sales genius. If the target tried to give the flower back, the Krishna always refused, kindly telling the person, "This is our gift to you." Only after the gift was accepted did the solicitor try to sell the target a book or magazine. With free gift in hand, many passersby now found it easier on themselves to hand over a contribution to the smiling devotee than to feel guilty every time they got a whiff of the flower. This gimmick made the Krishnas a wealthy organization.

Over time, inevitably, people caught on to the flower scam. Many targets began cynically walking past the solicitors and then tossing their flower into the nearest trash bin. Some resourceful Krishnas adapted cleverly to this turn of events. For a while in San Diego—which has a high concentration of military personnel and retirees—devotees turned to pinning little American flags on people's jackets. It was interesting to watch pedestrians freeze as they realized it was an American flag they'd almost thrown in the trash. As long as the gift was in their possession, the rule of reciprocity remained active.

The free-gift technique is used widely. As a little experiment, I recently decided to save my own unsolicited mail for two weeks. I conducted my study in early December, at the peak of the gift shopping season. Excluding newspaper-type fliers, my pile ended up just over a yard (thirty-eight inches) high. Most of these envelopes (just under thirty-one inches) contained one or more unsolicited gifts. They included, for example, a box of Christmas cards from a veteran's group, Claude Monet masterpiece cards from an Alzheimer's association, a ballpoint pen from an organization serving the handicapped, a book from a cystic fibrosis charity, lots of personalized address labels from lots of organizations, a penny from a federation for the blind ("Lisa wants *you* to have this shiny penny"), and a nickel from a school for special children ("Our retarded children desperately need your nickels"). (Some solicitations tried to grab me with the "winker" approach by poking fun at their competitors. One of my favorites was an antigift solicitation from a group that fights world poverty, which announced in large letters on the front of its envelope: "Enclosed: No Address Labels to Use, No Calendars to Look At.")

Open the newspaper or check a bulletin board and you'll find more people waiting to give you gifts than you'd know what to do with. Perhaps you'd like a free weekend vacation for sitting through a speech about buying into a time-share or a free hat or a case of soft drinks for test-driving a new car. "Robert V. Levine, bring this letter for admittance and receive, just for attending, a 50-piece tool kit, ABSOLUTELY FREE," read a typical recent invitation. These aren't bonuses you get for making a purchase but gifts you get just for considering a purchase. Hey, you've got a million friends out there.

Despite its evolutionary heritage, however, the free-favor strategy hardly guarantees an automatic sale. All the gift-giving competition on the market makes for a cynical group of consumers whose initial response to the offered present, unless it comes from someone they trust, is suspicion. As the Krishnas eventually learned, it's difficult to get a wary public to accept your gift in the first place. More challenging yet is to make people believe that the gift was delivered with anything in mind other than blatant manipulation. This doesn't mean the free-gift strategy is on the wane. For it to be effective, however, marketers need to stay a step ahead of the target's suspicions.

One solution to this problem is camouflage. Door-to-door vacuum cleaner salespeople, for example, may try to convince you that you'll be doing them a favor by accepting their gift. A saleswoman I encountered knocked on my door, cold call, and offered to demonstrate her remarkable machine by cleaning my house free of charge. I told her I had no interest in a new vacuum cleaner, didn't want to be a freeloader, and, so, respectfully declined her generous offer. She was ready for me. "Actually, I get paid for each demonstration," she said. "So you'd be doing me a favor to let me clean your house." I accepted her request. (This occurred before my Cutco training.) She spent the next half hour furiously cleaning corners of my house I'd never looked at before. Meanwhile, I was becoming increasingly uncomfortable watching her do my housework for free. But I couldn't see a graceful way to end it. By the time this hardworking, low-key saleswoman, a single mother of two young children the age of my own (it's amazing how many salespeople tell me they have children the same age as mine), brought out her brochures, my guilt was in full bloom. I didn't buy a vacuum cleaner. But I did purchase her cheapest product, a $20 bottle of carpet spot remover I'll never use. After all she'd done, I *had* to buy something. (She also cleverly applied the contrast principle—see the next chapter—by leaving a dirty strip across the middle of each room "just to show how well the vacuum works.")

Another challenge faced by practitioners of the reciprocity principle is to avoid creating an obligation that's too burdensome for their target to repay. This can lead to a persuasion problem we might call the "justification leak"—when, rather than reciprocating the persuader's offering, the target restores his self-image of fairness by simply rationalizing. For example, employers sometimes give substantial raises to workers with the intention of reinforcing their hard work and, more important, motivating them to work even harder. Studies show, in fact, that if the raise is large enough, it does activate a brief feeling of obligation to please the employer. In the long run, however, it rarely leads to more output. Instead, it encourages the workers to rationalize why they deserve the raise. They might, for example, tell themselves that their job is more difficult than they'd previously thought, or dwell on how little they'd been paid in the past. As a result, if the raise is too steep, and the justification leak isn't plugged, the initial favor can backfire. The persuader may create new standards of entitlement, subsequent disgruntlement, and, ultimately, lower production than before.

When applied with skill and subtlety, however, the free-gift strategy remains an extremely potent means of manipulation. "Despise the free lunch," warn Robert Greene and Joost Elffers in their book, *The 48 Laws of Power*. "What is offered for free is dangerous—it usually involves either a trick or a hidden obligation. What has worth is worth paying for. By paying your own way you stay clear of gratitude, guilt, and deceit." This is perhaps a bit overcynical, but, clearly, the reciprocity norm is a force you should watch out for.[7]

The Gift of Time

One of the most subtle but effective manipulations of the reciprocity norm involves gifts of time. We live in a culture where time is money. In a remarkable feat of measurement, humans have converted the most ambiguous and amorphous of all entities, time, into one of the most objectively calibrated of all commodities, money. I can tell you how many days, hours, and minutes of my time equals the value of any object, including the computer I'm typing on. Since time is an economic commodity, it can be bought, sold, traded, saved, and wasted. If my time is worth more than yours, it may be profitable for me to pay you to watch my children or clean my house or do my shopping. In some countries, there are people whose job it is to waste their own time for people who can afford to pay not to waste their own. If you need to obtain a visa in Mexico, for example, it usually requires lining up outside the consulate the night before to secure a viable position when the doors open the next morning. The well-off, however, will find professional waiters-for-hire (*gestores*) in front of the consulate who are willing, for the right price, to stand in your place overnight. An entire family can even be hired to wait in place of your own. You literally buy their time. In the United States, you can hire people to do your shopping, run your errands, pick up your children at school—virtually any task for which it's less expensive to buy someone else's time than to use your own.

When time is conceived as a commodity, it becomes fair game for the reciprocity rule. If you're made to feel you've been given someone's time, you feel obligated to give something in return. If this happens to be a sales situation, giving usually translates as buying. Otherwise, the customer has wasted the salesman's time.

Gifts of time are less transparent and, so, more readily accepted than tangible commodities. A salesman casually sidles up to you and asks if you need assistance. You're "just looking," perhaps, but the unhurried salesman follows you around, anyway. After a while you ask a question that leads him to expend more effort than you anticipated as he shows you product after product. If enough time passes, the norm of reciprocity sets in. "I really should buy something," you think. Otherwise you've taken advantage of this helpful person. You've stolen his time.

The reciprocity pressure is a function of the perceived value of the other's time. We feel more obligated if we've taken the time of the owner or a salesman working on commission than that of an employee paid by the hour. Time, importance, and value are tightly related in our culture. The more important a person, the more valuable his time. Mostly, this follows from the law of supply and demand. There's more demand for important people's time and, so, it's more expensive. The rule also works the other way around: the scarcer people's time, the more important they appear. The fee for a lawyer or a performer is enhanced by the simple fact that she's booked well in advance. This leads to even greater demand for her time, and so the cycle continues.

A good salesman may manipulate the perceived value of his time by creating the appearance that he's in demand. He'll make it known that he's taken time out from an important phone call or a critical meeting or canceled another appointment to make time for you. If the impression of scarcity is conveyed convincingly, you're left bearing the burden of the reciprocity norm.

The reciprocity norm is also activated when someone saves our time. If the maître d' lets you move to the front of the line, or a ticket scalper saves you from waiting in a line, it's understood they deserve something in return. When I lived in Brazil several years ago, I became all too familiar with a group of paraprofessionals known as *despachantes*, who serve as intermediaries between citizens with money and the endless bureaucratic red tape. To get an exit visa, for example, I'd have had to wait in several lines in several buildings. The entire process would have taken three weeks. The *despachante*, however, got me the visa in two days without my waiting on a single line. Similarly, if you need to renovate a building in New York City, you're likely to hire an appropriately named "expediter" to save you time and waiting in lines for a building permit. The fee for a *despachante* or an expediter is determined by how much time they save you.

When I was training to sell Cutco knives, we were taught delay tactics. You may recall how, on initial contact, we encouraged friendly referrals to let us visit their homes by telling them it wasn't really a sales call, that we'd get paid for simply giving a demonstration. Once arriving, however, we made it known that we felt it was our responsibility to show everything in our catalog. With this established, we'd prolong our presentation as long as possible. Along the way, we made it clear that we were paid on commission and, on top of that, could win prizes and scholarships for making sales. Finally, we demonstrated how much time our razor-sharp, ergonomically engineered tools would save the customer in their food preparation. In other words, we (1) gave them as much of our time as they'd accept; (2) let them know that our time was valuable—it's how we make a living; and (3) explained that we were doing all this to save them time. If it became clear, by the end of the presentation, that the customer wasn't going to buy one of our more expensive sets, we'd exploit his sense of fairness by offering him a compromise: perhaps he'd consider one of the less expensive stand-alone items, maybe our vegetable peeler (only $21) or pizza cutter ($26). By this time, we hoped, the increasingly guilt-ridden customer was thinking he really should buy something.[8]

Killing You with Kindness

Another gift that may slip under the radar is kindness. I observed an artful application of kindness-as-manipulation in, of all places, my neighbor Nancy's living room. The event was a "candle party," another Tupperware-type affair. Nancy, our "hostess," had invited nine of us to a presentation by representatives of a company that sold candles and candle paraphernalia—products billed in the company's brochure as the "the last affordable luxury." The candles, the company assured us, were of such high quality that "they're used at the White House and in soap operas."

The proceedings were conducted by two "consultants" from the company who worked the triad of trustworthiness expertly. Both were attractive and personable and, they told us, engaged to be married. The woman, whom I'll call Barbie, was extremely bubbly; she just *loved* meeting new friends at these events and she *adored* candles. Her fiancé—let's call him Ken—was the designated expert for all technical questions. When he explained how different oils and scents affect the behavior of heat and wax, it sounded like he'd discovered the fourth law of thermodynamics.

All nine guests were friends Nancy invited. Other than Ken, I was the only man in the room, a situation that drew many perplexed looks at first. I don't know how everyone else felt about my being there, but I couldn't have been more uncomfortable if it was a Tampax party. Fortunately, it wasn't long before my uniqueness lost its mystery, after which I was pretty much ignored. After the first few minutes, Ken and Barbie were addressing us as "you women."

Ken and Barbie let us know that their candles were much safer than those you'd buy off the shelf. Every fifteen minutes or so one of them recounted a story about an accident caused by cheaper brands. Barbie, for example, told how she and Ken were once putting on a party when a guest came running of the bathroom screaming that a votive candle (one of the stumpy ones) had caught fire. "Oh, Ken," Barbie continued, looking on the verge of tears, "you tell the rest." Ken then explained how he went into the bathroom and, in fact, found that the votive was burning like a torch and had set the doily under it on fire, too. He noticed right away that the candle was not, of course, one of theirs. It was apparently a cheap knockoff from a drugstore. As he was making this discovery, the evening's hostess and her young son ran in. The hostess apparently panicked and furiously tried to blow out the candle. Ken paused before going on with his story. He then lowered his voice and explained very sternly to us how he was fortunate enough to stop the woman in time, because blowing on a candle that is out of control can cause hot oil to fly everywhere. If the woman had exhaled, Ken observed, the hot oil would have gone directly into the child's face. I don't know about everyone else in the room, but my estrogen level was headed for the roof by then.

They related another story about a customer who nearly ruined her oak table with candle wax by blowing out the candle too hard. Many customers, we were told, complained about this problem. The perfect solution? A candle snuffer. It was only $23.95. ("Quite a bargain since it could prevent your furniture from getting ruined!")

Everything about the evening emoted knowledge, trust, and, more than anything, friendliness. Ken and Barbie were enthusiastic, knowledgeable, decent, amiable people, folks just like the rest of us. We knew, of course, they were earning money. But it was hard not to believe that they really wanted to be in that living room with us. It was as if they'd discovered these terrific candles at a party just like the one we were at tonight and became so inspired that they wanted to share the good news with as many worthy people as they could. Ken and Barbie didn't seem like *real* salespeople. They were more like friends advising friends. They were our candle mavens. By the end of the party, all of us—Ken and Barbie included—were exchanging phone numbers. The line between business and pleasure had become awfully fuzzy. Were these salespeople or friends? Was it a retail event or a party?

But the real sales pressure had little to do with the products. It played off guilt and social obligation. Nancy had obviously put care and money into the evening. There were drinks—wine, coffee, fancy mineral water—and a spread of beautiful hot and cold hors d'oeuvres. Everything about the situation called out, "Relax, you're at home, among tasteful friends."

We quickly learned how we could and should repay Nancy's hospitality. When Barbie began the presentation, one of her first topics was how hostesses receive free gifts and large discounts if their parties sell $200 in merchandise. If anyone had somehow missed the connection, Barbie added that this was "the same arrangement that Nancy has." The message was repeated again in our candle brochure with a bold-faced description of the hostess's deal. And again by Barbie at the close of her presentation. And once more in the *Candle Care Tips* brochure we took home. Even an insensitive water buffalo like me understood that anyone who didn't spend at least twenty-plus dollars (one-tenth of $200) was freeloading.

We were also set up to feel obligated to Ken and Barbie. Sure, it was their job. But it was obvious how hard and caringly they worked to transform Nancy's living room into an attractive display of candles. They also put on a very thorough and entertaining presentation. They'd spent their entire evening with us. They were getting married soon. And, Barbie let it be known, she had a couple of teenage children she was already supporting. We wouldn't make them work for nothing, would we?

Ken and Barbie gave us free things. Every time a guest asked or answered a question they were given a little ticket, like the kind kids get from amusement park games and then exchange for prizes. At one point, for example, Barbie excitedly announced that she'd just heard that candles are called "the universal gift." She then asked us, "What holidays would be good times for giving candles?" One woman said "Christmas" and was immediately given a ticket. Another answered "Easter" and got a ticket. One came up with July Fourth, for which Barbie got so excited she gave the woman two tickets. (Hanukkah came to mind, for which I might get eight nights' worth of tickets.) Then, at the end of the evening, the numbers on our tickets were drawn from a hat and the winners were given free candles. Almost everyone got them. Add these gifts to our tab.

Finally, obligation was used to seed future obligations. Ken and Barbie literally began their presentation with an appeal for new hostesses for the next candle party. They dangled rewards—that you could "win gifts" (How's that again?), just as Nancy was doing that night, for simply hosting a get-together for your friends. But they also threatened us with shame—incessant reminders that Nancy wouldn't get all the gifts she was entitled to unless one of us volunteered to be a future hostess. If just one of us came forward, Ken and Barbie got to play mavens in a new living room filled with new trusting customers. If more than one of us volunteered, the circle of customers, and yet more potential hostesses, multiplied exponentially.

The Good Cop

The reciprocity-of-kindness effect may be enhanced by contrasting it with meanness. There is, for example, the well-known "good cop–bad cop" routine.

One of the most remarkable mind control texts I've come across is the 1963 CIA interrogation manual titled *KUBARK Counterintelligence Interrogation*, recently made available through the Freedom of Information Act.[9] The manual was designed to teach operatives "noncoercive" techniques for eliciting confessions and intelligence information from uncooperative detainees. What makes KUBARK so frightening is that it has no references to electric shocks or rubber hoses or other methods of torture. It's 100 percent applied social psychology.[10]

The KUBARK manual teaches a notable version of good cop–bad cop that it calls the "Mutt and Jeff " technique. One interrogator takes a "brutal, angry, domineering" stance while his partner plays the friendly good-guy role. The performance begins with the angry interrogator ranting and raving, shouting down anything the subject says, cutting off his every answer, smashing his fist on the table. He accuses the subject of other offenses—"any offenses, especially those that are heinous or demeaning," the manual instructs. The bad guy "makes it plain that he personally considers the interrogatee the vilest person on earth."

During the harangue, the nice interrogator tries to appear a little afraid of his colleague. At some point, seemingly having had enough, the nice guy breaks in. "Wait a minute, Jim. Take it easy," the manual instructs him to say. The angry interrogator explodes at this. "He shouts back, 'Shut up! I'm handling this. I've broken crumb-bums before, and I'll break this one, wide open.' He expresses his disgust by spitting on the floor or holding his nose or any gross gesture," the manual instructs.

Finally, red-faced and furious, the bad-guy interrogator storms out. He shouts at the subject that he's going out for a few drinks and that when he returns, "You better be ready to talk." As soon as the door slams, the second interrogator tells the subject how sorry he is. He explains, the manual states, how "he hates to work with a man like that but has no choice, how if maybe brutes like that would keep quiet and give a man a fair chance to tell his side of the story, etc., etc." At this point, the interrogator hopes, his subject will be so grateful that he'll do anything asked of him in return.

The manual also describes a variation on the technique in which the interrogator works alone: "After a number of tense and hostile sessions the interrogatee is ushered into a different or refurnished room with comfortable furniture, cigarettes, and so forth. The interrogator invites him to sit down and explains his regret that the source's former stubbornness forced the interrogator to use such tactics. Now everything will be different. The interrogator talks man-to-man." Obviously, it's now the subject's turn to reciprocate.

Interestingly, virtually the same technique was applied during the brainwashing programs conducted in Korean POW camps. A former POW described this during his postcamp debriefing:

> I went in and there was a man, an officer he was . . . he asked me to sit down and was very friendly . . . It was very terrific. I, well, I almost felt like I had a friend sitting there. I had to stop every now and then and realize that this man wasn't a friend of mine. . . . I also felt as though I couldn't be rude to him. . . . It was much more difficult for me to—well, I almost felt I had as much responsibility to talk to him and reason and justification as I have to talk to you right now.

The CIA manual adds that the Mutt and Jeff technique is most effective with women, teenagers, and timid men.[11] Oh.

The Love Bomb

"The deepest principle in human nature is the craving to be appreciated," the great psychologist William James observed. We've already seen how people let their guards down for people they like. But, even more so, we're susceptible to people who like *us*. There's no stronger aphrodisiac than to be liked, to be esteemed—to be loved! It's a feeling hard to resist. Unfortunately, it sometimes should be.

When persuasion experts employ the liking principle, the best of them aim the arrow both ways. We're encouraged both to like them and to believe they like us in return. Pairing the two is simplified by the reciprocity norm—more specifically, what's known as the reciprocity-of-liking rule: when people like us, we're inclined to like them back. Salespeople are good at exploiting this principle. "Are you feeling unwanted? Need a friend to talk to?" an experienced auto salesman I interviewed asked me. "Just go visit a car lot. They're filled with people who want to be your friend. In fact, they'll fight each other for the privilege."

Some of the most effective exploiters of the reciprocity of liking rule are cults. When I began investigating cults, I shared the common stereotype that most joiners were psychological misfits or religious fanatics. Certainly, many who become active cult members arrive with their share of personal weaknesses and unusual religious leanings. But I found that if there's any generalization you can make about why people join these organizations, it's the attraction to what appears to be a loving community, an extended family. It's no coincidence that cult members so often address each other with family labels—brother, sister, father. Even those groups that eventually become destructive begin their appeal at the emotional level: they promise acceptance and love. The religious ideology is almost always reserved for later. Although extreme mind control may be the end result, emotional acceptance is the beginning.

Perhaps the most blatant exploiters of the liking principle I've observed are the Moonies. Until recent setbacks, Reverend Sun Myung Moon's Unification Church was one of the most successful cults (or progressive religious movements, depending on your point of view) of the twentieth century.[12] The term *Unificationism* refers to Moon's vision of an ideal world in which all other religions are abolished and absorbed into one religion—the Unification Church. During their heyday, from the 1970s until very recently, the Moonies had a worldwide membership by various estimates at somewhere between several hundred thousand and three million people. The organization accumulated enormous wealth. The church today holds a vast empire of properties, including the *Washington Times* newspaper, UPI (United Press International), the University of Bridgeport, and the New Yorker Hotel (which the Moonies operate as a Ramada Inn franchise). They not long ago spent billions of dollars constructing an automobile plant in China.

Most of the wealth accumulated by Moon and his inner circle was produced by dedicated members willing to work around the clock, often in mobile fund-raising teams, selling small specialty items like flowers and ginseng tea. The disciples receive no monetary reward for their work. They've become renowned for their totalistic, seemingly zombielike devotion to the man they call True Father and the teachings of his Unification Church. Moonies are often described by outsiders as tape recorders mindlessly reciting the doctrine of True Father.

The Unification Church achieved its success with what sociologist and cult expert John Lofland described as "one of the most ingenious, sophisticated, and effective conversion organizations ever devised."[13] But for most recruits, joining had little to do with Moon's ideology, or even religion at all. Most former members instead described a sequence of events that sound more like a seduction. The specifics varied depending on the time and place. In general, however, they fell into three steps: the pickup, the first date, and the love bomb.

Stage 1: The Pickup

Devotees spent considerable time cruising around public places, managing tables for front organizations and picking up hitchhikers in search of promising new recruits. "Hey, you look lost. Can I help?" or "Hi! Where you from? . . . Wow! My cousin's boyfriend (sister's roommate, maternal grandmother) came from Pasadena (Patagonia, Plymouth, England)."[14] College campuses were, and continue to be, particularly active targets. After a few amicable exchanges, during which you discover the friendly stranger has an extraordinary amount in common with you, there's usually an invitation to a dinner or a lecture or both. Gordon Neufield was twenty-three when he left his native Canada for a planned two-week trip to California. "On only my second day," he recalled, "while sight-seeing in Ghiardelli Square in San Francisco, I was approached by two young men who vaguely promised me a free dinner with a bunch of friendly people. They didn't say it was the Unification Church of the Reverend Sun Myung Moon. They didn't even say it was a religious group. So I went."[15] Neufeld was an active member for ten years before finally quitting.

Some ex-members recall pickups that sound scripted out of a bar scene. One Moonie center, for example, specialized in sending voluptuous women to visit male professors at colleges in the area. After a little innocent flirting, the professors were invited to a get-together for a group called United Science.[16] (At one time this approach was also adapted for purposes of political lobbying on Capitol Hill, when Moon assigned three attractive women to each U.S. senator. "Let them have a good relationship with them," Moon stated in 1973. "One is for the election, one is to be the diplomat, and one is for the party.")[17]

The recruiters were not only nice to you but, it seemed, just plain nice people. The front organization they represented always claimed that it was working for some noble cause. You might be invited to meet members of the International One World Crusade or the Creative Community Project. "What does the group do?" you might ask. "We go out and take care of young kids." "We do projects for the elderly." "We work for the environment." "We try to clean up the city." You didn't sign up for a cult. You went along because these were fine people. And usually they were. One of the ironies of cults, in fact, is that the craziest groups are often composed of the most caring people.[18]

Stage 2: The First Date

The newcomer arrives at dinner to encounter fifty or more friendly, smiling people running around busily doing various chores and, most strikingly, having an apparently wonderful time. The social atmosphere, one observer recalled, "exuded friendliness and solicitude." You're assigned to a "buddy" who never leaves your side. While you're eating, one person after another stops by to introduce him or herself and talk. "They seemed to be circulating like sorority members during rush," one woman observed. Another commented, "It certainly felt wonderful to be served, given such attention and made to feel important."[19]

As the evening draws to a close you might hear the beginnings of a vague, generic group philosophy—how everyone present is bound by principles like sharing, loving, and working for the good of the community and humankind. But the real purpose of the dinner is to get you to a retreat. Allen Tate Wood was a tourist visiting the University of California, Berkeley when he agreed to attend a dinner in the 1970s. He ended up spending six years and serving in upper-echelon positions in the church. "The purpose of taking that person there [to a dinner]," he said, "is to get them off to a training center, run them through a training regimen of seven, or twenty-one, or forty days. When that's complete, that person's going to be on a bus for the next seven years working sixteen hours a day."[20]

Stage 3: The Love Bomb

And so you're off for a weekend of games and social events, perhaps at "Camp K" or "the Farm" in northern California. One hundred or so people are there, over half of whom are church members. Your schedule is filled from 7:30 in the morning until 11:00 at night. A new buddy is assigned to watch over you, shadowing your every move, even accompanying you to the bathroom. You become the buddy's "spiritual child." The day is filled with collective activities: chanting, cheers, dancing, singing, garden work, games, exercises, group eating, lectures. Sex is prohibited, but you're constantly being hugged and patted by members of the opposite sex. A lot of what you see seems silly, but it all has a good feeling. Anthropologist Geri-Ann Galanti attended a weekend retreat undercover as a research project. "My overwhelming response to my experience that weekend was that I was having fun," she recalled. "It was like being a child again. Most of the time spent in lectures was passed by eating, playing games, and singing songs. No wonder it's called *Camp* K. . . . It was nice to be a child again, with no responsibilities except to have a good time and learn a little."[21]

At this point the Moonies' unleash their most powerful weapon: "the love bomb." "Love," recruiters are told, "is more important than truth." The job of a trainer is to be a "happy maker." Group leaders who slacken in their enthusiasm are sternly reprimanded. As one recruiter later testified:

> You must really love people. You must "love-bomb" them. [We] have a staff of about twelve people who are the best "love-bombers" in the whole world. Sometimes when I'd be having trouble with one of my

guests—they weren't responding—I could give one of them a look and they'd come over. Their ability wasn't in anything they said but it was loving that person. Finally the person's heart would melt.[22]

All weekend long members will "spontaneously" come up and give you compliments: "You know, you're one of the most open people I've met." "Everyone's talking about how much they like you." "We need people like you." When you contribute to a conversation the entire group bursts out in applause. It doesn't matter what you say, they'll shower you with praise. "Whenever I would raise a theological question," one prospect recalled, "the leaders of my group would look very impressed and pleased, seem to agree with me, and then give me a large dose of love—and perhaps say something about unity and God's love being most important. I would have an odd, disjointed sort of feeling—not knowing if I'd really been heard or not, yet aware of the attentive look and the smiling approval."[23] At least once during the weekend the group will break into a "spontaneous" song directed at you:

> We love you, Zach [or Andy or Ben, or whomever],
> We love you more than anyone,
> We don't want you to leave us—
> And we don't mean maybe!

Trainers would meet during the weekend to plan "love-bombing" strategies. They'd target the recruit's most vulnerable points: the need to feel useful, to belong, and to feel loved. One guest recalled overhearing a session very early on Sunday morning: "I heard a cheer: 'Gonna meet all their needs.' And that did seem to be what they tried to do. Whatever I wanted—except privacy or any deviation from the schedule—would be gotten for me immediately and with great concern. I was continually smiled at, hugged, patted. And I was made to feel very special and very much wanted."[24]

Recruits reacted to these bombings by wanting to please in return. "But you quickly learn that the only way to please is to conform," another ex-member observes. "You succumb many times to small acts of conformity without realizing it. You feel guilty when you hold back, and you're told that wanting to be alone is a symptom of fear and alienation."[25] With time, recruits surrender total control of their lives to the church.

Eventually recruits are exposed to the extensive, elaborate teachings of the Unification Church. These are the principles they learn to recite like tape recorders. This doesn't come, however, until the emotional bonds are established. And when thought conversion begins, it plays heavily on these bonds. Ex-member Craig Maxim explained to me how the lectures utilized a well-orchestrated support cast of Moonies:

> For instance, I was once asked to help out at a lecture, and when I went, there was only one real recruit. I looked around the table and there were six or seven other Moonies and I recognized all of them, but they were just sitting through the lecture as if they were new recruits. I never once heard one of them say to the guest that they were members, but they would talk after the lectures like: "Wasn't that fascinating? So let me see, the four position foundation. . . ." And they would ask questions of the lecturer as if they didn't know the answer, when I knew that they had to have.[26]

In the end, total conversion consists of accepting the opinions of your friends. This includes not just your new Moonie friends but, whenever possible, the friends you started the weekend with. One former Moonie, whom I'll call Wendy, recalled her decision to join. It began with a typical love-bombing. "I was being treated with a lot of favor: praised in meetings for my 'great' presentations, held up as someone from the working class who managed to get a college education and yet was about to give up 'easy living' for the life of a dedicated political activist." But although she enjoyed the praise, Wendy believed that what ultimately caused her to stay was the approval of her friends: "I thought to myself that this was all pretty weird and I probably wouldn't have joined except I knew that two of my best friends were going through the same investigation and were expecting and hoping to join. They were both mature and level-headed individuals whom I respected, so I thought it must be all right and worth a try." It was social proof.

Loving and liking—these are the magic potions of cults. Few guests understood much about the Unification religious philosophy at the end of the weekend, but they knew they were among happy, friendly people who really liked them and wanted them to stay and find out more. What's not to like? When anthropologist Geri-Ann Galanti left the camp she'd entered two days before as a cynical researcher, she was amazed by how her defenses had collapsed. "Most telling was a remark

I made to the friend I had arranged to pick me up from Camp K: 'I had a great time. Remind me what's so bad about the Moonies.'"[27]

The Creditor

When it comes to exploiting reciprocity, there's a certain personality type to especially watch out for. These are individuals who thrive on having others indebted to them. Much of their lives are spent on the twin tasks of assembling indebtedness from others and avoiding being in debt themselves. They're addicted to the power advantage indebted people give to them, secure in the knowledge that they can cash in at their discretion. They are the psychological equivalents of what economists might call a chronic "creditor." Idries Shah, the Sufi writer, observed: "A man who takes money may be greedy for money, or he may not. But a man who takes nothing at all is under the gravest suspicion of robbing the disciple of his soul. People who say, 'I take nothing,' may be found to take away the volition of their victim."[28]

Here are six characteristics that define the creditor type:[29]

- Creditors are great proponents of the principle that people are not only obligated to return a favor but should give back more than they receive.
- Creditors work hard to stay on the dominant side of the reciprocity equation. Creditors don't like being on the receiving end unless they're in a position to quickly repay their debt anytime they want.
- Creditors are uncomfortable when a debt is repaid and immediately search for ways to get the other person back in their debt again.
- Even when others try to make repayment, creditors try to make it appear that it's not enough. There's an old story about a stereotypical Jewish mother who gives her son two shirts as a present. The first time he wears one, she looks at him sadly and says, "The other one you didn't like?" Creditors use this approach to maintain their advantage.
- Creditors are suspicious of gifts and favors. They're wary of becoming victims of the reciprocity norm. Creditors would

endorse La Rochefoucauld's observation, in 1678: "What seems to be generosity is often no more than disguised ambition."

• Most critically, creditors go out of their way to exploit the reciprocity norm. When they give to others, it's usually with the expectation of later receiving more in return. To a creditor, generosity is a manipulative scheme.

"A creditor is worse than a slave-owner," Victor Hugo once wrote. "For the master only owns your person, but a creditor owns your dignity, and can command it."

If you hang around hucksters, swindlers, and con men too long—as I have in writing this book—it's easy to begin seeing everyone who offers you a gift or performs an act of kindness as some kind of creditor or control freak. It often seems, as a Malian proverb says, that "one does not give a gift without motive." It's important to remember, however, that the reciprocity norm has developed its hold because, more often than not, it serves society extremely well. The essence of the norm isn't abusive power and manipulative control but to avoid inequality and exploitation. Usually, it has less to do with mean-spirited creditors than the advice of Winnie the Pooh: "When someone does something nice for you, you're supposed to do something nice for them in return. That's called friendship." The reciprocity norm has become a universal driving force because it usually generates fairness.

The Japanese emphasis on *giri*, for example, evolved out of social and environmental conditions that required a spirit of communitarianism. Japan is made up of small, isolated islands with a long history of limited resources and crowded living conditions. (Four hundred years ago, the population density of Japan was already twice that of the present-day United States.) Given these confinements, mutual cooperation and trust become a necessity for Japanese survival. The rules of *giri* helped choreograph a crowded populace so people wouldn't walk all over each other.[30] Similarly, in China, another country with a long history of limited resources, there is a system of rules known as *guanxixue* (pronounced "guan-shee-shwe"), meaning "doing favors for people." *Guanxixue* prescribes rules for exchanging gifts, favors, and even banquets. The goal is to cultivate personal relationships, create networks of mutual dependency, and, ultimately, meet everyone's needs and desires in everyday life.[31]

The reciprocity norm not only allows trade and transactions to proceed in good faith; it lays the foundation for cooperative, prosocial, unselfish human relationships. It reminds us to balance giving and receiving, to share. At its best, the norm both induces generosity and provides the psychological security that our generosity will be returned in due course. The creditors among us are the occasional deviants, the freaks in the system. As Sigmund Freud once said, "Sometimes a good cigar is just a good cigar"; and, more often than not, an act of kindness is simply an act of kindness.

It's noteworthy that the reciprocity norm is much less prone to abuse by allies. In a study of gift giving around the world, anthropologist Marshall Salins captured an uncanny universal trend: the closer the kinship between the person giving a gift and the one receiving it, the less scrupulously the reciprocity rule was enforced. Within one's family there was what Salins called "generalized reciprocity," meaning that no one kept count of who gave what or how much the last time around; or, you could say, essentially no reciprocity pressure at all. Gift giving between tribes, Salin found, was an entirely different matter. Exchanges between rivals were characterized by "negative reciprocity"—another term for theft, if you will—whereby people tried to get back more than they gave out in the first place. True reciprocity—value for value—only appeared between unrelated allies. Within their village or tribe, for example, people were expected to be relatively exact in returning a gift.[32]

There's nothing inherently manipulative about giving or receiving. The challenge is to separate the manipulators from those with good intentions, the enemy tribes from your allies. In our own modern-day villages, unfortunately, this can get awfully complicated.

FOUR

The Contrast Principle

Or, How Black Gets Turned into White

The background has as much to do with the likeness as anything else. . . .
The spaces on either side of the head and above the head can do so many
different things good and bad to the head that it is remarkable how little
attention is generally paid to them. A figure can be dwarfed by its placement, and if there is no sense of distance back of it and on this side of it it
will most surely be flattened. . . . There are backgrounds so well made that
you have no consciousness of them.

—Robert Henri, *The Art Spirit*

Matisse, it was said, could create any color in a painting without
touching the color itself. All he asked was to control the colors around
it. Similarly, look closely at a Van Gogh or a Monet or virtually any
other impressionist work and you'll have a hard time finding an accurately depicted color or clean brush stroke. These paintings are populated by oddities like people with bright orange hands and green faces;
with irregular globs of paint that represent flags and trees; and with
what appear to be accidental brush drippings that pass off as stars and
steeples. Every detail on the canvas, seen in isolation, is inaccurate. But
it all looks right when you stand back and take in the whole painting.

In perception, context is everything. Colors and shapes are elastic
creatures that change with their surroundings. A black picture frame
will make a gray painting look lighter; a white frame turns it darker. Put
the same gray painting against a green background and it becomes pink.
If you want to see a total color change, place a strong blue up against a
red and watch the red turn orange—not orangish, but actual orange.
Now vary the size, the shape, or the placement of any of these objects

and everything changes again. You don't have to squint or make an effort to see the changes. If your vision is normal, they can't be seen any other way. The changes are so dramatic that to the unprepared viewer, they can seem like magic.

The impressionists understood that the appearance of an object is controlled by the background as much as by the features of the object itself. Background forces are so powerful, in fact, that artists need to learn the seemingly absurd skill of knowing what "wrong" color will make a color look right. If you're working against a dark background, for example, you need to paint the objects darker than they actually are to make them look like they actually are. When I studied art, we were taught not to overly intensify a color by surrounding it with a dull one, or to suck the intensity out of the color by surrounding it with an intense one. You even need to watch out for combinations that electrify each other. Try alternating strips of turquoise next to orange, for example, and you'll see the two colors vibrate. Separate the colors and they both quiet down. Is the color *really* light or dark, red or orange, vibrating or still? Unless you live in an isolation tank, these are meaningless questions.[1]

The human brain is wired to see relationships, not detached elements. The artist Heinz Kusel, who taught color theory for twenty years, explained: "Color by itself doesn't exist. All that we see as color is created by relationships—what the color is next to, what surrounds it. A name for a color is absurd, because its appearance is constantly changing as a result of its environment. There are no fixed colors. In a different context it's changed completely."[2]

The creation of context is also the art form of persuasion professionals. Advertising, in particular, is all about background. There's an old Madison Avenue axiom that every ad should include at least one dog, child, or sexy person. When in doubt, toss in another. Products are placed in the company of beautiful people and happy families, under cool waterfalls and tropical skies, in luscious mansions and manly wilderness—whatever casts the best light on the merchandise. Skim any magazine and count the ads that don't use evocative background. I challenge you to find more than a handful. More attention, in fact, is usually paid to the context than to the product. This has been the case for many years. In 1917, Cyris Curtis made this observation about the then-popular ads for Arrow Collars and Pierce-Arrow cars: "They are almost all picture. It's the *atmosphere* in these that sells . . . the quality that gives prestige, the little imaginative sure touches that bring the thing before you."[3]

Some advertising is *all* background. Nissan, for example, introduced their then-new line of luxury cars, the Infinity, with a huge campaign that made a point of not showing the car. The visuals in these ads were Zen-like images intended to establish a feeling, a mood, for the sort of person who would want to own the new car. There were scenes of raindrops striking the surface of a pond, Japanese rock gardens, a flock of geese against an ethereal sky. One magazine ad showed a large granite rock—nothing else—on half the screen, with the question "What kind of person would drive an Infinity?" on the other half. Some ads strove for intellectual profundity about the meaning of the car; for example: "There are differences in philosophy between a car designer raised in Bavaria and one raised in Kyoto. Not so much on what is fundamentally good engineering, but on what luxury is."

Nissan ran ads like these for six months, never showing the car or offering details about its mechanics (leave that toilet talk to the Bavarians), and certainly never stooping to vulgar matters like price.[4] By omitting specific information, says Don Easdon, who codesigned the ads, "the scene becomes a frame for the message."[5] The message—that owning an Infinity will bring peaceful transcendence, or affirm your Zen-like presence, or God knows what salvation it's supposed to offer you—would have assumedly lost its impact from the sight of the car itself.

Advertising's ultimate triumph of background over content may have been recently achieved in New Zealand, where graphic designer Fiona Jack conducted a peculiar billboard campaign to market her new product, Nothing.[6] "I was thinking about advertising and all its strangeness, its coercive ability to sell the most completely bizarre things to people who usually don't need them," Jack observed. "I realized that the ultimate nonexistent product would be nothing." New Zealand's Outdoor Advertising Association became interested in her idea and agreed to feature the slogan "Nothing—What you've been looking for" on twenty-seven billboards around the Auckland area. The billboard company soon began receiving calls from potential customers wanting to know where they could buy some of that Nothing. "The majority of the population," Jack says, "seem to be convinced that it is either a teaser for a campaign, or a new cosmetic product of a similar nature to the 'Simple' cosmetic range."

The success of her campaign, Jack told me, "illustrates the absurdity of advertising and how it has established a kind of pseudo-authority which enables it to sell *anything*, even absolutely nothing, and consequently leaves the public in a vulnerable and gullible position." The means of communicating this pseudoauthority is context. In the Nothing campaign, Jack pointed out, "the mere fact that people were very aware that 'those billboards must have cost a lot of money' means that what they're advertising must be worthwhile. It couldn't possibly be nothing, could it?" In an ironic postscript, Jack reported that "many people have been absolutely adamant that we make a product and call it Nothing. 'You'll make a fortune,' they say. All I can wonder is, what could we make? Battery operated Zen gardens? Handy meditation kits? New Improved Satori—with an introductory offer of 30 milliliters extra free?"

While living in Brazil several years ago, I watched a variation on the Nothing strategy set to a campaign for the presidency. The country was, at the time, conducting its first free elections in many years. As you might expect, there was a great deal of excitement. Campaign ads were all over television. The streets were often filled with rambunctious caravans of vehicles blaring music and carrying beautiful women holding up signs for their candidate. The only thing people didn't hear were the candidates themselves. The reason for this, it turned out, was that the ruling military government had banned the candidates from making public statements. I wondered how voters made their decisions. ("I liked the smile on the guy followed by the car with the blonde." Or maybe, "I'm not voting for some jerk in a Volkswagen.") To my surprise, few Brazilians I spoke to seemed bothered by the no-talking rule. "When the politicians start saying things," one of my friends explained, "it just confuses people." *Muito bem, Brasileiros.* (The Brazilian authorities might have pointed to the municipal elections that had taken place two years earlier in the town of Picoaza, Ecuador. Just before those elections, a product called Pulvapies Foot Deodorant had launched an opportunistic ad campaign with the slogan: "If you want well-being and hygiene, vote Pulvapies!" To everyone's embarrassment, the product was elected mayor through write-in votes.)

The most fundamental of context effects is the principle of contrast. The principle relies on the fact that human minds magnify differences:

when two relatively similar stimuli are placed next to each other, they'll be perceived as more different from each other than they actually are. Contrast is not only the most basic of context effects but probably the easiest to achieve. "I don't paint things," Matisse said. "I only paint the difference between things."

The effect is well established in psychophysics. In a classic experiment, for example, psychologist Donald Brown asked subjects to lift various weights and judge how heavy each was. Some subjects were also asked to lift an anchor weight that was lighter or heavier than the target weight. Consistent with the contrast principle, subjects asked to lift a heavy anchor judged the target weight lighter than they had before lifting the anchor; lifting a light anchor led to judging the target as heavier.[7] Of course, any baseball player who's warmed up by attaching a weight to his bat could have told you the same thing.

On the sensory level, this magnification occurs physiologically. In vision, for example, we distinguish objects in space by seeing edges and boundaries. To make these edges stand out more clearly, the visual system oversharpens them in the mind's eye through a process called lateral inhibition. When a sensory receptor cell is excited by a light source, it sends out two sets of messages. First, it sends impulses upward to the brain that announce the presence of the light. But it also sends inhibitory messages sideways to neighboring receptor cells to keep them from becoming excited at the same time. The more strongly the target cell is lit up, and the closer the two cells are to each other, the more the adjacent cell is inhibited. As a result, a light that is turning brighter may actually appear to get dimmer—that is, if its surroundings are brightening at an even faster rate. Lateral inhibition fools the visual system into seeing more contrast than actually exists.[8]

The contrast effect occurs not only across space but over time. Our perceptions are affected by what occurred beforehand. This is called successive contrast. A loud noise on a quiet night sounds even louder. A cool breeze on a hot day feels that much cooler. Both spatial and temporal contrast apply to virtually every input that can be scaled from high to low. Boundaries seem sharper, brights look brighter, and darks turn darker. Our perceptual systems are like a big Clorox commercial.

When we move to the level of social experience, the contrast effect is even more pervasive. The human brain finds it extremely difficult to comprehend social cues outside of a context. How we respond to a person or a request—whether it seems reasonable or excessive, important or trivial—depends on what came before and what other information sits beside it in the picture.

Say you receive a registered letter from the Internal Revenue Service. You tear it open and see the words "Back taxes owed" across the top. After skipping a few heartbeats—and perhaps mentally bargaining with your preferred deity about how you will change your life in return for this letter going away—you read they are asking for a total of $75. Thank you, God. But suppose later that day, when checking out a movie at the video store, the clerk informs you that your son has run up a late-return bill of $75. Perhaps you now have a different message for your Lord. It's a matter of context.

I have a friend, Lenny, who has a habit of answering every question of judgment with the retort "Compared to what?" It's an extremely annoying habit. But the question has great psychological wisdom, for almost any aspect of our lives worth evaluating is a matter of relativity. Are you happy with your life? Your marriage? Your job? Your dinner? There can be no meaningful answers to these questions before establishing the great human baseline: "Compared to what?." Lenny doesn't let me forget this. Whenever I express joy he bursts my bubble with the question "But are you *really* happy?" (I *really* don't like Lenny.) After all, outside of the extremes of euphoria and depression, how do we evaluate life's ambiguities other than by comparing ourselves to others? H. L. Mencken defined wealth as "any income that is at least one hundred dollars more a year than the income of one's wife's sister's husband."

Social psychologists call this process "social comparison." Cognitive psychologists refer to it as "framing." To me, it's basically Lenny's law: compared to what?

Which brings me back to advertising. To say advertising takes advantage of the contrast principle is something of a redundancy. The fundamental aim of most advertising is to make your product stand out from the field. Marketing talk is saturated with terms like *product differentiation*, *positioning*, and *finding a niche*.

Consider toothpaste advertising, for example. With all the toothpastes on the market, companies need to somehow make theirs appear different. Once upon a time, Crest set itself apart by advertising that it—implying it *alone*—had stannous fluoride and was recommended by the American Dental Association. Now shelves are filled with competitors who fight cavities with fluoride. Since each has pretty much the same cavity-fighting formula, advertisers are challenged to find some other "differentiator" that will establish a "position" for their product. In other words, how do they create a visible contrast between their product and the competition? If the toothpaste aisle were a painting, it would be like challenging Matisse to make a small patch of color in the corner jump out to capture the viewer's attention.

I recently conducted a survey of toothpaste packaging. (My study engaged the classic scientific methodology of walking down the tooth-paste aisle in my local Long's drugstore and reading the labels on each product.) Every toothpaste, I learned, touts its differential by high-lighting one or two ingredients or a specific benefit that is its alone. Arm & Hammer tells you it's the baking soda + peroxide toothpaste. Listerine toothpaste kills germs that cause bad breath. Tom's of Maine is the natural toothpaste (with calcium to boot). Rembrandt is the whitening toothpaste. Metadent has fluoride, baking soda, and perox-ide and—lest you confuse it with Arm & Hammer—adds that it has "the ingredients dentists recommend most for the care of teeth and gums." One brand just calls itself by its differential: Plus + White Toothpaste. My own favorite is a Colgate toothpaste that contains "micro-cleansing crystals." Take that, Mr. Tooth Decay. Crest, mean-while, hasn't stood still. It now promotes a series of toothpastes, each with its own special formula. The entire Crest line is contrasted not only with competitive brands but against itself. One Crest toothpaste features sensitivity protection, another has tartar protection, a third offers cavity protection, a fourth has gum care protection. Would it really be so difficult, one wonders, to mix all those protections together in one tube? (Maybe toss in a couple of micro-crystals while they're at it, too.) All these pitches strive for the same goals: sharpen the edges, magnify the differences, and—most important of all—make consumers aware there is something you have for them that they need and don't yet possess.

The most direct application of the contrast principle in advertising is what is known, literally, as "contrast advertising," whereby your product is directly compared to specific competitors. For example, if you show a Big Mac next to your brand of hamburger while explaining how yours is cooked fresher, has more beef, and costs thirty cents less, this is contrast advertising.

Contrast advertising has a history of controversy attesting to its potential effectiveness. For years, the dominant trade groups and large advertising agencies aggressively fought for its prohibition. The critics' overt argument was the technique is uncivil and unprofessional. Their real fear, however, was it offered a weapon that small, aggressive competitors could use to cut into their share of the market. As a result, the major television networks initially banned the method. Consumer groups and the FTC, however, argued that contrast advertising held the potential for communicating relevant information. The best of these ads offered consumers hard, verifiable facts instead of the usual vague puffery coming out of Madison Avenue. NBC finally lifted its ban on contrast advertising in 1964. ABC and CBS didn't relent until 1972, when they were under threat of FTC lawsuits over restraint of trade. By 1980, 25 percent of advertisements on ABC were drawing pointed comparisons with other products.[9]

Contrast advertising often focuses on images as much as it does facts. LOT Airlines, the airline of Poland, for example, not long ago set out to persuade more tourists to visit that country. The company designed an advertising campaign that emphasized the Europeanness of Poland. One typical ad showed a picturesque outdoor café in the old town of Warsaw with two happy tourists being fawned over by an eager, Continental-looking waiter. But how do you convince foreigners that la dolce vita awaits them in a country best known for wartime horrors, political repression, and economic depression? To show that Poland's finest wasn't just worthy by Polish standards, LOT set up a clever contrast with the established real thing in European charm—Paris. In one series, the ads showed cafés in Poland that easily passed as Parisian look-alikes. They then took advantage of the stereotype that French people are unfriendly to tourists. The slogan read: "Quaint little Parisian cafés without the Parisians." In your *visage*, Maurice.

Still, some advertisers question the sensibility of naming or showing competitors' products. They argue that it both can be demeaning to your own commodity and gives your rival free publicity. But contrast advertising has an impressive history of success stories. As a case in point, Madison Avenue giant Amil Gargano has used contrast advertising in breakthrough advertising campaigns for some of the world's largest corporations. The criteria for using comparative advertising are simple, he says: "You have to compare reasonably like products. If you are in the market for a car at—let's say—between $12,000 to $15,000, what are your choices? What would you look for? What cars are selling in that price category and are they of comparable performance characteristics? Of course, you must also have the superior product. Otherwise, why make the comparison?"

Gargano recently designed an advertisement for his client MCI that showed two pictures of the same woman side by side. In front of the first picture was a sign saying "Bell $8.20." In front of the second picture was the sign "MCI $4.98." The implied message: everything is the same, except MCI is less than half the price. "That's a superior product benefit—a significant point of comparison," he observes.

One of Gargano's most notable campaigns, for Hertz rental cars, challenged the Avis "When you're number two you try harder" slogan. Avis's catchphrase was classic contrast advertising, even if it never did actually mention Hertz by name. Gargano built a countercampaign under the slogan "For years Avis has been telling you Hertz is No. 1. Now we're going to tell you why." The advertisements, which ran for ninety days, effectively killed off the long-standing Avis campaign. As Gargano observes, "If comparative advertising is done correctly, it can be enormously effective."[10]

In persuasion, contrast gets exploited in at least two ways. One is to convince you that what a company is selling is a better deal than what the competition has to offer. The second is to alter your expectations, or what's known as your "anchor point." Perhaps you're shopping for a certain camera. Your friend tells you he just bought one for $200. You see the same one in a discount store for $175. Good deal, right? But say, instead, the friend had told you that he thought the camera should cost $150. That $175 price isn't so attractive anymore.

It works something like a thermostat. Say your air conditioner is set to turn on at seventy-five degrees but the temperature in the room is only seventy degrees. Either of two events will start the air conditioner: the temperature in the room goes up five degrees or you lower the thermostat five degrees. Likewise, in persuasion, you can manipulate either a person's anchor point or the features of the product you're selling. Both achieve the same effect.

Anchor points are remarkably malleable. I like an observation Terry Prothro, the former director of the Center for Behavioral Research of the American University of Beirut, once made about his chaotic, war-torn years there: "There is a test we used to do in class to see how easily living things can adapt. You put a frog in a pail of water and gradually turn up the heat. The frog just keeps adjusting to the new temperature, until it finally boils to death, because it is so used to adjusting that it doesn't think to jump out of the pail. I feel like that frog."[11]

Sometimes salesmen up the ante so slowly and over such an extended period of time that we fail to recognize how much more they're asking. A good example is the evolving advertising campaign for Michelob beer. Imagine how you'd react if a company came right out and told you to drink beer every night. Why not just preach the virtues of becoming an alcoholic? This is pretty much what the good people at Michelob have done. But they've been clever enough to up their requests in small increments. In the 1970s, Michelob's slogan was "Holidays are made for Michelob." Apparently limiting drinking to special occasions didn't sell enough beer because a year later the slogan became "Weekends are made for Michelob." Next thing we knew it stretched to "Put a little weekend in your week." Eventually it became "The night belongs to Michelob." Who knows what's next? "Breakfast is Michelob time"? "Put a little weekend in your oatmeal"? Taken as a whole, the ad campaign sounds frighteningly like a tutorial written by drug dealers: get a little of the chemical in people's systems, let them adapt, and then gradually up the dose until they're hooked. But you don't notice because no single step registers a noticeable difference.

Because our anchor points are so readily manipulable, they're often easier to change than the product itself. Here are three traps to watch out for.

The anchoring trap. Consider these two questions:

1. Is the population of Turkey greater than 30 million?
2. What is your best estimate of Turkey's population?

Most people's answer to the second question, studies find, is heavily influenced by the figure of 30 million—which is, in fact, an arbitrarily selected number.[12] But, now, what would happen if I substituted 100 million for 30 million in the first question? Almost without fail, the answer to the second question increases on the order of many millions. This is an example of what's known as the "anchoring trap."[13]

The anchoring trap may be used to make a high price appear lower. For example, when Storer Cable Communications wanted to raise its rates to subscribers in Louisville, Kentucky, the company mailed out this notice: "It's not often you get good news instead of a bill, but we've got some for you. If you've heard all those rumors about your basic cable rate going up $10 or more a month, you can relax: *it's not going to happen!* The great news is . . . the rate for basic cable is increasing only $2 a month."[14] In other words, Storer wasn't charging you $2; it was saving you $8. What a swell company.

Our anchors are easily manipulated through distortions like this. We're especially vulnerable when our initial baselines are weak. This is often the case when entering a novel situation or a suddenly threatening one. When unsure of our bearings we look to others for clues. Sometimes we get good information, but other times we don't. One thing's for sure: you'll find no shortage of manipulators happy to set your expectations for you.

The base rate fallacy. Not only is the level of our anchor point subject to manipulation, but we sometimes use the wrong anchor completely. Consider the following statements.

Benjamin Harper is best described as a meek, unassertive person. He's either a salesman or a librarian. Which one do you think he is?[15]

The almost unanimous answer to this question is that Benjamin is a librarian. When people are asked to set odds that he's a librarian, the average estimate is in the neighborhood of 90 percent. The obvious reasoning behind the choice is that Benjamin's personality fits the stereotype of a librarian and is contrary to the stereotype of salesmen. The logic sounds sensible. But it's completely wrong.

The problem is your anchor, or what in this case is called your base rate. Benjamin's personality may match that of a librarian, but the number of male salesmen in the United States outnumber male librarians by about one hundred to one. In other words, before even beginning to consider information about Benjamin's personality, you should have recognized there's only a 1 percent chance he'd be a librarian. Let's assume the stereotype of the two professions turns out to be wildly accurate and that 90 percent of all male librarians are, in fact, meek and unassertive while 90 percent of salesmen are not. Even then, this works out to more than ten meek salesmen for every meek librarian.

I watched the base rate fallacy manipulated often by car salesmen. When I was training to sell at one dealership, one of my fears was how I'd be able to learn enough information about every car and model to give credible sales presentations. I explained to one of my managers that I was (and am) virtually illiterate about cars. He told me not to worry, that lots of the other salesmen were, too. A few facts, he explained, would go a long way.

The manager assigned me to shadow one of the more experienced salesmen on a "walk around." This is when the salesman slowly walks the customer around a specific car and points out as many attractive features as he can. The primary goal here is to make the car appear sufficiently special to warrant taking it out for a test-drive, a step which most salesmen consider the watershed commitment in the sales process (see chapter 7). The salesman usually begins his walk by pointing out features under the hood, then circles the chassis and trunk, and finally sits the customer in the driver's seat. The walk around requires the salesman to be as specific as possible about the features of a car.

The salesman, whom I'll call Lou, put on an impressive performance, firing a rat-tat-tat of facts as he moved the customer around the car. Under the hood, for example, Lou explained how this car had specially designed gauges for convenient reading. He moved quickly to the halogen headlights and how crisp and clear they were. After a few minutes of information like this, he ended the walk around with the safety features, stopping to emphasize the remarkable way the hood on this car was designed to crumple in predesigned areas during a frontal impact to "keep it from decapitating the driver and passenger."

I was astonished by the volume of knowledge Lou had about this car. This couldn't be one of the fellow automotive illiterates my manager was talking about? I asked Lou how he could possibly memorize so much about all the brands and models on the lot. It was easy, he said. You basically say the same thing about every car. Sure the fluid gauges in the car he'd shown were specially designed for easy reading. But the thing is, every car manufacturer does something to make fluid checking easier—one uses color coding, another uses icons, and so on—so you make the same statements about convenience no matter what the car. Similarly, it was true that the car he showed had crisp, clear halogen headlights, but so did every other car on the lot. The predesigned frontal-impact crumpling? This, too, was a fact. What Lou didn't tell the customer was that by law, the hood on every automobile sold in the United States is required to fold up on frontal impact.

You see the base rate fallacy exploited a great deal in the advertising industry, too. Consider, for example, the Bayer aspirin ads that used to brag how the product was "100% pure aspirin." They then went on to say that "government tests have proved that no pain reliever is stronger or more effective than Bayer."[16] What they failed to mention was every aspirin is 100 percent aspirin, and so why in the world would you expect any brand to be more effective than the others? (Bayer's duplicity was enhanced by the fact that they were among the most active critics of contrast advertising. When a competing aspirin compared its prices to Bayer's over the air, the director of Bayer's advertising agency, Frank Hummert, sent a venomous threat to NBC: "If this continues any further I personally will see to it that every relationship between us and National Broadcasting Company is impaired to the best of my ability and I think you know that I make good on these things.")[17] Bayer's competitors over at Anacin were even craftier. They added a little caffeine to their pill and then, rather than calling the product aspirin, simply announced that "Anacin contains the pain reliever doctors recommend most." The pain reliever they referred to was, of course, none other than good old aspirin.[18]

If you don't begin with an accurate base rate, the contrast effect will just lead you further astray.

The decoy. Another application of the contrast principle entails showing the customer options he won't buy but which will reset his base rate so that other products look more attractive. A Realtor, for example, might first show you a house that is similar but slightly inferior to one you're interested in—a little smaller or more expensive, perhaps. Auto dealers might start off with an overpriced car, or the same car they hope to sell you but with fewer features, or one that is less comfortable or the wrong color. These setup items are decoys.

The decoy may be embedded in a manufacturer's product line. Recently, for example, I went shopping for an espresso machine at a well-known gourmet cooking store. The saleswoman steered me to a quality German brand which she carried in three models, list priced at $199.95, $299.95, and $499.95, respectively. The $199.95 machine was being offered at a $25 discount. The saleswoman first spent a few minutes selling me on the virtues of the brand. "My customers say it makes better coffee than Starbucks" was her precise tag line. This was basic self-serving contrast advertising, of course.

She then turned to differences within her own product line. These contrasts were less blatantly self-serving and, as a result, more persuasive. The only difference among the three models, she explained, were features. The two more-expensive machines made more coffee (up to twenty cups) on one tank of water than the $199.95 machine. The big feature of the $499.95 machine was that it used—in fact required—prepackaged packets of coffee rather than loose scoopfuls from a bag. These coffee packets had to be purchased from the manufacturer. "To tell you the truth," the saleswoman said, "very few of my customers ever need to make twenty cups of espresso at one time. Besides, it only takes a couple of minutes to refill and heat a new tank of water if you do. And everyone I've talked to hates the idea of a [$499.95] machine that limits you to prepackaged coffee packets." All three models, she explained, made the same quality coffee. "If you can live without the twenty-cup water tank," she observed, "you're buying all the best features of a $500 coffee machine for less than half the price."

After pausing to let that sink in, she added, "You may want to know that almost everyone who comes in buys the $199 machine. I've seen a few customers take the $299 model, but that $499 machine—I haven't sold one of them in the two years I've worked here. I don't know why we even carry them." When I inquired further, she told me the $499 machine rarely went on sale. How strange, I thought. Here was a store with limited and very expensive floor space, with professional buyers who carefully select their offerings from a highly competitive product line, and the store carries a coffee machine that nobody has bought for two years?

To understand the presence of the $499 machine, I might have looked to an experiment by Itamar Simonson and Amos Tversky that studied consumer responses to different microwave ovens. Half the shoppers in their experiment were given the choice of either a $179.99 Panasonic oven or a $109.99 Emerson oven, both of which were being offered at a 35 percent discount. The other half were also given a third option—a $199.99 Panasonic at a mere 10 percent discount. Results showed that very few shoppers (only 13 percent) selected this expensive third option. But that shouldn't have bothered the good people at Panasonic. When the expensive Panasonic was not an option, more buyers (57 percent) chose the Emerson than the $179 Panasonic (43 percent). But when the expensive Panasonic was an added option, the results were reversed: 60 percent now selected the $179 Panasonic and only 27 percent wanted the Emerson. In other words, the addition of the relatively expensive, low-value microwave sold more of its sister Panasonics than it did of itself.[19]

And here lies the true value of the $499 espresso machine, which, for all I know, is still gathering dust on the shelf in that same store. Its critical function had less to do with selling itself than to provide contrast with the rest of the product line. How many of its more reasonably priced colleagues did that awkward $499 model help sell? A good decoy is a team player—it makes everything around it look better.

Of course, salespeople must avoid being too obvious with decoys. One strategy is to set up the decoy with another item—a decoy for the decoy. One clothing store I visited did this cleverly. They began with a come-on to get customers in the shop: at the entrance, about ten feet inside the doorway (thus avoiding the decompression zone just beyond the entrance), they placed a large sign with the seductive message "Save 10% when you open an instant credit card account." A few feet beyond the sign and maybe thirty degrees off to the right (thus taking advantage of shoppers' inclination to move toward the right), the customer's eye was drawn to a small, sloppy table of name-brand cashmere sweaters at 40 percent off, of which only odd sizes remained. This was the decoy to set up the decoy. A few steps farther down the aisle, again slightly to the right, was a small table with the main decoy: name-brand cotton sweaters which were priced 20 percent to 30 percent higher than the cashmeres. Just beyond that was a large, neat, colorfully displayed table with the real catch of the day: "This Week's Featured" sweaters, discounted generic-brand clones of the name-brand cashmeres, priced even lower than the sale-priced cashmeres and much lower than the decoy. You're in the store, you're down the aisle, your wallet is open.

A question marketers frequently face is how much difference a person requires to see contrast. How high, for example, can they raise the price of a drink before customers perceive it to be significantly more expensive? How much has to be shaved off the size of a candy bar before people notice a drop in value? How much sugar needs to be added for a cereal to taste sweeter?

In psychophysics, these critical points are called "just noticeable differences," or JNDs. Scientists have been studying JNDs for a long time; in fact, since before there was even a field of psychology. In 1834 (the first psychology laboratory was established by Wilhelm Wundt in 1879), Ernst Weber published the results of a series of experiments in which he asked observers to lift a standard weight and a comparison weight and to then judge which was heavier. By carefully varying the difference in heaviness between the pairs of weights, Weber was able to quantify the smallest difference that could be detected at each weight level. Weber's crucial discovery was that the greater the weight you begin with, the more must be added to see a JND. If you begin with a standard weight of ten pounds, for example, the addition of about two pounds is just noticeably different. A fifteen-pound weight, however, requires an additional three pounds to see a JND, and a twenty-pound weight requires an additional four pounds. A JND is defined as the point at which two stimuli are recognized as different half the time.

After a long series of experiments, with many types of sensory inputs, Weber discovered that the JND between any two stimuli is based on a precise ratio between the size of the increase and the size of the beginning standard—what is known today as Weber's law. The particular magnitude of this ratio depends on what you're comparing. Studies have shown, for example, that it requires on average less than half a percent change in the pitch (frequency) of a tone for the change to be noticed, a little less than 2 percent in the brightness of a light for it to be recognized as brighter, a 14 percent change in pressure on the skin surface to be felt, and 20 percent more salt to be added to food before it tastes saltier.[20]

Marketers, naturally, are very interested in JNDs. Their focus is on perceptions of price and product quality and how these data can be applied to maximize their profit margin. To put it cynically, the question marketers want to answer is this: how much less value can I give you before you notice a difference?

Let's return, for example, to the question of how much a price must be altered before it makes a difference. Strictly speaking, measuring JNDs in price perception is ridiculous. Prices, unlike sensory experience, come to us in the form of numbers. You don't need to run experiments to figure out that two numbers that are different will be noticed as different. But there's the more challenging—and potentially profitable—question of subjective meaning: How different must prices be before they affect a purchase decision? Do buyers really care whether the product costs ninety-nine cents or a dollar? Is there a JND when it's dropped to ninety-five cents? Where are the cutoffs?

As with all JND questions, the answers begin with the rule of proportion: a $1 difference obviously has a bigger impact when we're choosing between inexpensive items (say, two cereal brands) than if we're comparing expensive ones (for example, new cars). The specific ratio? This is where it gets messy. As a beginning, however, we might turn to the results of an experiment by marketing researcher Joseph Uhl and colleagues that measured people's reactions to various price changes for a range of products. Uhl found that on average, something on the order of a JND occurred when prices varied by 5 percent. Variations of at least 5 percent made a difference to 64 percent of the consumers he tested. (This is about half the change [10 percent] needed for the loudness of a tone to be noticed as different.) This means that all things being equal, more than half of us will perceive a meaningful difference when a $1 item is dropped to $0.95: ninety-five cents is a sale, ninety-six cents is not. The higher the base price, the more absolute change required to make a difference. A $5 item must be reduced to $4.75 to achieve a JND. A $20,000 automobile needs to be discounted to $19,000.[21]

But this 5 percent figure is only a rough generalization. Studies show that the ratio required for a price change to produce a meaningful difference for consumers is considerably more elastic than the JND ratios for weights or sounds in a laboratory. Research has found, for example, that:

- We're more sensitive to price differences when shopping for necessities than for luxuries.
- Women are more discriminating of price differences than are men.[22]
- It takes a smaller price increase to deter poor shoppers than rich ones.[23]
- Price drops are weighted more heavily for name brands than for generic store brands. For example, a name-brand product requires a smaller discount to be perceived as a bargain than does a generic store brand.[24]

In other words, the percentage of change needed to create a JND for prices depends on a host of factors, ranging from the nature of the product to the context of the purchase to the resources of the consumer.

Equally important is the slippery problem of the appearance or "surface features" of the numbers themselves. These can be as influential as the actual magnitude of the prices. This has led to a practice sometimes called "psychological pricing." There is evidence, for example, that:

- Odd-number prices (like $199 or ninety-nine cents) tend to be perceived as significantly lower than the next highest even, round numbers ($200 or $1).[25] In other words, the "ninety-nine cents" strategy works. On the other hand, an equal price drop, when it goes from an odd to an even number, has less impact. Dropping a price from $201 to $200 or from $199 to $198, for example, doesn't create a JND.
- Prices ending with odd numbers create the impression of being more different from each other than do pairs of prices ending with even numbers. Consumers perceive the difference between $5.99 and $7.99, for example, as significantly greater than the difference between $6.00 and $8.00.[26]
- For many products, we typically don't look past the second digit in the price. This is more likely to be true for high-priced items, but it is also the case for many low-cost articles, such as grocery items. For example, consumers don't discriminate price-wise between a can of tuna selling for $1.59 and one selling for $1.53.[27]

Given these and many other quirks, there's clearly no single, invariable ratio that defines JNDs for prices. What makes for a meaningful difference in the consumer's eyes depends on many factors, all of which must be taken into account.

If you want to observe cutting-edge JND research nowadays, there's no need to visit a psychophysics laboratory. You'll find all the specimens you need in your mailbox. The ones I find most interesting are the solicitations from charitable organizations because they don't simply look for a yes or no sale, but are out to obtain the largest gift possible. Contributions are theoretically limitless.

Many of these solicitations are haphazard. The National Federation for the Blind, for example, recently sent me a letter with the request to "send $55.00, $27.50, $37.25, $12.50, $17.25 or as much as you can share with us." There's not a lot of psychophysics in that machine-gun fire. Other organizations, however, are more systematic. The typical strategy is to first win a minimal commitment and to then apply the contrast principle from a reverse perspective, with the express goal of pushing you just short of a JND to a larger commitment. The surface features of the numbers are often key elements in this strategy.

Recently, for example, I received a donation request from Special Olympics. To be more specific, it was a "sponsorship request" from their spokesperson, ex-football great Roger Staubach. Even more specifically, it was my "SECOND NOTICE" (Roger's capitals) of his sponsorship request. "Dear Dr. Robret Lemine," he addressed me. (Roger is one of several "friends" who write for my money who call me "Robret Lemine." Ed McMahon does, too. Robret Lemine also happens to be the misspelling that was transcribed when I signed up for a subscription to a popular magazine. It doesn't take Sherlock Holmes to figure out that this magazine is the source, or at least the source of the source, from which Roger and Ed both bought my name. It seems that Special Olympics and Publishers Clearing House work from the same mailing list. Go know.)

Roger went on to say, "Any amount you decide on or whatever you can afford will help tremendously and be deeply appreciated." Stuffed in the envelope was my "SECOND NOTICE Reply Form," which confronted me with the following statement:

I have enclosed my contribution of:
( ) $20   ( ) $24   ( ) $28   ( ) Other $___

How did Roger arrive at these numbers? First off, he needed to decide on a baseline. This was a no-brainer. His computer knew I'd donated $20 to Special Olympics the year before. Roger was relying on a common strategy. Begin your request at the highest level the purchaser has committed to in the past. If there's anything we've learned in psychology over the years, it's that the single best predictor of how a person will behave in the future is how he behaved in the past. It's like fishing. With all the possible spots on the lake, how do you decide where to drop your bait? As a general rule of thumb, you begin where the most fish were caught the last time around.

After establishing my most likely acceptable baseline point at $20, Special Olympics goes on to ask me to dig a little deeper this year. This is where JNDs come in. The graduated solicitations are designed to avoid the perception of contrast. It's their hope I'll see all three as reachable, giveable amounts and I'll opt for the highest one.

But the magnitude of the upward requests is a slippery business. On one hand, they should be high enough to be profitable. Aiming too high, however, can put your solicitation—literally—in the trash. This is because a request falling outside our latitude of acceptance is not only rejected but may lead to a paradoxical effect. If we're pushed too hard, we react with everything from suspicion and annoyance to anger and dislike. Research has shown the entire solicitation then loses its credibility, and people are less likely to give anything at all.[28] It sets off one of the great banes of solicitors—the boomerang response.

How effectively has Special Olympics played to my JND? Consider its first suggested increase, to $24. On one hand, this 20 percent increase (from $20) seems a bit steep, at least compared to what Uhl found for the JND of retail prices. On the other hand, it works nicely when you consider surface features: most people are going to weigh the increase of $4 against a second standard—the round figure of $5. You've got to assume that almost any donor who chooses to raise his contribution level is thinking in minimal increments of $5. Anything smaller seems chintzy. By that standard, the suggested $4 increase seems a bargain—a full 20 percent less than $5.

All in all, then, the $24 request is a reasoned attempt to exceed the limits of my JND without moving into my range of rejection. In addition, how many people will actually write out their check for an awkward figure like $24? It's safe to assume that many of the contributors who are willing to take the leap to $24 will, in the end, toss in another buck, rounding their donation up an additional less-than-JND increment to $25.

Another approach Special Olympics might have taken here is to separate the payments into smaller portions. This is the "How much does it cost a day?" strategy. For example, another nonprofit group, a school for special children, recently sent me a solicitation with a nickel pasted at the top of the cover letter. Next to the nickel was a large photo of a beautiful, angst-faced little boy who looked like he could have played the lead character in *Angela's Ashes*. Below that was the appeal: "Only a nickel a day helps you give a child like Frankie a new chance at life." Hey, brother, are you going to tell me you can't spare a lousy nickel? Try explaining why you said no to that pitch.

The small payments strategy isn't, of course, limited to nonprofits. Cellular phone companies, for example, typically offer you a deeply discounted or free phone if you commit to an extended service contract. If you're a moderate user, perhaps you'd consider signing up for $39.00/month for the next two years. The phone is thrown in for free. How would you feel, however, if the company hung a $959.76 price tag on that new phone, which is at least what you'll be paying before your contract expires?

But back to Roger Staubach. His next suggestion, for yet another $4 increase, to $28, is even more reasonable than the first. It's asking an even smaller proportional increase (16.7 percent) from the previous level ($24) while at the same time remaining 20 percent below the $5 reference standard. But there's also a flaw in this solicitation. If Special Olympics thinks $4 is the lower limit of my JND at the $20 level, then they're too far under a JND at this one. The absolute dollar increase should go up at each level. If there's a 20 percent increase at the first level, there should be another 20 percent at the next. You get the picture.

Of course, the fund-raisers from Special Olympics could care less whether they get high marks from an academic theorist. They're not taking a class in research methodology. Salespeople—no matter whether they work for profit or nonprofit causes—are probably the most empirical of all professionals. "It is an immutable law in business," supersalesman Harold Geneen observed, "that words are words, explanations are explanations, promises are promises—but only performance is reality." The bottom line is always the same: does it sell? By that criterion, I would grade the Special Olympics appeal a clear success: I ended up writing a check for $30. After all, Roger's my bud. Then again, I signed the check "Robret Lemine."

FIVE

$2 + $2 = $5

Or, Learning to Avoid Stupid Mental Arithmetic

Money isn't money in a casino. At home, you might drive across town to save a buck on a box of Tide, but at the table you tip a waitress five dollars for bringing a free Coke. You do both these things on the same day.

—Frederick and Steven Barthelme, *Double Down: Reflections on Gambling and Loss*

Afew years ago my wife and I decided to sell our house. We hadn't the faintest idea how much to ask, so I called a Realtor friend. She told us two comparable houses in our neighborhood had recently sold. One around the corner had gone for $175,000, but it stayed on the market for almost a year. The other house went for $130,000, just hours after being listed. We had our range. Now we had to decide on a figure. Should we offer the house at $130,000? At $150,000? Or maybe $180,000? We started thinking in multiples of tens of thousands of dollars. One moment we were preparing to ask another twenty or thirty and anticipating a lower offer, the next moment we'd decided to bring our asking price down ten but to hold firm. The numbers were dazzling. We settled on an asking price of $149,000, practically on a coin flip.

The first offer came in low, at $110,000. We not only rejected it but felt insulted. After all, we knew the absolute rock-bottom value of our house was $20,000 higher. Mind you, three days earlier our Realtor might have told us our house was worth 50 percent less or more and I'm sure we'd have just as easily accepted that range. But forget that. The anchoring process had begun.

Other offers trickled in—none at our asking price, but all above the lower limit. When considering these offers, we now found ourselves thinking in scaled-down units. Usually we spoke in terms of thousands of dollars. One buyer's offer came in ten (thousand, of course) below asking. Should we counter at five more? Or go up eight and expect them to come back four, and then we could counter for two more? Perhaps we should hold to our original price but offer them three in credit for new carpeting? We decided to ask for five. They came back at three less, leaving us two apart. We nodded to our agent, as we assumed the buyers were at the same moment doing with theirs, and suggested in a civilized tone just to split the difference at a thousand each. We offered this thousand as casually as if it were a stick of gum.

That night we received a visit from our Realtor. The buyers had refused our compromise. They were holding firm and, their Realtor had sent word, would probably call off the deal if we demanded a penny more. In tandem—and surprising each other with our voracity—my wife and I barked back, "Absolutely no." Who did these money-grubbers think they were, trying to milk us for a thousand bucks? Neither we nor the buyers budged for close to a week—they at one forty, we at one forty-one. I'm sure they had no clearer idea how they'd arrived at their last-ditch figure than we did about ours. But we all were obviously now certain exactly what this house was worth.

The stalemate was eventually broken by the Realtors, both of whom volunteered to give up $500 of their fees. Later, in fact, our Realtor told us these impasses were rather common. "At some point in these nego-tiations people seem to get a bottom-line figure in their head and, once they do, there's no getting past it," she observed.

Looking back, what I find most remarkable about these events was how, in my mind, there was no relationship between the amount of money at stake and how important the decision felt. After the first couple of days, it didn't matter whether the particular involved $20,000 or $1,000. I always seemed to expend the same effort and care, and our successes and failures affected me with the same inten-sity of pleasure, regret, or (more than occasionally) anxiety. This was especially true when it was money leaving our pockets. When I felt gypped, I felt gypped, no matter for how much. Losses were losses, period.

There is something marvelous about how effortlessly a human mind can switch scales like this. But there is something equally ridiculous. Literally minutes after we closed our deal, I went to a supermarket to buy groceries. I discovered that cauliflower was $1.99 per pound, twice what I paid elsewhere the week before. Unfair! Without a second thought, I indignantly put the cauliflower back and continued down the aisle to find a better value. Forget that it would be my second choice and that I'd reacted with more emotion to paying an extra ninety-nine cents for the cauliflower than I had to the $10,000 decisions I was making two weeks earlier.

We like to think of ourselves—not necessarily other people, but ourselves—as rational decision makers. It's comforting to believe that we reach our conclusions through an objective calculation of costs and value, logically concluding what will be in our best interests. But we don't. Not even close. By accepted business standards, we're awful mental accountants. Study after study reveals that my own ridiculous arithmetic is completely normal behavior.

Imagine you're lying on the beach on a hot day. All you have to drink is water. You can't stop thinking about how much you'd enjoy a nice cold bottle of your favorite brand of beer. A companion gets up to go make a phone call and offers to bring back a beer from the only nearby place where beer is sold—a fancy resort hotel. He says the beer might be expensive and wants to know how much you're willing to pay for it. He says he'll buy the beer if it costs as much or less than the price you state but won't buy it if it costs more. You trust your friend and understand there's no possibility of his bargaining with the bartender. What price do you tell him?

Now consider a slight change in the scenario. What if the only nearby place to buy beer is at a small, run-down grocery store? What price would you tell your friend this time?

If you're like most people, you'd offer a lot less at the grocery than at the hotel bar. This is what marketing professor Richard Thaler found when he posed the two questions to executives who said they were regular beer drinkers.[1] When they had to purchase the beer at the fancy hotel, the executives were willing to pay an average of $2.65. At the run-down grocery, they were only willing to pay $1.50. It made no difference that the product was identical in both cases—the same beer, consumed in the same surroundings.

This finding runs totally contrary to traditional microeconomic theory. A basic assumption of economics is that equal amounts of money and/or equal products are fully interchangeable—what's known as the principle of fungibility. After all, isn't $1 equivalent to every other dollar? At a bank, perhaps, but not in the world of mental arithmetic.

Like so many principles in this book, our ability to shift scales to meet the context is usually adaptive. But like the other principles it, too, has a gaping flaw: it's easily manipulable. Persuasion artists understand that in the buyer's mind, the value of an absolute number is arbitrary, ambiguous, and malleable and that as a result, consumers can be easily induced to pay more or less for the same product. Effective salespeople knows how to frame the sale so it will seem like a gain, rather than a loss; or, even better, so that not buying will itself be a loss, an opportunity forgone. It's all in the setup. Here are ten rules of framing that salespeople may exploit you with.

Rule One: Separate Gains

Say you win $75 in lottery prizes. Which would you prefer: to win the whole $75 in one prize or to win the same $75 split into two different prizes on different occasions? Most people, studies find, opt for the two smaller prizes. It's been shown, for example, that people are happier when they win a $25 lottery *and* a $50 lottery—especially when it occurs in that order—than if they win a single $75 lottery. This is because we respond less to the cumulative total of the gains than the fact that it is a gain. Every gain brings pleasure.

One way marketers take advantage of the "separate gains" principle is to offer consumers a free gift with their product instead of just giving them more of the product itself. *Sports Illustrated*, for example, sometimes offers new subscribers a free videotape or other gift instead of simply adding a few bonus issues. Or look at the advertisements for cosmetic companies in almost any Sunday newspaper. Lancôme, for example, recently ran ads offering a free present with any $18.50 purchase. Estée Lauder bettered this by offering a free eight-piece gift with any $19.50 purchase. In all of these cases, the company wants you to file the gift in your unexpected windfall account, where its perceived value is psychologically inflated, rather than mentally bunching it together with the other products into one big purchase.

As one marketer put it, a salesperson "shouldn't wrap all the Christmas presents in one box."[2]

Rule Two: Separate Small Gains from Larger Losses

This is a corollary to rule one. Any profit is pleasant, of course, but it gets buried when it's filed alongside a bigger loss. If *Sports Illustrated* or Lancôme simply reduced their asking prices a couple of dollars, the reduction would have been lost in the total cost of the transaction. The companies would have to offer a handsome discount—certainly much more than the value of the gift—to make it significant to consumers. This is especially true when the asking price is perceived as malleable. When it comes to magazines, for example, there are so many deals going around that who can keep track of what's a good price for *Sports Illustrated*? But the free gift will always stand out.

Supermarkets have become good at applying this rule. There's no getting around the fact that food bills are expensive and difficult to predict with precision. As a result, even the best of deals tend to get lost in the final tally. To highlight their discounts, many markets now give you "savings" information separately. After paying and bagging your groceries, the clerk hands you your receipt and informs you exactly how much money you've saved today by shopping at her store: "Thank you, Mr. Levine, you saved $3.24 on your Safeway card today."

A variation on this principle is that a small reduction in loss should be kept separate from the higher loss. This is the silver-lining rule. The practice of automobile rebates applies this concept nicely. It's said that the automobile rebate program originally developed because of the threat of government price controls. Dealers didn't want to officially reduce prices, fearing that the prices might get permanently frozen there without notice. By offering rebates, cars could be attractively discounted without this long-term risk. Arithmetically, the rebate idea doesn't make a lot of sense for consumers. Consumers usually pay taxes on the rebate, meaning they would come out ahead with an up-front discount. And it's been decades since anyone talked about price controls, so it shouldn't matter one way or the other to dealers. Yet the practice continues, and it continues to sell cars. Why? It's the allure of the silver lining. The small reduction in loss is perceived as a gain. This strategy is most effective when the lining stands out—for example, when the rebate arrives as a separate check from corporate headquarters rather than as a reduction in the down-payment price.

Rule Three: Consolidate Losses

Which would upset you more?

1. The IRS sends you a letter saying you made a minor arithmetical error on your tax return and owe $100. Later that day you receive another letter from IRS saying you made a second error and owe them an additional $50.
2. The IRS sends you a letter saying you made a minor arithmetical mistake on your tax return and owe $150.
   (Note: There are no other repercussions from your mistake in either case.)

More than 75 percent of people who are asked this question say they'd be more upset by the two small bills than the single large one.[3] This is because every loss stings no matter how much the total. As is the case for gains, the number of losses has greater impact than the actual amount of the loss.

Effective marketers apply this principle by bundling losses whenever possible. For example, it's easier for an auto dealer to sell a car stereo at the time the auto is purchased than to sell the stereo separately later. After all, $300 is a lot of money to spend when you're shopping in a stereo store, but it gets lost in the shadow of a $20,000 automobile price. And the $300 turns almost invisible when the whole auto package is spread over five years of payments.

The principle doesn't only apply to money. In my own profession of academics, for example, rejection is a way of life. The odds are stacked against us every step of the way—getting into graduate school, obtaining a job, having a grant approved, having a paper accepted for publication. The probability for success in any of these activities usually begins at around one in ten and gets worse from there. With no false modesty, I feel confident saying I'm a true expert on being rejected.

In an informal study, I asked a group of my fellow experts how they prefer to be rejected. The professors I interviewed were offered the options of either receiving several rejection letters the same day or having the letters spread out over several days. They were unanimous (a rare event on any issue for my colleagues) in choosing the first option. As one observed, "Get it over with at once. That way I only have to go through the process of feeling incompetent and unwanted one time." Another commented, "I can just be depressed one day instead of several. One cry and I'm done." Bundle those losses in one neat package and move on.

I then asked these same colleagues how they'd prefer to receive the letters if they contained news of acceptance. Again my colleagues were unanimous. In this case, however, they wanted the news spread out. "I'd want to squeeze every last crumb out of each word," one observed. "It would be better than a month on Maui." These responses were consistent with rule one: we prefer to receive many small gains separately than all together.

One of the least effective strategies is to make separate solicitations in close temporal proximity. Movie theaters, for example, sometimes run appeals from charities during the coming attractions. The problem here is that most customers are still conscious of the costs of admission and probably the snack bar. They may have anticipated these costs, but nonetheless still feel their sting. This is not a good time to ask them for more money, no matter who you represent. Too often, people's first reaction is to ask "If it's such a good cause, why don't the theater owners just donate some of their own profits?" From a marketing perspective, this isn't a bad question. Why not just bundle the losses together in the admission price?

Rule Four: Bundle Small Losses into Larger Gains

This is another corollary to rule one, rounding out the four involving bundling. Since large gains are subject to the rule of diminishing returns, there's not that much psychological difference between a big gain and a pretty big gain. This offers salespeople a way to minimize the impact of a small loss. If a small loss can be packaged with a larger gain, the loss will be less noticeable than if it stands by itself.

A popular application of this rule is to encourage employees to pay for items through automatic payroll deductions. It's been shown that people are more likely to buy savings bonds or contribute to United Way or pay for life insurance when it comes out of their monthly paycheck than when they're asked to write a big check for the year.[4]

The principle works even more effectively when it comes to payroll deductions for health insurance premiums. Workers believe that this loss, or part of it at least, is assumed by their employer. If someone else is writing the check for my HMO premium then it's not coming out of my pocket, is it? We unfortunately forget that every dollar our employer pays in our name is part of the same compensation package.

Even the IRS applies this principle. Right after asking for your name and address, Form 1040 inquires whether you want to contribute a few dollars to the Presidential Election Campaign Fund. Say what? "Hi, glad to meet you. Before you figure out how many thousands of dollars you owe us this year, we want to offer you the opportunity to give money to politicians." Most taxpayers would probably puke at this suggestion in any other context. But how many want to bother worrying about a few bucks when preparing a tax return?

My own state of California takes a slightly different approach. On our state form, taxpayers are currently offered the opportunity to contribute as much as we want to any of nine nonprofit organizations, ranging from a fund for the study of Alzheimer's disease to an endowment for public libraries. Unlike the federal return, this request comes at the very end of the form. One expects that taxpayers who have just calculated they will receive a refund contribute considerably more money to these charities than do those who've just learned they have to write a check to the tax board, regardless of how much withholding tax they might have paid throughout the year. In fact, from the standpoint of a fund-raiser, there is probably no moment in time that so divides these two groups of people. Asking the people who owe taxes for a contribution is like tapping your dad for a loan after he just got a speeding ticket; let's just say it opposes the principle of consolidating losses. But there will never be a better occasion to approach those expecting a refund. The request (1) neatly bundles a small loss into a large gain; (2) leaves the amount of gain in doubt until the last moment, so that potential contributors enter with a fluid frame of reference; and (3) makes sure unless the taxpayer is either a saint or a great repressor, he's probably feeling more than a little guilt and perhaps fear by the time he signs the tax form. All in all, it's an exquisite moment for soliciting philanthropy.

Bundle losses, separate gains.

Rule Five: Appeal to Risk Taking for Losses, to Safety for Gains

One of the most robust idiosyncrasies of mental arithmetic is that people experience more pain from a loss than they do pleasure from an equal gain. We get more upset over losing $100 than we feel happy about gaining $100. This is true not only for money but for our lives in general. It's been shown, for example, that bad emotions feel bad more than good emotions feel good: people try harder to escape bad moods than they do to prolong good moods and they remember their bad moods longer than their good ones.[5] "We find pleasure much less pleasurable, pain much more painful than we had anticipated," Schopenhauer observed.[6] As one of my clinical psychology colleagues estimated it, the average person needs five good experiences to balance out a single bad one.

From an evolutionary viewpoint, a bias toward the negative makes perfect sense. The survival of our species has always been more closely linked to avoiding disaster than to finding happiness. We're primed to see threats. People pick an angry face out of a happy crowd much more quickly than they pick a happy face out of an angry crowd.[7] Potential danger signals action needs to be taken. The only action positive events usually call for is celebration, and nobody's ever died from forgetting to plan a party.

Hyperreactivity to loss and pain underlies most people's risk-taking strategies. When it comes to gain, we tend to be conservative. People usually prefer a small certain gain over a less secure larger one—your basic bird in the hand over two in the bush principle. It's been shown, for example, that most people are unwilling to bet $10 of their own on the outcome of a coin toss; one experiment found that the majority of people weren't willing to make the bet unless they were offered at least two-to-one odds.[8]

When it comes to losses, however, we're more willing to gamble. Because even moderate losses are so painful, we go to extraordinary lengths to avoid or reverse them. Most people will risk an uncertain large loss rather than accept a more certain smaller one. For example, one study found that when given the choice between an 85 percent chance of losing $1,000 or accepting a sure loss of $850, the vast majority of people choose the 85 percent gamble. Casinos, of course, have capitalized lucratively on this mentality. The willingness of losers to take risks is why gamblers often go deeper and deeper into debt in the hope of "just getting back to even." This is the double-or-nothing mentality.

This rule—that people are more willing to gamble when they face a loss than when they risk giving up something they possess—can lead to distorted decision making. Consider this scenario.

Imagine that the United States is preparing for the outbreak of an unusual Asian disease, which is expected to kill six hundred people.

Two alternative programs to combat the disease have been proposed. Assume that the exact scientific estimates of the consequences of the programs are as follows:

If Program A is adopted, two hundred people will be saved.
If Program B is adopted, there is a one-third probability that six hundred people will be saved and a two-thirds probability that no people will be saved.

Which of the two programs would you favor?

In a study by cognitive psychologists Amos Tversky and Daniel Kahneman, 72 percent of the respondents chose the sure savings offered by Program A. Only 28 percent were willing to gamble on Program B, although the odds were that more people would be saved under this program.

But responses change dramatically when the options are framed just a little differently. Which of these two programs would you favor?

If Program C is adopted, four hundred people will die.
If Program D is adopted, there is a one-third probability that nobody will die and a two-thirds probability that six hundred people will die.

Programs C and D offer the exact same odds as Programs A and B, but they phrase their outcomes in terms of losses instead of gains. This simple change in framing produces an almost 180-degree reversal. Tversky and Kahneman found that only 22 percent chose the sure savings of Program C—the very same sure savings selected by 72 percent of the people in the first go-around under Program A. Seventy percent opted for the gamble of Program D—the same gamble endorsed by only 28 percent of the people under Program B![9] One of my art teachers used to say that the frame is as important as the picture. In persuasion, it can be even more important—the triumph of form over content.

If these sound like the type of questions you hear from insurance salespeople, be assured this rule hasn't escaped that industry. It used to be that insurance agents promoted policies as protection against losses. My father used to tell of salesmen coming into the living room and frightening him with questions like "What's going to happen to your family if you get in your car tomorrow and get smashed to death by a truck?" or "What would your children do if you come home tomorrow and your house is burned to ashes?"

Insuring against losses, however, goes against the grain of the risk principle. It asks people to accept a sure loss (the cost of the policy) rather than to gamble on an uncertain larger loss. Since we like to gamble on losses, this can be a difficult sell.

Most insurance companies today avoid this problem by phrasing their messages in the positive. Insurance is now described not so much as a buffer against unpredictable loss but, instead, as a way of protecting the valuables you possess. Even if you don't currently have valuables to speak of, the companies encourage you to insure against losing the good things you're hoping will come your way in the future. Why gamble on losing your hopes? One company advertises: "Whether you want to secure your family's future or safeguard your auto or home, Prudential has the insurance products to help you achieve your goals." A television commercial for another tells us: "Is it possible to secure a dream? At The Hartford, we do just that." Allstate's motto (right below the "good hands" shtick) goes straight for the buzzwords without bothering over sentence structure: "Succeeding today, planning tomorrow." I doubt anybody has the faintest idea what that actually says, but, for a few cents a day, who wants to gamble with success and tomorrow?

Automobile salespeople are masters at this spin. The sales manual for one large auto dealer I studied has a section on how to overcome buyers' objections to an extended service agreement. The most common objection, the manual observes, is "I bought it before and never used it." When you hear this, the salesperson is advised, "Explain to the customer that it's great that they had a good experience with their car, but a car has 10,000 moving parts and buying the added protection will give peace of mind." This company has learned that most of us will gamble over a bad transmission, but we will pay generously to insure our mental serenity. *Om mani padme hum.*

Rule Six: Let the Consumer Buy Now, Pay Later

We hate giving up what we possess. We're also quick to assume psychological ownership. Salespeople try to capitalize on these entwined forces by encouraging buyers to live with the product before making a commitment, to create the feeling of ownership: "Walk around in it."

"Look at yourself in the mirror." "Bring the sofa home for a few days." Only later does the salesperson try to close the sale. By then, he hopes, the consumer frames *not buying* as a loss.

Some companies, for example, encourage you to buy "on approval." Or, there is the enormously successful cousin of this approach, to "buy now, pay later." Many magazines insert subscription cards asking you to check either of two boxes, one marked "Payment enclosed" and the other marked "Bill me later." The return card is prestamped. If you choose the "Bill me later" option—which, given the two choices, is pretty much an automatic for most people; it even saves the cost of a stamp—then you simply drop the card in the mail. In case the strain of marking a box is too much of a burden, the card often includes an even larger default box marked "YES" which has been prechecked for you. Some magazines offer a free first issue. One typical come-on I recently received read: "100% Risk-Free Guarantee. If I'm not thrilled with [the magazine] I'll write 'cancel' across the invoice I receive, return it and owe nothing. My FREE issue will be mine to keep no matter what." What's there to refuse? But how many people like me will forget to write "cancel" across that invoice a couple of months from now?

Another advertisement sent to my home hit the quiniela for ease of possession. The letter—which was addressed to my then fourteen-year-old son!—brought several pieces of good news:

1. "Mr. Levine, you have been selected to receive a FREE $20.00-value gift" (a desk clock)
2. " . . . just for trying our merchandise" (a VCR with a "total value of $320")
3. for a "no charge 30-day home trial"
4. which "could be sent to you FREE and CLEAR" ("All that's required on your part is a little fast action!" it was explained later.)

And, if all this were not enough, there was yet an additional good tiding: "Standard credit approval procedures have been waived for you, Mr. Levine." (This was a truly remarkable piece of banking. My son has many wonderful qualities. But—call me an overcritical father—a good credit risk is hardly one of them.) This meant, they concluded, there was no need "to fill out any long complicated forms or wait for someone to approve your credit." Just check a box and it's all yours.

Needless to say, I hid the offer from my son.

The buy now, pay later approach has many variations. Another common application is to allow consumers to delay payment for thirty days or ninety days or maybe to make "no payments this year." One Maryland auto dealer I studied advertised, "No money down, Zero % interest for 36 months and a $500 customer rebate coupon." (He also displayed a fascinating slogan: "Bad credit, slow credit, bankruptcy, military personnel welcomed." It sounded like something Bob Dylan might have written for the credit company who preapproved my fourteen-year-old son for the VCR.)

An advertisement for a Washington, D.C., mattress store pushed the principle even further. The ad began, in very large letters, with the word *NO* written three times and the word *PLUS* written four times. The subtext read: "NO money down, NO monthly payment for one year, NO interest for one year, PLUS free delivery, PLUS free set up, PLUS a free bedframe, PLUS free disposal of your old mattress." In other words, just phone the store and sweet dreams.

Many service providers allow a free or inexpensive trial period to new members. This is a common technique used by groups ranging from weight-loss clinics and health clubs to cable television companies and Internet providers. Sometimes the consumer is informed he was "selected" for this privilege. "We are writing to you, Mr. Robert Levine, because we know you are a person who appreciates good health," one clinic wrote to me. Other companies have written to me because I'm "a connoisseur of fine wines." Or I "recognize the value of a dollar." Or "care about the future of my children." Or "the future of my environment." I guess I'm just an all-around special kind of guy.

A famous mail-order book club addresses the no-commitment appeal squarely, with the slogan, "4 Books, 4 Bucks, No commitment, No kidding." (My friend Martin said he used this line when he proposed to his wife.) The last offer the club sent me—because, they said, I am a person "who appreciates good books AND a good deal"—added a free booklight if I accepted their $1 books. This was followed by the reminder that I had "no commitment ever."

In all of these examples, salespeople hope that the trial period will stimulate our ever-eager juices of psychological ownership. We'll then assimilate the products or activities into our baseline of normal life, so that no longer having them would feel like a loss.

Finally, these appeals put customers in the position of needing to exert more work to not own the product than to just give up and buy it. Returning the products or the membership card or the monthly "I don't want this month's book selection" card means physical effort to get it back to the store or into the mailbox. It may entail paying shipping costs. More significantly, it often necessitates psychological work. If the salesperson met with you personally, you're left needing to rationalize the cost you're inflicting on that nice, hardworking seller by taking home a new product and returning it in secondhand condition; or why you knowingly took advantage of the seller's generosity by accepting a free gift when you never intended to buy the product. If, in fact, you can easily afford the product, it makes you a cheapskate to boot.

Taken together, the forces of inertia, possession, and loss often make paying up and making it yours the easiest course of action.

Rule Seven: Frame It as an Opportunity Forgone Rather Than an Out-of-Pocket Loss

Our aversion to loss leads to another basic rule: out-of-pocket losses are more painful than opportunities forgone.

Which of these incidents would upset you more?[10]

1. You're expecting a Christmas bonus of $300. When you receive the check it is indeed in the amount of $300. A week later you receive a note saying there has been an error. The check was $50 too high. You must return the $50.
2. You're expecting a Christmas bonus of $300. You receive the check and find it's for $250.

Nearly everyone finds the first scenario more aversive than the second. This is because it hurts more to part with what we hold in our hand than with possessions we expect to obtain in the future. There's a well-known legal rule of thumb that possession is nine-tenths of the law. The same might be said about psychological possession.

Several years ago, for example, some banks were offering customers the choice of either paying a $5.00 per month service charge for a checking account or of keeping a minimum balance of $1,500.00 and paying nothing. Since interest rates on savings accounts were about 5.8 percent at the time, anyone choosing the minimum balance option would be giving up $7.25 in monthly interest income to avoid the anguish of paying $5.00 in out-of-pocket costs. Yet, consistent with the opportunity forgone rule, the banks found most people who could afford the minimum balance selected the free-checking option.[11]

Salespeople take advantage of this quirk in various ways. Every spring, for example, advertisements appear for products you can buy with no-interest credit using your forthcoming income tax refund. Automobile, home improvement, and stereo salespeople are particularly inclined to use this appeal. They understand it's less painful to part with money you don't yet possess than with money in hand. This is particularly true when you're purchasing luxuries. Until the refund check arrives, it's funny money.

Rule Eight: Emphasize Sunk Costs

Our aversion to loss not only makes us vulnerable to manipulation but often leads to just-plain-stupid decisions. For example, almost every stock market investor has heard the widely cited portfolio advice to cut your losses short and let your profits run. But, in fact, investors usually do the opposite. When management professor Terrance Odean tracked the trading history of 10,000 investors over the seven-year period 1987 to 1993, he discovered a strong preference for selling winners rather than losers: investors were one and a half times more likely to sell stocks on which they were ahead than those on which they were losing.[12] There was no evidence that these decisions were motivated by rational fiscal considerations, such as a desire to rebalance portfolios or avoid the higher trading costs of low-priced stocks. The only explanation seemed to be that people are simply unwilling to swallow a loss. As stock market journalist Mark Hulbert observed: "As long as they avoid selling a loser, they can rationalize that it will recover someday, thus vindicating the original decision to buy. By contrast, once they sell a stock, investors cannot avoid the fact that they lost money."[13]

But in the context of a portfolio this behavior makes no sense. The only question for an investor should be which stock will go up most in the future. And, in fact, the inclination to stay with losers turned out to be quite costly for the investors in Odean's study. He calculates that after taking tax savings and capital gains into consideration, investors would have earned an average of about 4.4 percent more money a year each time they sold a loser rather than a winner.

Falling into this way of thinking is to succumb to the "sunk-cost trap," a problem I'll have more to say about later. Sunk costs are non-recoverable investments of time or money. The trap occurs when your aversion to loss impels you to throw good money after bad because you don't want to waste your earlier investment. Real banks are as likely to fall into the trap as we laymen. Cognitive psychologists John Hammond, Ralph Keeney, and Howard Raiffa, who have done considerable consulting with banks, have found that the bias shows up with disturbing regularity among those professionals. They offer an example.

> Fifteen years ago, we helped a major U.S. bank recover after making many bad loans to foreign businesses. We found that bankers responsible for originating the problem loans were far more likely to advance additional funds—repeatedly, in many cases—than were bankers who took over the accounts after the original loans were made. Too often, the original bankers' strategy—and loans—ended in failure. Having been trapped by an escalation and commitment, they had tried, consciously or unconsciously, to protect their earlier, flawed decisions. They had fallen victim to the sunk-cost bias. The bank finally solved the problem by instituting a policy requiring that a loan be immediately reassigned to another banker as soon as any problem became serious. The new banker would be able to take a fresh, unbiased look at whether offering more funds had merit.[14]

If professional bankers fall into the sunk-cost trap, it's no wonder amateurs get caught in it, too. Salesmen know that if they can persuade you to make a small investment, you'll be that much more likely to make a larger one later. To avoid the trap, try not muddle your decisions by agonizing over what you spent in the past. Your sunk costs are irrelevant to your decision today. See it through fresh eyes.

Rule Nine: List High, Sell Low

The system of fixed prices was first popularized a little more than a century ago when, in a revolutionary marketing vision, retailer John

Wanamaker decided to attach price tags to every product in his Philadelphia emporium. Until then, and still today in many parts of the world, prices were usually set by bargaining. Most stores were like used-car lots, with salesmen sizing up customers as they entered the store and then haggling to get them to pay the highest possible price. Wanamaker, a social-minded Presbyterian, wanted to create a more efficient and civil environment. His solution was to establish fixed prices. In the process, he also created the great American pastimes of discounts and sales.

Sometimes it seems like the entire world is on sale. When three-quarters of the products on the mall are discounted, this sets up a credibility question, so much that you no longer pay notice to the stated "list" or "suggested retail" prices. Right? Wrong.

In a study by marketing professor Joel Urbany and his colleagues, consumers were shown one of several variations of a supposed newspaper advertisement for the same RCA nineteen-inch television.[15] In all the ads, the TV was offered at a sale price of $319. The ads people saw differed, however, in what was given as the list price of the television. It was either $359, $419, a ridiculous $799, or, in some cases, no list price was indicated.

Urbany wasn't too surprised to find that buyers who were shown a plausible list price—$359 or $419—thought the televisions were a better value than people shown no list price. Or that the $419 retail price made the set even more attractive than the $359 price. This simply confirmed what contrast theory has said all along.

The unexpected finding was how far this rule could be pushed. People who saw the obviously inflated $799 list price were the most willing buyers of all. Consumers weren't exactly fooled by the price. In fact, those who read the $799 ad were considerably more likely to agree with the statement that "I do not believe that the amount of this advertised reduction is a truthful claim" than those shown the other retail prices for the set. But never mind. Compared with those reading the more reasonable ads, consumers presented with the inflated list price of $799:

- Estimated the price of the TV would be higher at other stores (the $799 group estimated an average market price of $449, compared with estimates of $389 from the $419 group and $363 from the $359 group)

- Believed the discounted price ($319) they were getting was a better value
- Were (in a computerized shopping simulation) less likely to take the trouble to telephone other stores for comparison prices
- Were more likely to go straight to the advertised store and buy the set

This study shows that a high reference price not only makes a dealer's discount look more attractive, but even when people are skeptical about the suggested reference price they may remain more willing consumers. Naturally, there are limits to how far discount seekers can be manipulated. There's a point where consumers' suspicions make them ignore marketers' supposed discounts. As Urbany found, however, it takes longer to reach this point than you might think. This is especially true for products you purchase infrequently or whose quality is difficult to gauge. Don't overestimate your ability to know where to draw the line.

A variation on this rule concerns the sequence with which you present different-priced items. Say you want to sell customers a $1 pen. Studies show that they'll be more likely to buy the pen if you show several higher-priced pens first; and they'll be less likely to buy the $1 pen if you show it before you show the higher-priced ones.[16] Salespeople frequently apply this order effect through a tactic known as top-down selling. Catalogs, for example, may display similar products from most to least expensive. Or, in a literal top-down maneuver, stores may display a more expensive product at eye level and then place a similar item that is on sale just below it.

It should be noted that Wanamaker's system of fixed prices has not been without problems for retailers. The fact is that any set price is arbitrary. Once attached to the product, however, it's static. As a result, the going rate may not reflect what a consumer who walks into the store is willing to pay. The price tag on a Compaq computer may remain exactly the same while the company's stock bounces up and down by the second. The fixed-price system can be costly for retailers: some enthusiastic buyers would be willing to pay more than the number on the price tag; other reluctant customers might be willing to buy at a lower price but won't pay the list price. "Hence," as one business writer observed, "the great challenge of modern retail: how to discount to the cheapskates without giving a free ride to the spendthrifts."[17]

Rule Ten: Never Exceed the Reference Price

This is the flip side of rule nine and another basic application of the contrast principle. There is no surer way to send a consumer out the door than to exceed their reference price. Marketing professors Gerald Smith and Thomas Nagle, for example, offer the following example.[18]

Imagine you need gas and have to pay with a credit card. You are confronted with signs for two adjacent gas stations. Which would you choose?

1. Station one, which sells gasoline for $1.39 per gallon but advertises a ten-cent discount if you pay cash.
2. Station two, which sells for $1.29 per gallon but advertises a ten-cent surcharge if you use a credit card.

If you're like most people, you'll drive into the first station. Dollars-and-cents-wise, of course, the options are identical. But by setting the reference point high, the first station offers the illusion of an opportunity for savings; the second station holds out nothing but an in-your-face loss.

One of the worst pieces of marketing I came across while research-ing this book was from a Yuppie-targeted, mail-order outdoor furni-ture company. Its catalog began well enough. On the cover was the company motto, "For those who appreciate excellence." Then, playing directly to us sophisticates, the first few pages contained not a word about price, doting instead on the quality of the company's products—how, compared with competitors, its product are made of better wood, are more comfortable, are more expertly constructed, require less maintenance, last considerably longer, and are backed by superior ser-vice. When I was selling cars, this is what my managers called "build-ing value." Anyone who read through those initial pages with even a modicum of attention should have been set up for high prices. In fact, the company's claims of superior quality would have seemed dishonest if not followed by high prices.

In this, the company did not disappoint. Prices turned out to be in the neighborhood of 50 percent to 75 percent higher than those in most competing catalogs I reviewed. The Adirondack chair I had my eye on was certainly much higher than I'd ever considered paying—about

$150 more than one I'd priced a few weeks before. But after reading page after page about the advantages of their "FEQ" (First European Quality) teak and genuine Honduras mahogany and how they only used "true mortise and tenon joinery" (unlike those other sleazebags who, I assume, fake their mortise and tenon), I started feeling that only a complete loser would buy anything cheaper. Asking my family to sit on knotty pine furniture would be like feeding them Spam on their birthdays. The catalog propaganda was, in other words, unfreezing my previous anchor point. This unfreezing is a critical first step when selling to reluctant buyers. The sale was halfway home.

Then the company destroyed it. Upon turning to the order form—and still feeling quite tentative about the purchase—I was confronted with a loose insert informing me that because of rising production costs, all catalog prices were now 10 percent higher. The Adirondack chair would cost on the order of $40 more than I'd been considering. Note that this wasn't the often-effective technique of warning that prices would be higher if the customer didn't order soon. The cutoff date had already passed.

The momentum I'd been building stopped dead. That the chair was initially priced $150 more than the company's competitors had been nicely framed as an opportunity for gain. I could file it both as a desirable luxury and a sensible long-term investment. In fact, if the company had listed it as $190 more in the first place, I probably would have paid that, too. But this $40 late fee was framed as pure loss, and this I couldn't accept. Never, ever overexceed the buyer's reference point.

The never-exceed rule has wide applications. When I first began teaching, for example, experienced colleagues offered me all sorts of advice. I heard tips about everything from how to explain difficult concepts and motivate a class to dealing with discipline problems. But the most useful bit of wisdom I received was from an eighteen-year-old sitting in the back row. Midway into the semester I'd assigned an article that was not on the original syllabus. The article described a great piece of work that I was certain would become a significant contribution to social psychology (which it has). I explained to the class with some pride that I'd been fortunate to obtain a preprint of the article, which would not be published for another week. They held in their hands cutting-edge research. I thought they'd be excited. But I looked up to a roomful of Sylvester Stallone sneers. I was confused. Was it because they

didn't like the article? That was when the eighteen-year-old patroniz-
ingly explained to me, "You don't add to the course requirements, you
only take away." Sound mental arithmetic.

The quirks of mental accounting are deeply ingrained, mindless, and
highly susceptible to manipulation. But once you recognize your
habits, there are ways to minimize losses.

First, remember that a dollar is a dollar is a dollar. A few years ago,
I was serving as department chairperson at my university, which is
funded by the state of California. Just as I began my term, California
went into a severe economic crisis that led to the deepest budget cuts
our university had ever known. We were short of everything.

With a few months remaining in the fiscal year, our department had
spent virtually all of its annual budget. About then I got a call from a
man in charge of building maintenance at the university. He informed
me that the carpeting we requested for our offices, two years earlier,
had suddenly been approved for funding. When the gentleman read the
list of offices approved for new carpets, I noted that a few of them didn't
need new carpets. This was fortunate, I told him, because we desperately needed the extra money for other items. A few days earlier, in fact,
I'd been begging our dean for funds to purchase basic office supplies,
but he told me that his office was broke, too. Maybe, I told the building maintenance man, we could now trade a little unneeded carpeting
for some paper and pencils?

The man looked at me like I was an embezzler. These funds came
out of a special office renovation account and were untransferable to
other accounts. They were approved for carpets and carpets only, he
told me. And, he emphasized, we needed to get the work done quickly,
because if the money wasn't spent before the end of the fiscal year, it
would automatically revert to the state. Anyone who has dealt with government budgets knows what that means: we'd not only lose our carpets but would send the powers that be a signal that our department
could survive without the extra money. This would lead to a reduction
in next year's budget, not only for our own department but, perhaps,
for other departments like us. Those reductions would become the
baseline (anchor, if you will) for the following year's funding, which
meant the cuts could spiral for many years to come. Ever the patriots,
we accepted all the carpeting.

Mental accounting can be just as idiotic. Watch out when anyone frames a dollar to look like anything but what it is. Don't think like the government.

Second, you should always consider financial matters in the context of your total needs and resources. What is the absolute value of a dollar to you? Recognize when the sales pitch is appealing to your psychological needs rather than your fiscal sensibility. Face it, on an emotional level you're mush for a good salesman. But at least in the upper chambers of your cerebrum, try not to corner yourself with mechanical questions like "Are they taking advantage of me?" or "Is this an offer I better jump on before it's too late?" Many times, of course, these are the very questions you should be asking. But not always. When the wrong frame dictates your arithmetic, it may lead to self-destructive decisions. Try to be aware of your larger fiscal picture and how your decision accords with these resources.

To define your own criteria of fiscal sensibility, I suggest a two-question self-test.

Question 1: Is it a good value *NOW*? Not compared with the price it was yesterday or what your friend paid for it. Not whether it concedes a loss on your investment. The question is whether the entity you're considering is worth its asking price. Period. "If you invest in a lousy company at a low price," a successful stock investor observed, "it only means it will take a little longer for you to lose your money."

Question 2: Is it worth the cost to *YOU*? To answer this question, you might consider the "What's it worth to Bill?" scale of measurement. I base this criterion on an enlightening analysis of Bill Gates's wealth conducted by the Internet journalist Brad Templeton.[19] As of January 2002, Gates's personal net worth was estimated to be an astounding $73 billion.[20] If we presume that most of this money was earned in the approximately twenty-five years since Gates founded Microsoft and that he's worked, say, twelve hours a day, six days a week since then, Gates's average earnings figure out to a staggering $9,000,000+ per day, $780,000+ per hour, and $215+ each second.

If we assume it takes about five seconds to bend down and pick something up, this means it wouldn't be worth Bill Gates's time to retrieve a $1,000 bill if he dropped it on the ground. The "too-small-a-bill-for-Bill" index has risen dramatically over the years. When Microsoft went public in 1986, the new multimillionaire would have lost out by leaving behind anything but $5 bills. In 1993 his time was clicking away at $31 per second.

And what is your own "too-small-a-bill" index? Imagine you're in a store buying a new $1,500 computer and your companion whispers that you can get the same computer across town for $15 less. Would you make the drive? Probably not, studies show. But let's say you're in that same store buying a $30 calculator and somebody tells you a store across town is selling it half price, for $15 less. Now would you take the drive? Most people would.[21] Psychologically speaking, this is normal mental accounting. But economically, if one drive across town exceeds your "too-small-a-bill" index, shouldn't the second?

What's it worth to you, Bill?

SIX

The Hot Button

Or, How Mental Shortcuts Can Lead You into Trouble

For every complex problem, there is a simple solution.
And it's always wrong.
—H. L. Mencken

Engineers refer to a condition called system overload that occurs when a structure is burdened by more demands than it's built to handle. Put too much weight on a bridge, for example, and it collapses. Social psychologist Stanley Milgram observed that humans face a parallel problem: there are more inputs than we're capable of processing.[1] Thousands of pieces of information are competing for our attention at any one moment—adding up to what Isaac Asimov estimated to be about 1,000,000,000,000,000 separate bits of information that are experienced in an average lifetime.[2] The burden is greater today than ever before. A recent study estimated that one week of the *New York Times* carries more information than a person in the sixteenth century digested in a lifetime.[3]

To adapt to the predicament, we simplify. Only the most relevant information gets processed; details are screened out. The process is profoundly imperfect. Sometimes we clutter our consciousness with unnecessary information while discarding the truly relevant. Often we confuse the present situation with a very different one from the past. One way or another, however, we need to simplify. The late clinical psychologist George Kelly put it well: "Man looks at his world through transparent patterns or templates which he creates and then attempts to fit over the realities of which the world is composed. The fit is not always very good. Yet without such patterns the world appears to be such an undifferentiated homogeneity that man is unable to make any sense out of it. Even a poor fit is more helpful to him than nothing at all."[4]

Perversely, traditional marketing theory holds to the credo that people want choices, the more the better. Consider food. I recently counted 171 different types of cold breakfast cereals on my local supermarket shelf. Ice cream parlors leave Baskin-Robbins' thirty-one flavors in the dust by allowing flavors and toppings to be combined in endless combinations. Burger King tells you to "Have it your way." The greater the number of choices, the happier the consumer—so it's assumed.

Nearly everyone would agree that some choice is better than none at all. But what happens when it goes too far? My father used to say that children should be given two choices: "Chocolate or vanilla?" In a recent series of experiments, social psychologists Sheena Iyengar and Mark Lepper demonstrated that my father wasn't far off the mark. In one study, a group of Columbia University chocolate lovers were given a choice between six different flavors of Godiva chocolates. A second group was asked to select between thirty different flavors. Subjects given the extensive flavor choices rated their selection as less tasty, less satisfying, and less enjoyable than did the limited-choice group. The thirty-flavor subjects expressed more regrets about their selection and were less likely to choose chocolate as payment for participating in the experiment.

In another experiment, Iyengar and Lepper set up a jam-tasting table in Draeger's Supermarket, an upscale grocery store in Menlo Park, California, with a reputation for extensive selections. It had, for example, approximately 75 varieties of olive oil, 250 different varieties of mustard, and over 300 varieties of jam. In one condition, the researchers offered shoppers tastes of 6 different exotic flavors of Wilkin & Sons ("Purveyors to Her Majesty the Queen") jam. In a second condition, they offered 24 different Wilkin & Sons flavors. Easy choices like strawberry and raspberry were left out. The displays were rotated hourly over two Saturdays. Once again, Iyengar and Lepper found, shoppers were won over more by the smaller selection. Sixty percent of the customers who passed by the 6-flavor table stopped for a sample, compared with 40 percent of the customers who passed by the 24-flavor table. Of those who did stop, there were virtually no differences in the number of flavors they chose to sample. Finally, the bottom line: 30 percent of the customers who stopped at the 6-flavor table subsequently purchased a Wilkin & Sons jam. Only 3 percent of those offered 24 flavors did so.[5]

These studies show how too many choices can be overwhelming. They create a feeling that psychologist Barry Schwartz calls "the tyranny of freedom." The resulting anxiety leads to a desire for simplicity. Unfortunately, this can become an invitation for exploitation.

Cults specialize at providing simple answers to big questions. All your old problems—food, housing, bills, taxes—become things of the past. Daily routines are choreographed by the leader, sometimes down to specific details. "No one is to use Crest Toothpaste," Jim Jones instructed followers at one point. "The only toothpaste that will make your gums resistant to atomic radiation [a great fear of Jones's] is Phillips Toothpaste." On other occasions he told them, "If you see a ladder with a spot of red paint on it, you are to put the ladder out of sight for two weeks" and "No one is to ride a motorcycle for a month."[6] Many cults extend these instructions to more significant life choices. They'll even decide whom you should marry. The Moonies have become infamous for their mass wedding ceremonies, where Reverend Sun Myung Moon arranges beforehand and then marries tens of thousand couples at once, most to spouses they've never met and who speak different languages.[7] In Jonestown, at one point, all marriages were dissolved, and Jones took control of who slept with whom.[8]

One's inner life becomes equally simplified. Members internalize the group doctrine as the "Truth," and from that moment on, every thought is guided by a clear, simple map of reality. The process becomes simpler yet when the leader filters all your incoming information and then strictly controls how you think about it. In Jonestown, Jim Jones's "news" broadcasts and other rantings (consisting of either Jones speaking live or, when he was away, playing tapes of his earlier broadcasts) were piped loudly over the microphone nonstop, twenty-four hours a day.[9] Any questions about right and wrong, good and bad, were unambiguously answered.

Jeannie Mills and her husband Al spent six years as key figures in Jones's People's Temple and, eventually, in Jonestown. Before defecting, Jeannie served as head of the temple's publications office, Al served as official photographer, and both were members of the prestigious planning committee.[10] In her book, *Six Years with God*, Jeannie Mills recalled:

I was amazed at how little disagreement there was between the members of this church. Before we joined the church, Al and I couldn't even agree on whom to vote for in the presidential election. Now that we all belonged to a group, family arguments were becoming a thing of the past. There was never a question of who was right, because Jim was always right. When our large household met to discuss family problems, we didn't ask for opinions. Instead, we put the question to the children, "What would Jim do?" It took the difficulty out of life. There was a type of "manifest destiny" which said the Cause was right and would succeed. Jim was right and those who agreed with him were right. If you disagreed with Jim, you were wrong. It was as simple as that.[11]

Even language is streamlined. In George Orwell's *1984*, the totalitarian authorities create a new language, called Newspeak, designed to diminish the range of thought by cutting the choice of words to a minimum. "Newspeak," Orwell explains in an appendix to the novel, "differed from almost all other languages in that its vocabulary grew smaller instead of larger every year. Each reduction was a gain, since the smaller the area of choice, the smaller the temptation to take thought. Ultimately it was hoped to make articulate speech issue from the larynx without involving the higher brain centers at all . . . in Newspeak the expression of unorthodox opinions, above a very low level, was well-nigh impossible."[12]

Destructive cults create their own "loaded language" of words and expressions. Simple labels are assigned to complex situations; every ambiguity is reduced to a cult cliché. "In the Moonies, whenever you have difficulty relating to someone either above or below you in status, it is called a 'Cain-Abel problem,'" recalled former member Steven Hassan. "It doesn't matter who's involved or what the problem is, it's simply a 'Cain-Abel problem.' The term itself dictates how the problem must be resolved. Cain must obey Abel and follow him, rather than kill him as was written about in the Old Testament. Case closed. To think otherwise would be to obey Satan's wish that evil Cain should prevail over righteous Abel. A critical thought about a leader's misconduct cannot get past this roadblock in a good member's mind."[13]

It's not just cult members who fall into the oversimplification trap. There are certain situations that encourage lazy thinking in all of us—situations when, instead of carefully considering the complexities of the problem, we revert to mental shortcuts. We're particularly susceptible to persuasion at these times. The following are six situations to watch out for[14]:

Situation One: When you believe the consequences of your actions aren't important. If your decision has trivial consequences, why waste mental energy thinking through details? I recently purchased a new car stereo, for example. Several minutes into the checkout process, between a barrage of queries about everything from my method of payment to my zip code, the salesman nonchalantly asked, "And will you be wanting the three- or the five-year warranty?" The difference in price between the two, he said, was only a few dollars. It sounded like a trivial decision, just another item in the checkout procedure. What he neglected to mention was I had an additional alternative: purchasing no extended warranty, which would have saved 15 percent off the purchase price. (It's noteworthy that salespeople typically earn a higher rate of commission for selling extended warranties than for the product itself.)

Inconsequential requests may not be as safe as they look. In a clever experiment, Robert Cialdini and David Schroeder sent students around asking for donations to a charity. The requests were always the same, with one exception: half the time the students added the phrase "even a penny will help." Which it did—at least as far as the fund-raisers were concerned. The "even a penny . . ." people were almost twice as likely to make contributions. More important, they gave virtually the same size donations on average as the other group.[15]

Be careful when salespeople make your decision seem less consequential than it is. Don't be disarmed by their casualness.

Situation Two: When you're pressed to act quickly. Urgency discourages careful thinking. Salespeople are famous for exploiting this principle by speeding you up with limited-time offers or trying to convince you that the product is so popular it won't be there for long.

One of my favorite cases is a New York department store that used to hold sporadic "five-minute specials." It would begin with a hysterical voice on the loudspeaker announcing, "It's time, lucky shoppers, for today's five-minute special." The announcer would then pause for twenty seconds or so while veteran bargain hunters positioned themselves near stairs, elevators, and escalators to await details. When the announcement came—say, "Hanes boxer shorts on Two North!!"—there would be a stampede to scoop up one of the bargains in the allotted five minutes.

Urgency activates what Robert Cialdini calls the rule of scarcity: We ascribe more value to items we believe are less available.[16] In an experiment conducted by Stephen Worchel and his colleagues, consumers were given a chocolate chip cookie from a jar. For half the people, the jar contained ten cookies; for the other half, it held only two. Those whose cookie came from the two-cookie jar rated their cookie as more desirable and more attractive and thought it should cost more.[17] When something is too easily available, in fact, it can seem less attractive. Who likes to eat in an empty restaurant? We tell ourselves we chose the busy restaurant because it probably serves better food but it may be the line that convinces us the restaurant is worth the wait. It's the psychological component of the law of supply and demand. If we can be persuaded that a product or service is difficult to attain, we want it more.

Home shopper networks have carried the urgency principle to the mass market. As virtually everyone in the United States must by now know, these stations feature a given product for a limited time, usually ten or fifteen minutes. They enhance the time pressure with a little clock in the upper corner of the screen that ticks off the remaining precious seconds before the particular gem is lost from your life forever. There's also often a counter on the screen that runs down with every sale. "We have just a limited number of these unbelievable between-the-toes down footwarmers and when they're all gone, you can kiss them good-bye," you might hear. The counter might then start at 10 and tick down with each purchase: 9, 8, 7, . . . "Act fast because the opportunity won't come around again."

Situation Three: When there's too much information to process. The more information there is, the greater our need for shortcuts. All things being equal, people are more likely to mindlessly trust the competence of long messages over shorter ones.[18] This is true whether the message contains a good argument or a poor one, or even if we don't read the content of the message at all. The influential advertiser David Ogilvy observed, "On the average, five times as many people read the headline as read the body copy. When you have written your headline, you have spent eighty cents out of your dollar."[19] With that established, Ogilvy went on to say that the most effective advertisements should include long, authoritative-looking copy. It's not important that people read the copy. It just has to be there.

Long ads often dwell on the "scientific" merits of a commodity. These technical treatises aren't limited to obvious products like drugs and medical treatments. You'll find ads masked as research reports for everything from miracle fabrics to new toothpastes. This is one of the most paradoxical of mental shortcuts: the more information you're given, the more impressive it seems, and so the less carefully you evaluate its merits.

When simplifying, it's important to focus on the right bits of information. Say you're at a store choosing from several brands of toasters. You've decided to buy the best-quality toaster available. There's no reliable salesperson around and all of the brand names sound the same to you. If you're like most people, you'll probably fall back on the mindless shortcut that "expensive equals good" and buy the one with the highest price tag. The fact is, however, there's a good chance that at least some of the different brands were made by the same manufacturer. The only difference between the machines may be the label and the price.

Situation Four: When you trust the person making the request. The surest way for a salesperson to disarm you is to appear trustworthy. You're less likely to question people you trust, and you're more likely to adopt the heuristic they hand you. I've already discussed the triad of qualities that most promote trustworthiness: authority, honesty, and likability. When any of the three appear, we're quick to put ourselves on automatic.

Situation Five: When you're surrounded by social proof. If everyone's doing it, it must be right. This principle derives from two extremely powerful social forces: social comparison and conformity. We compare our behavior to what others are doing, and if there's a discrepancy between them and us, we feel pressure to change.

The principle of social proof is so common that it easily passes unnoticed. Advertisements, for example, often consist of little more than attractive social models appealing to our desire to be one of the group ("They pick Pepsi, time after time"). Sometimes social cues are presented with such specificity that it's as if we're being manipulated by a puppeteer—for example, the laugh tracks on situation comedies that instruct us not only when to laugh but how to laugh. The worst of it is how well these techniques work. Studies show that audiences laugh longer and more often when a laugh track accompanies the show than when it doesn't, even though we know the laughs we hear are contrived by a technician from old tapes that have nothing to do with the show we're watching.[20] (In fact, some of the laugh tracks were recorded so long ago that we're taking cues from dead people.) More insulting yet, there's some evidence that canned laughter works most effectively for bad jokes.[21]

Even the most trusted groups may exploit social proof. Some churches, for example, practice what is known as "salting the collection plate," whereby faithful ushers throw several different bills or checks onto the plate before it's passed around. Even a little salt gets things going. And the heavier the salt, the greater the returns: research shows that salting with tens and twenties brings in more than salting with ones and fives.[22]

As P. T. Barnum once said, "Nothing draws a crowd like a crowd."

Situation Six: When you're uncertain and confused. In the first five situations our willingness to take lazy shortcuts derives from an illusion of invulnerability. But there is a very different type of situation in which we feel so vulnerable that we actively, even frantically, search for simple answers to get us through. One of the most common situations is when we're confused and unsure how to act. Confusion can lead to helplessness, and helplessness breeds a desire for quick fixes—anything to get our bearings. This is the uncertainty principle.

It's no coincidence that it is often when life is at its most confusing that people are most prone to the dogmas of fundamentalist religions or rigidly structured therapeutic programs. Cults, naturally, are prime examples of this. Studies have uncovered surprisingly little commonality in the type of personality that joins cults: there's no single cult-prone personality type. But there are similarities in the immediate circumstances that surround the modal joiner. First, people who join cults tend to be at an unhappy point in their lives at the time they're recruited. In many cases, they've experienced a recent loss or disappointment. Second, they're frequently in limbo between meaningful affiliations—they're between high school and college or school and a job, or they've recently been fired, jilted by a romantic partner, have just moved, or perhaps are generally unsure what to do next with their lives. These are people in the market for simple answers; and if you're a cult leader, they're just the customers you're looking for.[23]

Edgar Schein, who has studied a variety of totalistic mind control programs, ranging from Chinese Communist POW camps to all-encompassing therapeutic groups like Alcoholics Anonymous, has observed that all of them take subjects through a three-step process: unfreezing, changing, and refreezing. During the unfreezing stage, you're bombarded with lectures, information, and group pressures that make you question everything you previously believed in—your past attitudes and choices, your sense of how the world works, your entire self-image. The process leaves you confused about right versus wrong and uncertain about where to turn next. If sufficiently destabilized, you become more than ready to consider whatever mind-set the new group has to offer.[24] In other words, totalistic groups not only target people whose lives are in limbo; they also do everything possible to enhance the limbo state and to make you experience it as unpleasantly as possible.

A similar dynamic is exploited by persuaders closer to home. Consider the approach of the trendy Diesel jeans stores, where jeans cost between $115 and $200 a pair. A customer who walks into a Diesel store is met with mind-rattling inputs ranging from blaring techno music to inexplicable videos of Japanese boxing matches. What the customer doesn't enconter, however, is an accessible salesperson or even signs for finding the men's or women's department. If the customer manages his way to the heart of the store, the so-called denim bar, he encounters a bewildering display of more than thirty-five types of jeans with strange names like Ravix, Fanker, and Kulter. These options are explained on a technical placard that appears almost intentionally confusing, a guide which, as one observer commented, could be mistaken for an organizational chart for a decent-sized federal agency. By this point, the typical first-time customer is, to say the least, disoriented. Is this simply a terribly managed store?

Hardly. Just as the uninitiated customer may be slipping into a sort of shopper's vertigo, a salesperson sidles up to the rescue. The salesperson, who has completed a week-long course on the science of denim, guides the customer through Diesel's puzzling lexicon of styles and washes plus a network of textile terms like *warp* and *weft*. More important, as Diesel salesman Stephen Miranda commented, "I try to be their shopping friend." With the customer's confidence in hand, the salesperson may now suggest what pair of jeans to buy, not in the role of a self-motivated salesman but as a concerned friend and beneficient expert.

There's nothing haphazard about this process. "We're conscious of the fact that, outwardly, we have an intimidating environment," observes Niall Maher, Diesel's director of retail operations. "We didn't design our stores to be user-friendly because we want you to interact with our people. You can't understand Diesel without talking to someone." Success or failure, salesmen are taught, depends upon finding the customers who look most lost. "The more someone is overwhelmed, the better the connection is when you help them out," Miranda observes. The company has been extremely successful. A good salesmen like Stephen Miranda may sell an average of $9,000 to $10,000 worth of jeans a week. Diesel had $500 million in sales in 2001, up 40 percent from the year before.[25]

To simplify is to narrow one's field of vision. Sometimes, in fact, we react to just a single, isolated piece of information. In persuasion, this can be a very dangerous shortcut. It exposes what's known in sales vernacular as the hot button. "The hot button," Jeffrey Gitomer advises professionals in *The Sales Bible*, "is a bridge that can get you from the presentation to the sale."[26] For the consumer, it's a bridge you may want to stay off.

The process mirrors a phenomenon in animal behavior known as fixed-action patterns (FAPs). These are sequences of behavior that occur in exactly the same fashion, in exactly the same order, every time they're elicited—as if, as Robert Cialdini observed, the animal were turning on a tape recorder. FAPs are the heart of what we like to call social instincts. They're preprogrammed, unlearned, and untouched by reason. There is the feeding tape, the territorial tape, the migration tape, the nesting tape, the aggressive tape—each sequence ready to be played when a situation calls for it.[27]

The operations are so mindless that once a tape begins, it plays to the end even when going on is pointless. If you hold an egg near a female greylag goose, for example, she'll invariably rise, extend her neck until the bill is over the egg, bend her neck, and, finally, pull the egg carefully into the nest. On the surface, this appears to be an intelligent sequence of behaviors. But consider what happens if there's the slightest glitch. If you remove the egg once the goose begins her retrieval, she'll go right on with the retrieval movement without the egg until she settles back in the nest. Then, seeing the egg isn't there, she'll go through the retrieval maneuvers all over again. It's all eerily robotic looking, like a pitching machine at a baseball batting cage that's run out of balls but continues through its motions, throwing one blank after another.[28]

A notable characteristic of fixed-action patterns is how they're activated. At first glance it appears the animal is responding to the overall situation. For example, the maternal tape appears to be set off when a mother sees her hungry baby, or the aggressive tape seems to be activated when an enemy invades the animal's territory. It turns out, however, that the on-off switch may actually be controlled by a specific, minute detail of the situation—maybe a sound or a shape or a patch of color. These are the hot buttons of the biological world—what Cialdini refers to as "trigger features" and biologists call "releasers."

Biologists have identified hundreds of releasers. The female redwinged blackbird, for example, signals her readiness to mate by the angle of her tail. Wrong angle, no mates. A newborn herring gull chick must peck on a small red spot on her parent's beak to get fed. Push the red button, you get the food. Anything else, you starve.

Most of the time these shortcuts work. But occasionally they don't. In the spring, for example, the male three-spined stickleback lays claim to a territory. Any approaching male is met with a threat posture or maybe an aggressive attack. The releaser for the territorial response, it turns out, isn't so much the invading male as simply the bright red stripe on his underside (red is a popular color in biology). The great ethologist Niko Tinbergen discovered this when he noticed that a passing red postal truck sent the male sticklebacks in his aquarium into aggressive fits. In subsequent experiments, Tinbergen learned that the defenders would attack any object with a red stripe, even an amorphouslooking lump of wax with a red underside. But they'd completely ignore a carefully crafted replica of a male stickleback that didn't have a red belly.[29]

The effect can be exaggerated with supernormal releasers. The adult herring gull, for example, goes into a fixed-action pattern of egg retrieval when she sees an egg roll out of the nest. If a regular egg has such a strong effect, biologists asked, what might happen with a monster egg? To answer this, they painted a volleyball the colors of a gull egg. Sure enough, when the volleyball was placed next to a real egg, the gulls invariably tried to retrieve the volleyball. They also preferred to brood the volleyballs. Madison Avenue would love it.[30]

Trigger errors may be costly. A few years ago, for example, a team of biologists who were conducting bird experiments decided to keep track of the babies by attaching shiny metal identification bands to the babies' legs. But the biologists forgot that the parent birds have a strong instinct to keep their nests clean of all light-colored objects. Most of the time this means throwing out excrement or broken eggshells. But when the parents noticed the leg bands, they threw these out, too. Unfortunately, the babies were still attached.[31]

Of course, releasers usually serve the animal quite well. Because animals exist in a relatively consistent and predictable environment, these automatic, preprogrammed responses serve as efficient and generally accurate shortcuts. The stickleback rarely needs to worry about red clumps of wax in its native environment, and herring gulls only have to distinguish between eggs and volleyballs when intrusive scientists are mucking up their habitat. We humans, on the other hand, must deal with all sorts of intruders.

My students and I recently discovered the power of hot buttons in an unlikely context: while soliciting donations for a highly respected local charity, an organization called Poverello House that provides meals to the homeless. In an attempt to generate funds for this most worthy organization, Karla Burgos, Albert Rodriguez, and I decided to conduct a bake sale on campus. But fund-raising on a college campus is problematic. For one thing, students tend to be busy people. When they're walking on campus, it's usually to rush between classes, studying, and jobs. Besides this, fund-raising on campuses is extremely competitive. Pedestrian thoroughfares are crowded with competing tables and kiosks—for fraternities and sororities, student clubs, religious groups, businesses, and nonprofit organizations. It doesn't take long for a passerby to suffer sensory overload. As a result, it's extremely difficult for a solicitor to capture people's attention. This became clear to us the first time we conducted our bake sale. We'd simply displayed our goods on a table in the path of a busy pedestrian thoroughfare. The food was fine and the price was right, but the sale was a total failure. We sold almost nothing; in fact, passersby hardly seemed to notice us.

Our challenge, we believed, was to develop a come-on that would grab people's attention and communicate our request with maximum economy. It needed to include enough information so that our cause stood out from the competition but be sufficiently concise that the already overloaded passersby would take it all in. We designed an experiment to compare the effectiveness of various come-ons. In all cases, one of the experimenters—an attractive, neatly dressed coed— stood a few feet in front of our table and amiably asked passersby to purchase our cookies. Then we varied the wording of the appeal slightly in each condition.

First, our saleswoman tried the briefest of appeals. She approached people and simply asked, "Would you like to buy a cookie?" This was our control condition. As we anticipated, this fared little better than when we'd passively sat behind our table: only two of thirty potential customers in this condition made purchases.

In the next condition, we emphasized that the proceeds were going to Poverello House. We knew from a previous survey that the vast majority of locals were well aware of the organization and felt favorably toward it.[32] Our saleswoman approached people exactly as before, except this time she added a second sentence: "Would you like to buy a cookie? It's for a good cause, the Poverello House." With these additional cues, almost half (fourteen of thirty) of passersby now made purchases—a remarkably high hit rate considering the difficult sales context. Mentioning Poverello House had worked wonders.

Or had it? Many of the purchasers, it seemed possible, were making their way to our table before the experimenter had even said the words "Poverello House." To test this speculation, we approached the next group of passersby with the "good cause" phrase alone: "Would you like to buy a cookie? It's for a good cause." This was slightly less effective, but not by much: twelve of thirty in this group made purchases.[33]

Finally, we hypothesized that if people were shutting their attention off after the words "good cause," it shouldn't matter what organization we were collecting for. To test this notion, in the next condition we tried using the name of a completely fictitious organization: "Would you like to buy a cookie? It's for a good cause, the Levine House." Sure enough, the phony name—preceded by the words "good cause"— worked practically as well as the well-respected Poverello name: eleven of thirty people purchased cookies.

The key to engaging customers, quite clearly, was the phrase "for a good cause." The words were like a switch that simultaneously turned people on (to their sense of charity) and off (to listening to further details about the charity). No one in the "for a good cause" (alone) condition asked what the good cause was. Not one person in the "Levine House" condition asked what went on in that house. Not a single one.[34]

But the "good cause" phrase wouldn't be effective in just any context. The key in our experiment was the trustworthy social context. In a follow-up study, we tried varying the appearance of the cookie salesperson. This time pedestrians were approached by a college-age man. In one condition the man was neatly dressed and well groomed; in a second condition he wore reflector sunglasses, a bandanna, and a T-shirt with a Harley-Davidson logo, and looked generally up to no good. When he was neatly dressed, the "for a good cause" phrase worked the same wonders as it had in our earlier study: the salesman sold two and a half times as many cookies when he used the "for a good cause" phrase as when he didn't. When the solicitor was dressed to look like a delinquent, however, the "good cause" phrase had virtually no effect: customers were equally unlikely to purchase a cookie no matter how the request was phrased. In other words, people are less prone to rely on mental shortcuts in a suspicious situation. But when they feel like they're on safe ground—as was the case when pedestrians were approached by an engaging, charitable-looking student, in a university courtyard, surrounded by other nonprofit organizations—most of them are happy not to be bothered with any more details than a simple phrase.[35]

Uncritical acceptance of catchphrases is common. Many seemingly innocent words and terms operate like a toggle switch that opens and closes our receptivity to inputs. We mindlessly accept statistics based on *scientific* studies, or from *leading doctors*, or *university professors*. Research shows that ads containing the words *new, quick, easy, improved, now, suddenly, amazing*, and *introducing* increase product sales.[36]

A study by Ellen Langer (a *Harvard* professor) and her colleagues demonstrated how even the simple word *because* can be enough to send us robotically on to automatic pilot. Langer's subjects were people waiting in a crowded line to use a Xerox photocopy machine in a library. In the first condition, an experimenter walked up to the front of the line and asked for a favor: "Excuse me. I have five pages. May I use the Xerox machine?" Sixty percent agreed to the request. Not bad. But consider what happened next, when the researchers added a reason for the request: "Excuse me. I have five pages. May I use the Xerox machine because I'm in a rush?" Nearly everyone—94 percent—now let the crasher come to the front. It would be nice to think these sympathetic bystanders were responding to a good reason. They weren't. In the next condition, a new reason was substituted, one that made no sense at all: "Excuse me. I have five pages. May I use the Xerox machine because I have to make some copies." Once again, nearly everyone—

93 percent—agreed.[37] The on-off switch for these helpers was the word *because*. The context did the rest of the work.

Hot buttons have a large cultural element. Say, for example, you were a coach trying to get your team fighting mad for a football game. You'd want to know the right button to push in your locker-room speech. If your players came from different cultural backgrounds, you'd probably find there's no singular answer. It depends on how the players were raised and where they grew up.

If they're from the South, for example, the coach might find the button is their sense of honor. If they're from the North, however, this probably wouldn't work. This is what social psychologists Dov Cohen, Richard Nisbett, and their colleagues discovered when they affronted the honor of college students from different regions of the United States. In one of their experiments, northern and southern men walking down a hallway were bumped and called an "asshole" by a passing confederate. Eighty-five percent of the southerners reacted to the provocateur by confronting him with a kneejerk anger/fight response. Only 35 percent of the northern men, on the other hand, seemed to take the incident seriously. The majority acted mostly amused by the affront. The southerners' damaged pride remained inflamed for some time. In a subsequent experiment, they were almost twice as aggressive as northerners in a game of chicken, as measured by the number of inches it took before they gave way to a 6'3", 250-pound former college football player who came barreling down the hallway. Even the physiological responses of the two regional groups were different. Saliva samples showed that southerners reacted to the confrontations with increased levels of the hormones testosterone and cortisol; the former is associated with aggression and competition, the latter with stress and arousal. Northerners showed no such increases.[38]

When asked why they reacted as they did, neither group of men had much to offer in the way of cerebral explanations, as Dov Cohen observed.

> Debriefings with some subjects resembled a monologue that could have been written for a John Wayne movie. In many other cases, they produced a lot of confused blustering as subjects groped for why they did what they did or why it was important or not important to act tough.

For some subjects, after a number of probing questions, it was obvious that the bedrock answer was "just because." Their goals, actions, and definitions of masculinity were activated by virtue of the situation they were in. It was not necessarily a matter of conscious deliberation; they were just following the cultural script. Attempts to push the analysis to a more introspective level would have been meaningless.[39]

It's not that southern men are more violent in every situation. On surveys, they express no more approval for violence than do northerners. But their sense of honor is a hot button. As one sociologist brought up in the South put it: "Like the words to 'Blessed Assurance,' the technique of the yo-yo, or the conviction that okra is edible, it is absorbed pretty much without reflection. . . . [As a schoolboy], if you were called out for some offense, you fought. I guess you could have appealed to the teacher but that just—wasn't done."[40]

These cultural scripts appear so automatically that it's easy to confuse them with the instinctual FAPs of the animal world. Whereas the animal patterns are perpetuated genetically, however, human ones are passed through cultures. This occurs on many levels. Southern women, for example, communicate the value to their sons: studies find that they're much more likely than northern women to support culture-of-honor-type violence; the difference is as large or larger than that between southern and northern men. The media also perpetuate the value. In one study, journalists across the country were given facts for a story about a man who stabbed someone who had repeatedly insulted him. Southern reporters, compared to their northern counterparts, described the stabbing as more provoked, less aggravated, and were much more sympathetic toward the perpetrator. Even the legal systems in some southern states have treated honor-driven violent responses as if they were hotwired into human nature. Until the 1960s and 1970s, a man who killed after catching his wife in bed with another man was innocent according to the law in Georgia and Texas. These laws deemed murder to be an inevitable, "automatic" response to the circumstances.[41] Punishing the aggressor, according to the reasoning, would have as much logic as prosecuting a stickleback for attacking a red-bellied intruder fish.

Any time behavior is dictated by cultural norms there is a heightened vulnerability to manipulation. The danger is twofold. For one thing, cultural norms are extremely powerful. They govern through formidable psychological forces—shame, guilt, and rejection. As a result, defying these norms is reserved for the extraordinary.

Second, it's extremely difficult to recognize when we're under the influence of cultural forces. One of the defining characteristics of cultural norms is their invisibility to insiders. The more readily the norm is accepted, the more it's taken for granted. After all, it's not very interesting to talk or think about something everyone does. As a result, our cultural reactions become unconscious and automatic.

Advertisers love hot buttons. They understand that our minds are filled with scripts and their job is to trigger the right one. "Whether alone or with others, consumers play out their special roles in the drama of life," observe business writers Robert Settle and Pamela Alreck. "Society has written the script, some authority figure may be the director, the physical environment is the stage, the current situation the setting, the others in the group the players, outside observers the audience, clothing the costumes, each consumer a star actor. Consumer goods are merely the 'props.'"[42]

Advertising is about slogans, brand names, and images. A company may devote less attention to promoting the actual qualities of its product than to suggesting social images it wants you to associate with its product. If you're attracted to the image—if you want to play the role—the product becomes a prop in your performance. Consider the following examples.

Want to act like a real man? When Philip Morris began marketing Marlboros over seventy years ago, they were sold as women's cigarettes with an elegant, prissy image. The Marlboro name was written in a soft, fancy script. The cigarettes had a red beauty tip so the smoker's lipstick wouldn't show. From this came the slogan: "Cherry tips to match your ruby lips." Then, in 1955, Philip Morris decided to appeal to the heavy-smoking, male market. The name stayed, but the package was completely redesigned in stark red and white colors; a sharp, angular design; and the infamous "crushproof" box. And so began the Marlboro Man. (The trade publication, *Advertising Age*, designated the Marlboro Man as the number one advertising icon of the twentieth century.)

Want to be a world saver? Coca-Cola is for people who care about humanity. How do we know this? Because the company tells us so. Coke began shaping this image with its Hands Across America Campaign in the late 1980s. In one typical commercial, we see Grandpa and his young grandson watching a home video on a giant screen. Gramps explains they're seeing that great day in 1986 when Hands Across America raised "enough money so people wouldn't be hungry or homeless anymore." "People were hungry once?" the child asks. Gramps, looking wistfully out in the distance, replies, "Once."

Is limiting your altruism to America too provincial for you? Not to worry. A few years later the company heralded in the 1990s with an epic new version of its famous 1971 "hilltop" commercial, in which hundreds of teenagers dressed in native costume had sung out, "I'd like to buy the world a Coke," from atop an Italian hill. This time there were some four hundred of our brothers and sisters, many of whom were grown-up returnees from the old commercial now appearing with their children. The ad begins with the same blond British girl, now nineteen years older and with her own teenager, crooning, "I'd like to buy the world a home and furnish it with love."[43] Around the same time, Pepsi types were watching ads with the likes of Tina Turner, David Bowie, and Madonna.

Do you want to feel like a good mother and wife? When Nestlé developed the first instant coffee, Nescafé, it was marketed as a product that saved time, was inexpensive, and tasted as good as the real thing. Sales were awful. The company then asked groups of women, at the time by far the principal food shoppers, what it was they didn't like about the product. The women explained that serving cheap coffee to their husbands was not something a good homemaker did (think Mrs. Olson here). Nestlé then designed a new ad campaign showing housewives at breakfast happily serving and chatting with their husbands and children. The company's message: by spending less time over the stove, Nescafé women gained more "quality" time with their spouse and children. Sales increased markedly, and the instant coffee industry was here to stay.

(Nestlé is the same company that was later caught shipping huge quantities of "free samples" of their infant breast milk substitute to Third World hospitals—just enough freebies to allow time for a new mother's breast milk to dry out, making her dependent on buying the powdered formula. Unfortunately, when powdered formula is mixed with contaminated water—which is unavoidable in these countries—it often leads to malnutrition, disease, and death in newborns, about a million such deaths a year, according to UNICEF. A costly world boycott forced Nestlé to agree to change its marketing policy, but international watch groups later found that the company continued to ship as much of the free formula as before, and even more of it in some areas of eastern Africa. Talk about chutzpah—this is the company that told women what kind of coffee they should buy to prove they love their families?)

For many products, different companies target different social roles. The aim is to win over a segment of the market—what's known as niche marketing. Blue jeans are a good example. Want that honest, straight-forward cowboy feeling? You should probably buy Wranglers. The company's ads are set in the West, and are populated by sincere, virtu-ous cowboys, and lots of horses. Almost everyone is lean: Wrangler jeans are for straight-up-and-down people. Or do you prefer to think of your-self as an urban hipster? Levi's, as shown in the Levi's blues campaign, is for you. The company's 501 ads are populated by black bluesmen, rap-pers, guitars, and street music. You might see one guy with two girls, or two girls with one guy, hanging out on an urban sidewalk. Everything in the ads says casualness—which, of course, is what you will be in your 501s. (Levi's Dockers, which aim for an older and more upscale market, show almost no black people in their ads.) But, hey, ladies, maybe you've got something a little more daring in mind? Check out that young beauty in the Guess? jeans sitting outside the Italian café, surrounded by all those men in silky suits, all of them looking twice her age and into some kind of bad business. The girl's blouse is opened slightly; she's feeling a bit sensual, kind of irreverent, willing to take a little risk. If you watch these ads long enough, it's easy to forget that Wrangler, Levi's, and Guess? are all selling basically the same denim, just with different labels.[44] The products are just props in the performance.

It wasn't long ago that consumers' distrust of advertising focused on the accuracy of product claims. Did Coke really alleviate headaches? Did the bleach in the ad actually make your clothes whiter? In most ads today, however, there's no question of factual accuracy—because there are no facts. The ad is unlikely to even bother with the actual qualities of the product. Consumers aren't being offered special clothing or food so much as new images, new selves. The ads provide the theater; you read the script. "The philosophy behind much advertising," observed advertiser William Feather, "is based on the old observation that every man is really two men—the man he is and the man he wants to be."[45]

Different cultures call for different hot buttons. In cultures that value individualistic behavior—places like the United States and most of western Europe—advertisements are frequented by images of individuality and independence. For example: "The art of being unique" (Cartier watches); "It's time to express your opinion" (Chex cereal); "She's got a style all her own" (a cologne ad). Even collectivistic enterprises in these cultures may be promoted with individualistic images. The U.S. Army, for example, recently hired the Leo Burnett advertising agency, whose clients include McDonald's, Walt Disney, and Coca-Cola, to reverse disappointing recruitment figures. Instead of emphasizing traditional armed forces values like team spirit and unit cohesion, the new campaign promotes the army as an incubator of self-actualization. In one of the new spots, a real-life army corporal looks into the camera and says: "And I'll be the first to tell you, the might of the U.S. Army doesn't lie in numbers. It lies in me. I am an army of one."[46] He says this with a shaved head, too.

Slogans like this don't go over very well in cultures that emphasize collectivistic values, such as most of Asia and the Third World. Imagine how Apple's "Think Different" slogan would be perceived in a country such as Japan, where children are socialized to live by the motto "*Deru kugi ha utareru*" ("The nail that stands out must be hammered down"). In most collectivist cultures, showing a person alone implies that he has no identity and no friends, that he doesn't belong—hardly the right hot button to sell your product. A study by business professor Sharon Shavritt and her colleagues found that successful ads in these cultures are much more likely to use images of group goals ("It's so beautiful you want to share it with others"—Hermesetas; Portugal), interdependent relationships ("Prospering together"—Chiyoda Bank; Portugal), and not standing out from the crowd ("Harmony—the essence of Samsung's innovative spirit").[47]

There are subcultural differences within countries, even when the same language is used. An article in *Business Week* observed: "While [in the United States] the gritty, independent hipsters in Levi's '501 Blues' TV ads have drawn young customers like a strong magnet, they didn't click for Levi's Hispanic employees and customers. 'Why is that guy walking down the street alone,' they asked. 'Doesn't he have any friends?'"[48] The number of people in the image also needs to be considered. An advertiser targeting a traditional Anglo audience in the United States might try to trigger a sense of family unity by showing a mother, father, and two children laughing at the dinner table. But a recent arrival from India or Mexico might wonder why there aren't any grandparents or grandchildren in the picture.

Cultural differences aren't limited to ethnic groups. Marketers know, for example, that gay men and women tend to consume considerably more alcohol on average than straight people. (This is also the case for many other oppressed groups.) This makes them a potentially lucrative target for alcohol companies. The macho images in most beer and liquor advertising, however, are hardly appealing to the average gay person, so the companies have designed special campaigns for them. For example, Johnnie Walker Red Scotch wrote an ad around the slogan: "For the last time, it's not a lifestyle, it's a life." Naturally, the ad only ran in gay publications. In an advertisement aimed at lesbians, Bailey's liqueur showed two feminized coffee cups next to the copy, which read: "Our limited-edition coffee cups are available nationwide, though only recognized as a set in Hawaii." (The reference to Hawaii is a subtle reminder that it was the first state that tried to legalize same-sex marriages.)[49]

Demographic differences can be equally important. Women have different hot buttons than men. The rich are different from the poor; teenagers from adults. Marketers pay considerable attention to these differences and have plenty of information to help them along. They can, for example, buy "geodemographic" profiles of regions, cities, neighborhoods, or even individual blocks that break down their target group by age, gender, race, ethnicity, education, social class, and many other characteristics.

The hot button might be group consensus for one type of person while it could be antigroup consensus for another. What's important is reading the audience. My colleague Constance Jones recounts an example of what happens when a salesperson misses this. "A woman was shopping for a wedding dress in a secondhand shop while I was there. She said, 'I love those funky, old-fashioned dresses, and I love doing my own thing. I want to wear this at my wedding.' The saleslady responded, 'Oh, yes, many women are doing that now.' The shopper looked horrified and said, 'Oh, well, I guess I won't do that, then.'" (Jones's story reminds me of a headline I saw in the Sarasota, Florida, *Herald-Tribune*: "Nonbelievers Gather to Share Their Beliefs.")

Fortunately for marketers, researchers can tell them what their audience thinks about and what they value through what's known as their psychographic profile. The most widely used of these techniques is the Values and Lifestyles model (VALS2), which surveys consumers about their interests, opinions, activities (whether, for example, you're motivated by principles, status, or action), and buying power.[50] Consumers are then classified into "lifestyle" types: actualizers, the fulfilled, believers, achievers, strivers, experiencers, makers, and strugglers. With psychographic profiles in hand, marketers can tailor their come-on to the mind-set of the audience.

Direct-mail advertisers are particularly facile at customizing appeals. The next time you and your neighbor receive L. L. Bean catalogs you might want to compare them side by side. In all probability you'll find that the catalogs aren't exactly the same; each has been tailored to meet the company's profile of you. Internet marketers are even better able to get at information that targets your hot buttons. Matching strategies like these can be extremely successful. PRIZM, a marketing program that garners information about consumers from their zip codes, promotes itself in *Advertising Age* as "the targeting tool that turns birds of a feather into sitting ducks."

It's a vivid image and, if you're a consumer, one worth proving wrong. Unlike other animals, we have the capacity to decide which mental shortcuts are in our best interest and which are not and to choose when and where shortcuts are best suited. Realizing these choices, however, requires both considerable self-awareness and a willingness to rise above deeply ingrained reactions that often feel as natural and normal as the air we breathe. You need to be on the lookout for the hot buttons that set you off, the heuristics and fixed-action patterns that you're likely to respond with, and the techniques a clever professional may use to exploit the process.

Sometimes it's best, as Rube Goldberg once said, to "do it the hard way."

SEVEN

Gradually Escalating the Commitments

Or, Making You Say Yes by Never Saying No

Just because things happen slow doesn't mean you'll be ready for them. If they happened fast, you'd be alert for all kinds of suddenness, aware that speed was trump. "Slow" works on an altogether different principle, on the deceptive impression that there's plenty of time to prepare, which conceals the central fact, that no matter how slow things go, you'll always be slower.
—Richard Russo, *Empire Falls*

To learn the tricks of supersalesmen, I decided to take a course from the pros. Conveniently, a full-page newspaper ad announced that Peter Lowe International ("The success authority") was bringing one of his popular ("Over 300,000 people attend every year") business seminars to the main sports arena in my little corner of America. The teachers included experts ranging from Mary Lou Retton and Joe Montana to Larry King and Zig Ziglar ("The most compelling and inspirational speaker you will ever hear!"). The ad was full of testimonials to the program: "I have never been in a room with so many successful people—it was the ultimate experience," commented a previous attendee.

According to the ad, if I registered by the next day—the event was three weeks away—the one-day seminar was available for the "unbelievable early registration price" of $49. At the door it would be $225. Forty-nine bucks for the ultimate experience—such a deal. I call the 800 number at Peter Lowe International several times the next day, but the lines are always busy.

I try again a few days later and a woman answers with the greeting, "It's a great day at Peter Lowe International." She tells me there are three categories of tickets available, starting at $59 and going up to $89. (Those $225 tickets must have gone fast.) I inquire about the $49 offer, but I'm told that expired last week. I purchase a $59 ticket. After peppering me with questions, the woman has me registered and takes my credit card number. She then mentions that "incidentally" (salespeople are great incidentalists) "there's a one-hundred-twenty-page *Success Yearbook* that will be really helpful for following the seminars." (I need a program to follow Mary Lou Retton's lecture?) It costs $19.95 at the door but is available at the pre-seminar price of $9.95 if I order now. It's returnable at the arena if for any reason I decide I don't want it. I buy one. She says, "Thank you," I say, "You're welcome," and I realize I've just paid $69 for a $49 seminar. I found myself thinking about some advice a gambler once gave me: if you can't figure out which player in the poker game is the sucker, it's probably you.

A week before the event I receive a priority mail package. On top of the price of my ticket and *Success Yearbook* they've added a $9.95 "Order Processing Fee" and $5.16 in "Taxes and/or other fees." My total is now up to $84.06. I make my first big decision: I would definitely pack a bag lunch.

An "Urgent" message is written across my ticket instructing me to attach my business card on the back "to facilitate admittance and to be eligible for door prize drawings." (Hmm, they never asked for my business card at basketball games.) There's also a large ad for a man named Jay Mitton, "American's top financial authority." "He'll cut your income tax by 50% and cut your capital gains tax to '0.'" The secrets of success, tax cuts, and Joe Montana, too? This is going to be quite a day. I am discouraged, however, by a picture on the front of the ticket of a gentleman I assume is Peter Lowe. His eyes seem to be popping out of his head, which I guess is his way of trying to show what an enthusiastic fellow he is. All I can think of, however, is the insane-looking photos of Charles Manson the media kept showing after the Tate-LaBianca murders. Plus, Peter is wearing a terrible toupee. Either the man thinks he looks better in the photo than he actually does or he's preparing us not to expect Donald Trump next Thursday.

But, hey, I've got my ticket, a program, and my capital gains tax is a distant memory. (My wife, cynic that she is, points out that I've never paid capital gains tax. These women just don't understand business, do they?) Success, I'm ready.

The day of the event, a team of assistants—volunteers, it turns out—are outside the arena helping people staple their business cards to the back of their tickets for the amazing door prizes. Inside, a book-store/gift shop has been set up in the middle of the arena. A catalog list-ing the products in the store is waiting in our seats. About three thousand attendees have shown up.

Peter Lowe begins the introductions. The man looks as unhealthy in person as in his photos. He also talks with an incessant, monotonish elation that quickly gets on my nerves. My friend Lenny, who has accompanied me, comments that "this is the kind of guy who gives hyperthyroids a bad name." But if you add up the numbers there's no denying Peter knows how to put together a profitable event.

The teachers fall into two groups. Half are what is known in psycho-babble as inspirational speakers. Peter Lowe has brought in an impres-sive list of this type to events like these over the past decade: Ronald Reagan, George Bush Sr., Colin Powell, Henry Kissinger, Oliver North, Barbara Walters, Christopher Reeve, Mario Cuomo. The big names are paid between $30,000 and $60,000 for a half-hour speech.[1] Charlton Heston and Larry King were the stars this day.

Mary Lou Retton opens the program. She sets an upbeat tone, offering one bouncy cliché after another: "Take risks. Meet those chal-lenges head on." "To really succeed sometimes you have to go outside your comfort zone." "Don't be afraid to fail." "Seize the day." "Seize the moment." A few presenters are less well known. There was an inspi-rational singer, Leon Patillo, who performed during breaks. Leon was introduced every time he came out as "the former lead singer of San-tana." At one point Lenny leaned over and said to me, "This guy is per-forming for a bunch of Republican business wanna-bes, killing time between acts while people go to the bathroom. He's singing on a lousy sound system on a Thursday afternoon in Fresno. And he's preaching, 'I believe in my heart I can do anything'?"

The other group of teachers are salesmen. They're all very lik-able—smooth, witty, articulate. And they're wickedly effective at their craft. Each pushes his own products—books, audiotapes, videotapes—which are being sold at the makeshift store. My favorite is Tom Hop-kins, author of *How to Master the Art of Selling*, "the book that launched over 3,000,000 careers worldwide." Tom says that Peter asked him here to bring a message of "selling with integrity." Selling, he tells us, "is really the art form of helping people make their decisions." Tom spends awhile running through nine basic rules for leading an effective life. (*Every* business/sales/success program I've studied is built around a list of "rules.")

That completes the integrity part of Tom's talk. From then on, he sells. Tom launches into a twenty-minute infomercial for his books and tapes. We follow along with each of the descriptions in the product catalog. You can buy everything from his signature book (which is "guaranteed to help you serve more clients while boosting your bank account") for $30 up to a package of six audiocassettes and a thirty-page workbook ("Tom's pick for the most complete coverage of the selling cycle") for $95. There's even a book for children, *How to Make Your Dreams Come True*, which normally sells for $40, but today only it's $24.95. After permitting us a few moments to let these prices sink in, Tom shifts into high gear. He asks how many people in the audience don't have his whole library. Everyone's hand goes up. Then he asks, "Would you pay $350 for it all?" All the hands go down. Tom anticipates the resulting collective groan and meets it with good humor. "So, let's conclude the problem is money," he observes with a smile. Then he turns serious. "But because of Peter Lowe, we're selling it for $195 today. That's $16.25 a month, $3.75 a week, $0.53 a day." Besides, he points out, "it's an investment." He goes on like that for several minutes. The bookstore is extremely crowded after Tom's talk.

Others have even more to sell. Zig Ziglar peddles seven pages of products ranging from a $30 book up to *The Whole Shootin' Match*, a large package of audio- and videotapes, books, CD-ROMs, and "Ziggets, bite-sized" lessons for businesspeople short on time. "Total value of $2,611. Yours for only $1,595. You save over $1,000!"

When I analyzed the seminar afterward, it was clear the salesmen had used many psychological techniques—triggers to engage our trust, framing with contrast, and toying with mental accounting were some of the most obvious. One common denominator, however, stood out: they all began with small requests, gave us time to reset our acceptable anchor points, and only then escalated to their next request. I doubt anyone sitting in that auditorium would have committed to pay several hundred dollars for a seminar a week ago. But would you pay $49 for a full-day training session? Nine dollars and ninety-five cents for a yearbook? Fifty-three cents a day for Tom Hopkins to turn your life around? Never push too fast. Never ask for more than what seems reasonable. The principle of slowly escalating commitments can be thought of as the grammar of effective persuasion. It's the temporal dimension.

There was also a nonmonetary twist to these escalating requests. After lunch and Joe Montana, Peter Lowe comes on for his own presentation. He's introduced by a video describing him as a great businessman, a humble man trying to make a difference in people's lives. There's a lot of talk about how Peter Lowe International is a nonprofit organization. "This is a man in the image of Billy Graham," the video concludes. ("Uh-oh," Lenny mumbles. "I think I see the little train coming.") Peter delivers inspiration and selling. He offers us a free sample tape from his audio series, *Success Talk*, "so you can change your life every month." Peter makes it clear that he takes no royalties or profits on the series: "I do it because I care."

But Peter has something more important to sell than tapes. At the close of his scheduled talk, he offers us a free fourteen-minute bonus session. The session is optional, but he highly recommends that we take this extra step because it will be the first stride toward changing our lives. ("The train has pulled into the station," Lenny whispers.) Peter waits maybe ten seconds for anyone to leave. The pause is brief enough so that anyone trying to walk out is stared at by those remaining in their seats. Those who've stayed, of course, have claimed the moral high ground. This is the same inhibiting technique the Moonies often use to keep people from walking out on their lectures: tell people they're free to leave but generate peer pressure to keep them from doing so.

The bonus talk reveals what Peter Lowe International seems to really be selling—religion. Peter says he's not talking about any religion in particular, then goes on to tell stories about forgiveness, Good Friday, and Easter Sunday. He has us recite an affirmation, "Lord Jesus, I need you, I want you to come into the center of my life," a couple of times. When I pick up my free *Success Talk* tape, it's bundled with two brochures filled with articles like "Who Is This Jesus?" (Lenny exclaims, "Praise Allah.")

I'm not grumbling about advocating for one's preferred religion. The problem is deception. There's something wrong when a hidden agenda turns up six hours into the program. It's no different from cults who disguise the real name of their organization until recruits are two days into an indoctrination weekend. But, of course, it's effective social psychology—a classic application of slowly escalating commitments. Wait until everyone has committed little by little to the doctrines of the program, let inertia settle in, and only then pop the big question.

Postscript: A month after the seminar I received a letter from Peter inviting me, one of "a few people," to *apply* to participate in a new pilot program of personal instruction from specially trained business consultants. When I call ("It's a great day at Peter Lowe International," comes the familiar greeting), a very polished salesman—I'll call him Todd—tosses a battery of questions at me: "Are you teachable?" "Are you a decision maker?" Todd tells me that they're looking for people who want to obtain a high level of business and professional success. "Are you a person who is truly serious about the changes you want to make in your life?" Todd asks me a dozen of these questions. This method of cornering the customer is called the "Four Walls" technique. You're asked multiple rhetorical questions (classically, four) that wall you in, forcing the inescapable conclusion that you have no justification for not purchasing this product.[2]

Todd prompts and pushes me whenever my answers are vague or less than emphatic. Only after I serve up a string of consistent yes answers does he up the ante. The program, Todd explains, will require a large time commitment. During the first twelve weeks students have to be on the phone at least half an hour each week with their coach. I'll need to spend thirty to forty-five minutes each day, six days a week, to go and do whatever my coach has worked out for me. After that, I'll move from weekly meetings to monthly meetings.

"Is that time you have or time you'd make to make changes that you want in your life?" Todd asks. When I answer, "Probably," he insists I change it to a yes or, he says, there's no point in our moving forward. "I say this," he explains, "because a person who is confused will stay where they're at. Does that make sense to you?" "Yes," I stutter.

I'm not sure which question I'd answered yes to—that I'd be willing to commit the time or that what he said about confused people made sense to me—but Todd obviously takes it as blanket affirmation to all of the above because he immediately moves to the bottom line. Depending on how long I have to work with a coach, the program would cost between $1,700 and $3,000. "I'm not asking you to enroll," he says. "I'm simply saying if you saw this as worthwhile, and if I see this as win-win and invite you into the program, is that something you could do and would do now?" When I hesitate, he emphatically remarks that obviously few people have that kind of money lying around. Most would need to put it on a credit card. "Is that how you would do it?" he asks. That's an easy yes for me. "So that's possible for you to do?" he asks. "Yes," I answer. Todd has me write down a series of questions (e.g., "What three things would I need to change about me or how I do things to achieve my dreams?") to do as homework. I'm to call him back with my answers, at which time he'll decide whether he thinks I should be invited into the program.

No wonder it's such a great day at Peter Lowe International.

Automobile salesmen have honed stepwise selling into an artform.[3] I not only took jobs selling cars during my research but studied many other dealerships.[4] Some have converted to nonnegotiable, "no hassle" Saturn-type pricing. Most, however, have retained the classic methods of car sales to one degree or another.

I encountered vast differences in techniques. But I was struck by how many of the best salesmen employ the grammar of patient, stepwise sequences. In most dealerships, the staff is required to follow specific steps. I observed programs using everywhere from seven to twelve or more steps, all of which covered pretty much the same ground. Some agencies require sales staff to review the steps on a daily basis or at weekly meetings; that's because if they have to turn a customer over to colleague during the sales process, they can tell their colleague what step they're on. One of the most impressive salesmen I came across was Michael Gasio, who sold new cars for fifteen years. Gasio followed a ten-step procedure, which he explained to me.

The initial step, as in any sale, is getting a foot in the door. In the auto business, this means getting the customer on the showroom lot. Sometimes customers come on their own, other times the salesman needs to push in front of his competition. This may entail a bit of deception. There is, for example, a variation of the foot-in-the-door technique known in the trade as "throwing the lowball." "The lowball," Gasio says, "is when I give you a price that no one else can beat. I quote you a figure that's lower than invoice and tell you not to pay any more somewhere else. I know that no matter what price they give you at another place you're going to come to see me." (There's also what's called "throwing the highball," which is when the salesman offers an unreasonably high trade-in price for a customer's old car.)

When I myself was selling cars I heard a lot about a related technique called the bait and switch. In this case, the salesman quotes a low price for the exact car the customer wants. When the customer comes to the lot, however, he learns that the advertised car is missing an important feature. The salesman then finds another car on the lot with that feature—but at a higher price.

The lowball and the bait and switch are often thrown at customers who are in the "just looking" stage, such as when they're phoning around for price comparisons. Gasio's response when he gets these phone inquiries is "I'm pretty sure I can get it for you at ————" and then names a sub-invoice price. He tells the customer to come in and ask for him by name when he or she is ready. "I've dug a hole I'll have to work to get out of," he observes, "but I know the customer will come back." The lowball is phrased to elicit the first small commitment from the customer, Gasio says. "The big question I ask is 'If I could, would you?' That's the key to a telephone call. Knowing that I can't do it, I still ask him, 'If I could, would you?'"

Most important, it gets the customer physically on the lot. The moment the customer comes and asks for him, the lowballing salesman becomes entitled to split half the commission should another colleague eventually make the sale. This split is recognition from the agency of how crucial it is to get that first foot in the door.

The lowballer knows his deception will eventually work against him, so he makes a fast exit. "I immediately 'turn' the customer to another salesman," Gasio says. "I'll have a phone call. I'll have an emergency. I'll need to go to the bathroom. I'll have some excuse to turn you over to another salesman." Later on, the new salesman explains that the lowballer made some mistake when he quoted such a low price. During my research, I heard a multitude of excuses: "He misunderstood which model you were asking about." "He forgot to figure in the options you wanted." The new salesman might distance himself from the lowballer: "He's had a lot of personal problems lately." "Frankly, we've been having terrible trouble with him." My favorite explanation came from Gasio himself: "Because there's a contest here and he wanted to get you in so he could win a prize."

Once the customer is on the lot, the salesman proceeds to steps two and three: selling himself and the dealership. This begins with the "meet and greet." "There's a five-minute window to decide whether or not the customer likes you," Gasio says. "If they don't like you, they'll use you for the information you have and they'll dump you. If I don't feel I'm in control after the first five minutes, I'll turn you to a new salesman." If the customer was lowballed into coming in, this means seeing a third salesman. During those first five minutes, however, a good salesman would have sized up the customer well enough to decide whom to turn him to. Usually it's someone who has things in common with the customer. The "turner" tells the new salesman what step he's on in the sales process and then disappears.

A cardinal rule in sales is to avoid questions that may result in the answer "No." This is particularly true in the early stages of the process. A dangerous meet-and-greet question, for example, is "May I help you?" The invariable response is "No, I'm just looking," which stops the salesman cold. (Every salesman I interviewed said the most common opening words they heard from customers were "I'm just looking.") Instead, one manager I worked for instructed, I was to hold out my hand and say, "I'm Bob Levine. And you are . . .?" Virtually every customer will return the handshake, and the vast majority will respond with at least their first name. Similarly, later on in the sales process, instead of asking the customer a question such as whether she liked a particular car, the salesman might ask, "Would you prefer the economy of the four-cylinder engine or the power of the six-cylinder?"[5] Avoiding "No" answers discourages the chain of commitments from being broken.

The salesman then sells the dealership. "I want you to know you've made a wise choice in coming to my dealership," Gasio explains. "At the last place I worked, we'd tell you, 'The company has been here for twenty-seven years. The owner has a good name in the community. I may not be here when you need something, but he will.'" Another approach at this step is to bring up social proof. One dealer I studied would say, "I know your neighbors like us because we're growing twenty-five percent a year." Another dealership—one where I worked—made a point of letting the customer know that it was the biggest volume dealer in our city. The salesperson applauds the customer for choosing that dealership.

These early steps ask the customer for very small commitments— essentially to acknowledge the credibility of the agency. More important, however, they start the clock ticking. This is no small matter. One of the early goals is to slow the customer down. The passage of time, in fact, almost always works in favor of the salesman. For one thing, as we've seen earlier, the time spent with the salesman activates the reciprocity norm. We know that since the salesman is working on commission, the time he spends with us is, in a sense, costing him money. If he's established good rapport with us, we're left with a feeling of obligation (i.e., the reciprocity rule) to do something for him in return.

The passage of time also works against the customer in other ways. Since we live in a society where time is money, it means any time we spend at this dealership is an investment—a deposit of sorts. If nothing productive comes of the visit, we've wasted our time. We've blown our deposit. It's the sunk-cost trap.

"You have to stall them," Gasio observes. "The main thing in sales is you make it such a long process they don't want to go through it again." The customer is inclined to say, "Just tell me your best price. I'm in a hurry." But if the salesman does that, it rarely leads to a sale. "The salesman needs to cover all the steps in their precise sequence," Gasio observes. "Before we talk about price, I need time to get you to surface all your objections. As long as you're willing to express your reservations, I'll find a way to overcome them. Otherwise, I know you're not serious and I'm going to 'broom' you [sweep you off the lot]. The rule is 'If you don't have time to drive it, I'm not going to give you a price.'" You'll notice that many salesmen—Gasio included—don't wear a watch. Like casinos without clocks in Las Vegas, they want you to stay longer than you'd planned.

Now the salesman turns to the product. Step four is "the walk." "I'm going to take control now," Gasio says. "I'm going to have you follow me all around the lot. I show you every car. 'I don't want to look at trucks,' you might complain when we move in that direction. 'But I need to show you this Ranger,' I explain, 'because I want you to see the stereo since it's the same system I can get for you in the Maverick you want.'" The salesman gets you in deeper and deeper by "giving you" as much of his time as possible. Gasio points out that time also works for him in another way: "Maybe I waste so much of your time that the next dealership is closed."

"All the while, I'm establishing in you a mind-set of obedience to my authority. The walk begins when I say, 'Come with me.' I've given you an order. You can choose to follow it or reject it. But I can tell you from experience that almost every customer is going to come with me. I get you to follow me in as many ways like this as I can."

Some agencies teach salespeople to do the "turn and walk" whenever they start losing control. "If I see you fading off while I'm showing you a car," another salesperson told me, "I turn and walk toward a different car. Or toward my office. Ninety-nine percent trail right behind me. I walk. You follow."

Step five is the "walk around," sometimes known as the "seven-point walk around." You're getting closer to a car here. "I'm now going to find out if I'm still in control," Gasio says. "We start in the front of the car. I pop the hood and tell you to look under it. If you follow my instructions, I know everything's going fine. Then we go around to the passenger side. When I sold Volvos, for example, I'd emphasize the safety features, things like the childproof door locks. Eventually I work you over to the driver's side. I tell you to sit in the car and I show you the dashboard. During the walk around I explain everything I can think of about the car to you. Most people get bored by this, so I give you a reason to listen to me, maybe that 'Someday you'll have to know these things to resell the car.' I'm not selling you a car. I'm educating you. I'm your friend."

Step six, after the customer gets in the car, is the watershed commitment—the test-drive. When my student researchers and I went car shopping, we found that if we appeared the least bit reluctant at this point the test-drive might begin by surprise. Jenny Guticrrcz, for example, was being led on the walk around when the salesman told her to get inside and see how it feels. "Next thing I knew, he sat himself in the driver's seat, closed the door, and off we went. He never asked if I wanted to go for a test-drive." Gasio confirmed the common use of this approach. "When I worked for Ford, the front seat made it easy. You'd set the customer in the driver's seat and then you'd scoot them over and we were gone, off the lot and on the demo drive." For some customers, Gasio uses a softer approach. "Sometimes I'll say, 'I know you may not be ready to buy this car, but I'll get ten points if you go with me on a test-drive.' (There are no such points, of course.) Once we start, I always drive far enough away so you'll have a nice long drive back when I put you behind the wheel."

The overriding goal of the test-drive is to build "mental ownership." One of my sales trainers taught me to refer to everything about the car as "yours" during the test-drive: "Let me show you how to adjust your mirrors." "How do you like your sound system?" "These are the controls for your air conditioner."

Used-car dealers sometimes take mental ownership a step further by following the test-drive with a technique called the "puppy dog close." The customer is encouraged take the car home for a while with the expectation that the car, like a puppy, will grow on you and everyone else at home. A saleswoman from the used-car sales division of a large rental company told me that her agency aggressively encourages potential buyers to borrow the car.[6] "We try to generate attachment during the test-drive," she observed. "But if that doesn't work, we encourage them to take it home by themselves overnight, or even for the weekend. When they do, that usually makes the sale." If the attachment takes as planned, the idea of returning the car becomes as uninviting as returning your puppy to the pound.

But the test-drive itself is often attachment enough. "After the test-drive," Gasio says, "I do what we call 'the assumed close.' I'm assuming that one hundred percent of the people who have followed me to this stage are going to buy a car. Otherwise, you just wasted my time. So I'm assuming we now have an agreement to sell you a car." One agency I trained with taught us to test the assumed closed by stating/asking (auto salespeople are good at masking statements as questions), after the test-drive, "Looks like we found the right vehicle for you and your family?" If the customer doesn't immediately object, the salesperson becomes more assertive: "Bob, go ahead and park it in the sold line and I'll start the paperwork." "Bob, were you going to register this in just your name or did you want Vickie on the title, too?" "You folks are going to love your new van. Did you want us to install the roof rack today, or do you want to bring it back on Thursday?" The salesman may now do a turn and walk into his office.

Step seven is requesting a hypothetical commitment. "I ask you," Gasio says, "'how much would you be willing to pay for this car to buy it today? Give me an offer, even if it's ridiculous, to bring to my boss.' One of the rules in the automobile business is 'Don't come to the manager without a commitment.' Most of the time the customer's in a hurry and asks you to just go to your boss and ask the lowest price he'll take. If the salesman does that, he's lost control and isn't going to finish the sale. So I ask you again, 'What's it going to take today?' I want a commitment."

The customer usually responds with an impossible offer—say, $20,000 for a $25,000 car. The salesman doesn't challenge the offer. He explains that he's not authorized to change the marked price. Only the boss can do that. But if we work together, the salesman tells you, we can figure a way to convince the boss to agree to your proposal. "I turn to the trade-in now," Gasio explains. "'What if I can get you a good price for your old car?' I ask. I start very low. 'We took a car like yours in about a month ago. It wasn't quite as nice as yours'—we always say that, to give us flexibility later—'and I think they only gave him $500 for it.' I write the figure '$500' on the paperwork so you'll be aware of it the whole time we're negotiating." The customer is usually startled by the low price. The salesman calms him down and eases up in small increments. "You don't want to give the money away fast," Gasio says. "It's important to leave room for a lot of steps. Maybe I say, 'What if, instead of five hundred, I could go seven hundred and fifty?' I now put one line through '$500' on the paper—making sure you can still see the number—and write '$750' above it. 'No, no, I want $3,000,' the customer screams. In the corner of the paper, very small, I write '$3,000.' I say, 'Sir, if I can get the manager to go to $1,000, would that make us a deal?' The customer undoubtedly says no, again. But I've made some small steps here which set up my next move."

Now the salesman plunges aggressively for a commitment. "'You asked for a $5,000 discount on the new car. Is that correct?'" Gasio asks the customer. "I wait for them to answer 'Yes.' 'And you want $3,000 for the trade-in?' 'Yes,' they say. Then I ask, 'What if I can get you eight thousand for your old car? Will we have a deal today?' I proceed to negotiate the same way on the down payment and your monthly payments. I need to get a commitment about how much you can afford a month. I write the figure down. What I don't write down is the number of months of payments."

Eventually, the customer agrees to the proposal. The salesman, of course, hasn't committed to anything other than bringing the customer's offer to his boss. "Now we have the customer initial the page," Gasio says. But this round isn't over. "Since you've agreed to this offer," he tells the customer, "you shouldn't have any objection to filling out a credit application." The customer is made to fill out the application completely. If you don't have some required information about one of your references, the salesman may have you phone the person. (The dealer rarely has any need to call the references. When they do phone the references, it's sometimes to try to sell them a car by emphasizing the great deal their friend or relative just got.)

Some dealers squeeze you further during the credit check. For example, a finance manager may come out and ask how serious you are about buying the car. It costs money, he explains, to run a credit check. He might toss out a figure like $20 or $50 or whatever. You're getting in deeper and deeper.

Step eight—if you're trading in a car—is the appraisal process. Before turning your car over to the agency's appraiser, the salesperson may tell you that he needs to get some information about the automobile. He walks around the car taking down information like your license and vehicle numbers and the car's mileage and features. While doing this, he makes a point of touching, usually without making comments, every obvious flaw—scratches, stains, oil leaks. This is known as "trade devaluation." It's intended to lower your expectations for the trade-in price.

Other commitments occur during the appraisal process. "In order to appraise your car," Gasio says, "you're now going to give me two things you've probably given to no other salesman—the keys and registration to your car. Mentally, you're kissing that car good-bye. And if I'm successful, you'll never see these items again." Giving up your keys can also lead to other problems: if you decide to leave during negotiations, some devious agencies have been known to "misplace" the keys to hold you hostage while the salesman applies more sales pressure.

Some dealers use your old car to rub a contrast effect in your face. The buildings in most car lots have glass all around. The salesman takes advantage of this by parking the car you've just test-driven so you're looking right at it. When your old car comes back from the appraisal it gets parked next to the new one.

At step nine, the customer is asked to commit money. "You need to give me something to bring to my boss that shows him your offer is in good faith," Gasio tells them. "What can you give my boss to show you'll buy this car if he accepts your offer?" The salesman might suggest the customer write a check for $1,000. If the customer doesn't have a thousand, he's asked to come up with whatever he can. The dollar amount is less important than making some commitment. In dealer terminology, the salesman is now trying to "tie 'em in close." If the customer says he doesn't have his checkbook with him, the salesman might come up with some money himself under the assumption that just getting the customer to sign the form is a better commitment than nothing. (The salesman's money is removed from the order as soon as the customer leaves.) The salesman wants to "put the guy on paper." But it's most effective to have the customer commit his or her own money, no matter how little the amount.

The salesman now carries the offer to the manager. After an appropriate lapse of time, the salesman returns with the news, which you on some level expected, that your offer has been refused. The boss doesn't give a counteroffer. This sets the stage for step ten—the "bumps." The customer is asked if there's a way he or she can raise their earlier offer, perhaps by increasing the monthly payments or the down payment or accepting a lower trade-in price. "I don't set the size of the bump. You do," Gasio points out. "I ask you, 'What can you come up with?' And the size of your bump gives away something critical, because a big bump predicts another big bump." The sequence of bumps plays the rule of escalating commitments to the hilt: "As soon as I get a bump," Gasio says, "I write down the new figure, have you sign your initials, and I get up and leave. I'm not going to try for another bump right then. I'm only trying for one bump per round."

Other psychology may also be used here. The salesman may, for example, coerce you with limited-time, scarcity pressures. You might be offered limited-time-only rebates or told this price is *today only*. The salesman may emphasize that people who hesitate may lose their first choice. In an agency where I worked, there was a sign posted on the wall of every salesperson's office that read "The car you looked at today and want to think about till tomorrow may be the car someone looked at yesterday and will buy today." In another agency, one of my students, Amanda Morgan, was negotiating the price of a white '99 Ford Escort when a voice came over the loudspeaker announcing: "Congratulations to Mr. and Mrs. Marcus Smith on their purchase of a '99 white Escort." "The salesman's head jerked up," Morgan recalled. "'White '99 Escort? I hope that's not the one we were looking at!' He then punched in some numbers and breathed a sigh of relief as he assured us it wasn't the car we wanted."

Some salesmen exert more generalized time pressure. Tony Razzano, who works out of the Gold Coast of Long Island, is reputed to be the most successful salesman of used, ultraluxury cars (Jaguars, Rolls-Royces, Bentleys, etc.) in the country. ("I could sell ice to an Eskimo," he says about himself.) Razzano encourages reluctant customers with the carpe diem philosophy. In a world of anthrax and terrorists, he reminds them, "why would you wait for tomorrow to get what you want today, when tomorrow may never come?"[7]

The salesman hopes that some of this motivates you to up your offer. If you do, he then brings the new offer to the manager. But, alas, he soon returns with the news that it, too, has been rejected. Again the customer is asked if he can raise his offer. If so, the salesman gets your initials and immediately leaves. This process is repeated over several rounds. If the customer refuses to bump up to an acceptable price, he's turned over to another salesman or manager or whatever for another try. Some agencies are known as T/O (turnover) houses, meaning that at some point in the process every customer gets turned over to a higher-up who presses for a new bump.

The bumps continue until the deal is closed, which is the final step. As salespeople say, "Closers are the winners."

For Gasio, this is the end of the process. "Buying and paying for the car are different stories," he observes. "I just want you to sign to buy it. Someone else can figure out how you'll pay for it later. That's the finance manager's problem. As soon as we get that sold sticker in the window, we're done. We could care less about you."

What advice does Gasio have for potential car shoppers? "Buyer beware, always," he says. "You need to recognize that your hormones become imbalanced in this process and that this can make a difference between having a clear head and making the wrong deal. Be patient. Never forget that if it's a good deal today, it's going to be a better deal tomorrow. And there's no such thing as an absolute best deal. You have to decide when you're comfortable. Is the car something you can afford and something you like? If not, there's absolutely no reason to finish the transaction without sleeping on it. You'll have a better perspective in the morning."

And beware of the illusion that you can outsmart the dealer. "People almost always think they're good at negotiating," Gasio observes. "It's worst when they're with close friends or lovers—then the macho and ego feed their illusion even more. As a salesman, I'll let you look like a big shot for a while. Until I go in for the kill. The salesman will joust with you all day. I'll let you think you're in control at first. But when the time comes, I'll knock you off your horse. Even if I don't, you're not going to win the match. You can't. Because it's always the manager who decides when it's over—either when he gets his price or decides to broom you."

There's also a postscript to Mike Gasio's story—and it's an encouraging one. Gasio quit the auto sales business a few years ago and began a new career. He's now a teacher and counselor to at-risk youths in an inner-city junior high school in Fresno, California. But although the content of his message has shifted, much of its form remains the same. Gasio applies the same process of escalating commitments to effect change in his students that he did to sell cars to his customers. He doesn't confront students with the value of achieving good grades or other long-term goals until they're ready to accept these challenges, no more so than he would have quoted a bottom-line price to a customer before the end of the selling process.

"With these kids," he observes, "the motivation has to be something other than a letter grade. The grade has no value to them as a reinforcer because an F doesn't hurt them. You've lost that power over the students as a teacher because the grade has no meaning or consequence." Instead, Gasio has developed a point system that begins with short-term goals and builds from there. The points are written on a chalkboard—much like the paper he used to put in front of car buyers to tally offers and counteroffers. Gasio sets the students up in teams. This develops camaraderie and cooperation while at the same time taking advantage of peer pressure. If their team succeeds, they immediately see the points on the board. Students trade the points in at the end of the week for longer-term reinforcers—soda, candy, bus tickets, or whatever else has value to them. Eventually points are saved for even longer-term rewards.

More than anything, what Gasio learned from car sales is the importance of getting the customer on the lot. He translates this to the school environment by offering students the most points for just showing up on time. Then, to begin their work. The points for accomplishments diminish as the day goes on.

The great Taoist Lao-tzu once observed, "The journey of a thousand miles begins with a single step." Or, as Mike Gasio might say, get a foot in the door and you're halfway home.

Some techniques bring a paradoxical approach to the escalation sequence by pushing a request to or beyond its acceptable limit and then backing off. The two most common of these are the "door-in-the-face" and "that's-not-all" appeals.

A door in the face. In the door-in-the-face—sometimes called the reject-then-compromise—procedure, the salesperson begins with a large request he expects will be rejected. He wants the door to be slammed in his face. Looking forlorn, he now follows this with a smaller request that, unknown to the customer, was his target all along.

In one study, for example, researchers John Mowen, Robert Cialdini, and their assistants, posing as representatives of the fictitious California Mutual Insurance Company, asked university students walking on campus if they'd be willing to fill out a survey about safety in the home or dorm. The survey, students were told, would take about fifteen minutes. Not surprisingly, most of the students declined—only one out of four complied with the request. In another condition, however, the researchers door-in-the-faced them by beginning with a much larger request. "The survey takes about two hours," students were told. Then, after the subject declined to participate, the experimenters retreated to the target request: "Look, one part of the survey is particularly important and is fairly short. It will take only fifteen minutes to administer." Almost twice as many now complied.[8]

The door in the face works for several reasons. First, it activates the contrast effect. When I trained to sell Cutco knives, we were instructed to begin with our most expensive sets and progressively "drop down" with reluctant customers. If, for example, they rejected our "most popular set," which cost $760, we'd bring out a smaller, $555 set that "a lot of people are excited about," then retreat to a $410 model, and so on down to our $240 starter set. To add a second dose of contrast, we'd tell them how much more these knives would cost if they were sold in stores. We'd explain that the $760 set, for example, would have cost $2,500. As a third dose, we'd then show a picture of a supposedly comparable set made by Henckels that sells for $1,255. "Always use price comparisons before naming a price," our sales instructor taught us. "You can make any price seem lower by making the customer aware of other high-price brands." Additionally, we told the customer the Henckels knives weren't even as good as ours. We'd say, for example, that only Cutco—not Henckels and certainly not (Feh!) Chicago—has a "Universal Lamb Wedgelock" handle made of a "tough synthetic polymer called Celcon" and a "DD edge" blade made of the "same metal doctors and dentists use in surgical instruments." Eventually, as I've described earlier, we'd show the least expensive items in our catalog—a vegetable peeler, pizza cutters, pocketknives. Surely you can dig into your pockets and buy at least some small object here?

Second, and even more important, a well-executed door in the face sets up the norm of reciprocity. "I've made this concession to you," the salesperson implies. "It's your turn to give something in return." There's nothing unethical about compromise, of course. Most of the time it's not only productive but the cornerstone of good-faith bargaining. In the Middle East, for example, give-and-take haggling is a way of life. "If you don't give a little in bargaining, the other fellow will back up," an Arab businessman explained. "If he gives two steps, you have to give two steps. If you don't he'll back up four."[9] But there's a difference between this Arab marketplace scenario and the door-in-the-face technique: in the latter, customers are manipulated into abiding by rules of fairness in a game they never agreed to play.

The door in the face also plays on the formidable psychological force of guilt. The other person's not getting all he hoped for, so isn't it selfish of me not to compromise a little, too? On a rational level, we know we've done nothing wrong but, still, our inner Boy Scout can't avoid wanting to apologize for taking advantage of this nice person. Compromise becomes a comfortable exit.

In the Mowen and Cialdini study, the door-in-the-face technique doubled compliance rates even though the request came from an obviously capitalistic insurance company. When other triggers are added, such as if we're made to believe the solicitor represents a good cause, the technique can be even more effective. In another study, Cialdini and his colleagues posed as representatives of the County Youth Counseling Program. They went up to college students and described a day trip to the zoo they were planning for a group of juvenile delinquents. Would the college student be willing to act as a chaperon? Not surprisingly, most—83 percent—refused. For a new group of students, however, the researchers began with an even larger request. These students were asked to commit two hours a week for a minimum of the next two years to serve as counselors for the juvenile delinquents. When the students refused this request, the researchers came back with a compromise: to chaperon the delinquents on a day trip to the zoo. This time, 50 percent complied with the zoo request—virtually triple the rate the first time around. It's enough to make Madison Avenue envious.[10]

Most salespeople, when presenting a high-to-low sequence of requests, try to maximize profits with a modified door-in-the-face approach. They don't necessarily assume their highest request will be rejected, but they do prepare for rejection with a backup compromise. The Hare Krishnas, for example, begin by trying to sell their high-priced Bhagavad Gita, then the less expensive *Back to Godhead* magazine. Sometimes they make a sale. If the customer declines both, however, they're asked if they can at least manage a small donation, anything at all.

Asking for a small donation is a popular last retreat among fundraisers. You may not want a car wash, or a magazine subscription, or to let a stranger in your house to wash your windows, but can't you at least share a little of that spare change in your pocket?

Some solicitations cleverly combine the principle of gradually escalating commitments with the door-in-the-face technique. One of my favorites is a request I received from an established charity for cystic fibrosis. The appeal began with a sensitive letter from a respected writer whose daughter, Alex, had died tragically from the disease. Along with his letter, the writer enclosed a book he'd written about his daughter's struggles and untimely death. I had no doubt this was a sincere, intelligent appeal for a worthy cause.

But it was the format of the appeal that was pure social psychology. To begin with, the charity had initiated the reciprocity process by sending me a free gift. And the gift was a clever one—a college professor is no more capable of throwing a new book in the trash than is a military man of tossing out an American flag. Not only was the charity's foot in my door, but it had somehow become my turn to reciprocate.

Then the charity began the escalating-commitment process. Along with the book, there was a "Mail Receipt Verification/Contribution Form." The form, actually a postage-free reply card, was composed of four statements, each preceded by a box to be checked.

☐ *YES, I received a copy of* [the book] *"Alex, The Life of a Child."*

I checked this box, of course. And once I did, my psychological debt had become a written commitment.

☐ *YES, I want to help make your daughter's dream come true. Here's my contribution to help the Cystic Fibrosis Foundation find a cure so other young children can live.*

What's my alternative? "No. I don't want to help your daughter's dream come true. I'd prefer not to find a cure for cystic fibrosis so other young children can live." Naturally, I checked the yes box.

Below this statement were a few miniboxes asking how much I cared to contribute:

☐ $10　☐ $15　☐ $25　☐ $50　☐ Other _____

And below these were the reject-then-compromise options:

☐ *NO, I can't contribute $10 at this time, but I am enclosing $3.00 for the book.*

"At least let us break even" was the implicit message. "Won't you meet us halfway?"

☐ *NO, I'm sorry but I can't afford to send even $3.00.*

In other words, I'm such a cheap shmuck that I'll just steal this book right out of your charitable hands. This was reject-then-compromise, part two.

Whatever happened to that nice present they sent me?

And that's not all! The "that's-not-all" technique also begins with the salesperson asking a high price. This is followed by a several-second pause, during which the customer is kept from responding. The salesperson then offers a better deal by either lowering the price or adding a bonus product. That's not all is a variation on the door in the face. Whereas the latter begins with a request that will be rejected, however, that's not all gains its influence by putting the customer on the fence, allowing her to waver, and then offering her a comfortable way off.

The social psychologist Jerry Burger has demonstrated the technique in a series of field experiments.[11] In one of his studies, for example, an experimenter-salesman told customers at a student bake sale that cupcakes cost seventy-five cents. As this price was announced, another salesman held up his hand and said, "Wait a second," briefly consulted with the first salesman, and then announced ("that's not all") that the price today included two cookies. In a control condition, customers were offered the cupcake and two cookies as a package for seventy-five cents right at the onset. The bonus worked magic: almost twice as many people bought cupcakes in the that's-not all condition (73 percent) than in the control group (40 percent).

Burger, currently a professor at Santa Clara University, is an acknowledged expert on the subject of social influence. But he initially learned about the that's-not-all technique from the receiving end. "When we first moved back to California in the mid-1980s," he recalls, "my wife got the idea that we should join one of these health, Nautilus-type clubs. When we went to look at one, they gave us a little tour of the place and showed us all the facilities. Then they sat us down in the office with the salesperson or manager or whatever he called himself. The guy sat across from me at the table and was telling me about this marvelous 'deal' he could make, this package. For two years my wife and I could have unlimited access to the facilities, and on and on. He had a little index card on which he wrote the price. Let's say it was $600. He writes this down and slides it under my nose. I'm looking at this figure and he just lets me hang there. This is the interesting part of the technique. He made some kind of excuse, he was slick enough to pick up some book or a file or something, to stall for a few seconds. I felt myself going through this process thinking, 'Gosh, $600.' The thing is, I have no idea what this is worth." In retrospect, Burger observes, his lack of grounding at this point was critical to the process. The technique works best, he's found, when it concerns an item for which you have no previous anchor point—a good application of the uncertainty principle.

"So he throws this $600 figure at me," Burger continues, "and I found myself debating in my mind, weighing how often my wife and I would use the facilities. Maybe I could take up racquetball? But is it really worth $600? Then after about fifteen seconds, as if on cue, the guy picks up the card and turns it over. He says something like 'just for you,' or "today only." And, on the blank side of the card, he writes a new figure—$400. 'I'm prepared to give you that whole package for this much money right now,' he announces."

Instantly, Burger recalls, he felt his resistance weaken. "I could feel the persuasion process activated. Oh, my God, here I was trying to decide if $600 was worth it. I was right on the fence, going back and forth. He had planted that anchor point in my head and now, when he threw that $400 at me, I thought, 'Wow!' It might have been worth $600, but surely $400. It was very, very persuasive. Extremely powerful."

The that's-not-all technique is popular with television infomercials. This is the old "it slices and dices and, if you call right now, we'll throw in a free set of salad bowls" routine. Infomercials for golf clubs all seem to sell this way. Not only do they show you tests and interviews demonstrating that their club will drive your ball straightest and longest, but it's hard to find a company that doesn't—"that's not all"— toss in a free head cover or video ("a $70 value") if you pick that phone up right away.

Like all persuasion techniques, that's not all has its limitations. Burger's most recent experiments on the topic find that when the initial request is too high, the subsequent bonus is ineffective. Often, in fact, it sets off a boomerang effect. "If the health club salesman had started out at $2,000 or something well beyond reason," Burger says, "I would have been turned off right away." When the original request is outside the buyer's range of acceptability, it seems, a different switch is turned on in people's minds. It sets off a string of negative reactions toward the seller, ranging from irritation to distrust. Once this negative mind-set is activated, the that's-not-all appeal only makes things worse. It confirms the buyer's worst suspicions.

The critical element is to begin with just enough pressure to start the buyer vacillating. "It only works," Burger believes, "when you get the buyer to hang there for a few seconds, on the fence, trying to decide which way to go. If you don't get to that step, if people instantly say no, then they stop processing whatever information is forthcoming, because they've already got closure in their mind."

This is an important characteristic—and potential shortcoming— of all the principles in this book. There are many psychological forces that can be set in motion in any given situation. Subtle differences in context or presentation may precipitate a reactive effect rather than the intended one. But whichever force is activated usually operates at full strength. It tends to be a digital process.

Even the crudest influence attempts may achieve powerful results when they're sequenced carefully. Consider the most direct of all control procedures: demanding obedience to authority. By itself, making outright demands is a terrible technique. It rarely accomplishes its goals and, worse yet, it's prone to the boomerang effect. People simply don't like being told what to do.

But that's when they're told all at once. It's a very different story when the demands are escalated slowly. For a chilling example of this, let's turn to perhaps the most disturbing group of social psychology experiments ever conducted: Stanley Milgram's studies of obedience to authority.

Imagine you see an ad in the newspaper offering $25 for participating in an interesting psychology experiment.[12] You've never been in a psychology experiment and can use the $25, so you sign up. When you arrive at my lab at the university, you're paired with another subject who's also volunteered. I explain that I'm conducting a study to test the effects of punishment—specifically, electric shock—on learning. I need one of you to play the role of teacher and the other to be the learner. I flip a coin. You're appointed teacher.

The three of us walk into an adjacent room where we strap the learner into a piece of furniture that looks vaguely like an electric chair. I explain the task—memorizing word pairs—you'll be administering to the learner. Every time the learner makes an error you're to give him a shock. Each shock will be at higher level than the one before.

Before you and I leave the control room, I ask the learner if he has any questions. The man announces he has a history of heart problems and asks whether the shocks will be perilous to his condition. I assure him the shocks may be uncomfortable, but they're not dangerous. You and I walk back into the lab where we can hear but no longer see the learner.

I seat you in front of a sophisticated-looking "shock generator." The apparatus undoubtedly makes you question whether I've downplayed the dangers of the shock. There are thirty switches, beginning at a mild 15 volts and increasing in increments of 15 volts to potentially lethal doses of 450 volts. There are labels under groups of switches, beginning with "Mild Shock" on the lowest end followed by "Moderate Shock," "Strong Shock," "Very Strong Shock," "Extremely Strong Shock," "Danger: Severe Shock," and, under the 435- and 450-volt switches, the ominous letters "XXX."

The experiment begins. You shock the learner every time he makes a mistake. When you get up to about 75 volts he screams with pain. The screams intensify with each subsequent shock. At 150 volts—one-third of the way along—he calls out that his heart is bothering him and demands to be released. I won't allow that, I tell you, because it would ruin the experiment. The learner screams more and more hysterically about pain and his weak heart as you continue up the shock ladder.

If you resist at any point, I instruct you to continue. I don't scream at or threaten you. My strongest words are statements like "It is absolutely essential that you continue" and "You have no choice. You must go on."

At 300 volts, the learner screams out that he refuses to answer any more. At 345 volts, if you've continued this far, the learner stops responding. There's total silence. Since you can't see the man, you don't know what's happened to him. Something, however, is obviously very wrong. If you ask me to look in on his condition, I refuse. I tell you I'll take complete responsibility for the learner's welfare and instruct you to continue. "You have no choice. You must go on," I say to you. If the learner doesn't give an answer, I want you to treat his silence as an incorrect response. You're to ask the question, give him a few seconds to respond, and, if you hear nothing, shock him at the next highest level. You're to continue like that until you reach 450 volts.

How many psychologically normal people do you think would go all the way to 450 volts? When this question was posed to the general population, the average estimate was about one in a hundred people. A group of psychiatrists guessed one in a thousand.

How far would you go? Most people estimate they'd break off at about 135 volts—at the point just before the learner demands to be released. What are the chances you'd obey all the way to 450 volts? Zero, of course.

Wrong. Way wrong. When Stanley Milgram conducted this experiment with a group of adult men from a wide variety of occupations, a full 65 percent (twenty-five of forty) went to 450 volts. In fact, all twenty-five continued at 450 volts as long as they were told to. For all we know, some of them would have kept shocking the subject all afternoon.

Milgram carried out his research to understand perhaps the most pathological episode of human destruction the world has known, the systematic murder of millions during the Holocaust. Certainly there were psychopathic leaders—the Heydrichs and Goeths; Himmler and Hitler—who carry massive responsibility for the genocide. But how do we explain the tens of thousands of everyday German citizens who provided the manpower to carry out the massive killing program?

When cooperation exists on such a sweeping scale, no matter how evil the endeavor, the search for causes can almost always be found in elements of the situation. Milgram suspected that in this case, the toxic feature of the situation was obedience to authority. His initial experiment, conducted at Yale University, was designed as a pilot study that he then intended to replicate in Germany to understand what it was about German culture that made people so prone to obedience. But the frightening results he obtained with subjects in the United States—65 percent total obedience—made the overseas trip unnecessary. As Milgram later commented, "If a system of death camps were set up in the United States of the sort we had in Nazi Germany, one would be able to find sufficient personnel for those camps in any medium-sized American town."[13] Blind obedience is a defect that transcends cultural boundaries.

But Milgram's research demonstrates more than simple obedience. It's an illustration of the power of slowly escalating commitments. No one would electrocute a stranger if a psychologist came up and outright ordered them to. The real question is whether you'd accept an invitation to earn money for participating in an interesting experiment at a university. Because the moment you set foot in my laboratory you've generated a forward momentum I can use to suit my purposes. You're the one who's come to my lab, but it's my foot that's firmly in your door. Red flags may go up when the particulars of the experiment are explained to you, when your cosubject is strapped into electrodes, when he mentions his bad heart, and certainly when you see the XXX on the shock generator. But your initial commitment makes it extremely difficult to reverse course. You take a wait-and-see attitude. By not saying no, however, you've said yes.

The commitments snowball when the shocks and the pressure to obey begin. The first shock—15 volts—is mild and elicits no reaction. Nor do the next four. It's not until 75 volts that you hear groans from your colleague. The heart complaints don't appear until five shocks later, at 150 volts. But every flick of the switch makes it that much less likely you'll stop at the next level.

The most profound lesson of Milgram's experiments is a paradox: what little disobedience there was took place before the shocks became most dangerous. Most of those who quit—eight of the fifteen—did so between 135 and 180 volts, when the learner was just beginning to complain about his heart. No one walked out during the next six shock levels, even though the screams and complaints were escalating. A few (five) subjects quit between 285 and 315 volts, when the screams became hysterical and the learner announced that he was no longer part of the experiment. But what happened when the eerie quiet descended at 345 volts, when the learner seemed to have passed out or maybe died? How many of the remaining twenty-seven subjects refused to continue with this by now obviously sadistic and even felonious experiment? A grand total of two.

It isn't that the subjects were unconcerned with their actions. In fact, Milgram reported that virtually every obedient subject appeared to be in torment while administering the shocks. Many pleaded with the experimenter to let them stop. They groaned, perspired, trembled, stuttered, dug their fingernails into their flesh, and bit their lips. But by the time the subjects had reached 345 volts they'd already complied with the experimenter's orders twenty-two times. They'd persisted through the learner's cries of pain, refusals to continue, and a possible heart attack. What could happen to make them stop now? As Milgram observed, "People become integrated into a situation that carries its own momentum. The subject's problem . . . is how to become disengaged from a situation which is moving in an altogether ugly direction."[14] It's a problem that most people are clearly unable to resolve.

Reactions to Milgram's study are almost as noteworthy as subjects' behaviors. Nearly everyone's first response when hearing the results is to psychologically distance himself from the obedient subjects. Typical comments are "There was something pathological about the people Milgram tested" or "It wouldn't happen today" (Milgram's initial studies were conducted in the 1960s). Wrong and wrong again—textbook cases of the fundamental attribution error. Milgram's subjects were prescreened for psychological normality. And in the years following his original studies, the obedience experiment was replicated dozens of times—on men and women,[15] adults and children, across many ethnicities and in many countries throughout the world. In virtually none of these experiments has total obedience dipped below 50 percent. Look to the right of you and then to the left; one of those people would probably go to 450 volts.

I've described the Milgram study to underscore how dangerously susceptible we are to carefully crafted sequences. The insidiousness of slowly escalating commitments, almost by their very definition, is they put you in situations that catch you off guard. You don't recognize the sum total of your actions until after the fact, by which time it may well be too late.

It's especially important to guard against the sunk-cost trap. Recognize when your most profitable course of action is to swallow a loss and move forward. Remember that it's normal to loathe a loss and that your inclination will probably be to persist until you've gotten back to even. But while persistence may be a virtue in some situations, it can invite disaster in others. Consider the advice of the billionaire investor Warren Buffett: "When you find yourself in a hole, the best thing you can do is stop digging." Practice saying, "I made a mistake." Or: "I was wrong. Thanks for the learning experience."

EIGHT

Winning Hearts and Minds

Or, the Road to Perpetual Persuasion

God said it.
I believe it.
That settles it.
—Saying on a bumper sticker

Much of this book has been about overt compliance. We've looked at techniques that get you to buy kitchen knives, give a donation, or obey orders. Many times that's all the persuader cares about. The bottom line in these situations is getting you to take out your wallet or cast your vote or perform some other onetime behavior.

There are some situations, however, in which mere compliance isn't enough. With sufficient force, for example, all parents can get a child to do a homework assignment. But how do you get him to work hard time after time, when you're not around to hold discipline over his head? What you really want him to do is internalize discipline, to become self-disciplined. How do you move a person from mere overt compliance to private acceptance?

It's the same issue faced by any organization that thrives on group commitment, be it a business organization, a religious group, a sports team, or one's family. Cults epitomize the problem. Almost any huckster can offer sweet perks to get you to come by for a weekend. But cults don't thrive on people who simply show up. They're in the market for true believers: people who will devote their entire selves to whatever is required for the cause.

Winning hearts and minds carries the principle of escalating commitments to the hilt. Think of this chapter as the advanced lesson to the principle. The process requires a long, patient sequence of demands. It also, however, necessitates the demands be framed in particular ways. There's no absolute template for this level of mind control. Ultimately, it's an artform that, like any exercise in persuasion, must be adjusted according to the characteristics of the persuader, the audience, and the message in question. But the following eight general principles are good basic guides for what to watch out for.

Watch Out for the Invisible

The esteemed social psychologist Elliot Aronson likes to tell about a baseball game he once umpired. The day after the game he met an acquaintance who'd been in the stands watching the entire game. When Aronson asked the man what he thought of his umpiring, the man was surprised. He said he hadn't noticed that Aronson was the umpire, or noticed much about the umpire at all. To Aronson, this was the ultimate compliment of a job well done. He'd successfully steered the game without getting in the way.

The most dangerous mind controllers are a little like invisible umpires except, unlike Aronson, they control events to meet their needs, not yours. They know how to pull the strings so subtly you don't realize they're doing it.

The Moonies are often held up as contemporary examples of the spellbinding power of brainwashing. The media has portrayed members as already-vulnerable weaklings who are overcome by insidious, hypnotic, even Satanic-like programs of mind control. But if the Moonies are brainwashed, it's far from the popular stereotype.

Moonies almost invariably deny that POW-type coercive brainwashing had anything to do with their conversion. "When I was in the Moonies I 'knew' I hadn't been brainwashed," recalls ex-Moonie and now anticult activist Steven Hassan.[1] Brainwashing, Hassan imagined, "would involve being tortured in a dank basement somewhere, with a light bulb shining in my face. Of course, that never happened to me while I was in the Moonies." But the fact that he wasn't being brainwashed didn't mean there was no mind control. "When I was under mind control, I didn't really understand what it would be all about," says Hassan. Only years later did he see that subtle psychological pressures were insidiously altering his belief system more powerfully than torture and brainwashing ever could have.

Hassan didn't see pressure because he was looking in the wrong place. The most effective mind control is channeled through peers, other recruits, and members—people who seem like colleagues, not bosses. A smart leader suppresses his ego and remains quietly in the background like an invisible umpire. In the Moonies, this is easy because everyone else you interact with encourages you to convert.

To begin with, the recruit encounters an army of enthusiastic members. "For the average person, talking with an indoctrinated cultist is quite an experience," Hassan observes. "You have probably never met anyone else, friend or stranger, who is so absolutely convinced that he knows what is best for you. A dedicated cult member also does not take no for an answer, because he has been indoctrinated to believe that if you don't join, he is to blame." The member feels enormous pressure to succeed in winning you over.

On top of this, you're surrounded by social proof. It seems that every other recruit is impressed by what they see. Little do you know that this unanimity, too, is manipulated. At the beginning of a Moonie workshop, members sometimes set up teams to quickly evaluate and divide recruits into the "sheep"—newcomers who are "spiritually prepared"—and the "goats"—stubborn individualists who are less likely to become good members. The goats are kept at a safe distance from the sheeps to be sure their "negativity" doesn't rub off. Goats who can't be "broken" are asked to leave. "When I left the group," Hassan recalls, "I was amazed to learn that entirely different cults were doing the same thing. We thought we had invented the technique."

Moonie leaders even exploit the term *brainwashing*. When outsiders denounce members as brainwashed—a regular occurrence in the life of a Moonie—the condemnation is spun to produce a counterproductive effect. "It's too bad the word 'brainwashing' is used so loosely by the news media," Hassan observes. "It evokes a picture of conversion by torture. Those inside a cult know they haven't been tortured, so they think critics are making up lies. I do remember, however, Moon giving us a speech in which he said a popular magazine had accused him of brainwashing us. He declared, 'Americans' minds are very dirty—full of selfish materialism and drugs—and they *need* a heavenly brainwashing!' We all laughed." Most Moonies, in fact, are proud of their new identity. Ex-members describe wearing T-shirts and drinking from coffee mugs emblazoned with the slogan "I'm a Moonie and I ♥ it!"[2] Accusations of brainwashing increase this wish to belong. "Whenever people yelled at me and called me a 'brainwashed robot,'" Hassan says, "I just took it as an expected persecution. It made me feel more committed to the group."

Force: Less Is More

We resent being controlled. When a person seems too pushy, we get suspicious, annoyed, and often angry, and yearn to retain our freedom of choice more than before. Psychologist Jack Brehm called this the principle of "psychological reactance."[3] Or, if you prefer, it's what the social psychologist Joseph Masling labeled the "screw you effect."[4]

Anyone who's encountered a willful child is familiar with the scenario. Tell the child something's prohibited and he becomes obsessed with nothing else. In an experiment by Sharon Brehm and Marsha Weinraub, two-year-old boys were placed in a room with a pair of equally attractive toys. One of the toys was placed next to a Plexiglas wall, the other was set behind the Plexiglas. For some boys, the wall was one foot high, which allowed the boys to easily reach over and touch the distant toy. Given this easy access, they showed no particular preference for one toy or the other. For other boys, however, the wall was a formidable two feet high, which required them to walk around the barrier to touch the toy. When confronted with this wall of inaccessibility, the boys headed straight for the forbidden fruit, touching it three times as quickly as the accessible toy.[5]

Research shows that much of that two-year-old remains in adults, too. The most effective way to circumvent psychological reactance is to begin the demands so gradually that there's seemingly nothing to react against. Steven Hassan recalls how, in the Moonies, "behaviors are shaped subtly at first, then more forcefully. The material that will make up the new identity is doled out gradually, piece by piece, only as fast as the person is deemed ready to assimilate it. The rule of thumb is 'Tell him only what he can accept.'" When Hassan was a lecturer in the Moonies, he'd often discuss this strategy with other lecturers. "To rationalize our manipulations we would use this analogy: 'You wouldn't feed a baby thick pieces of steak, would you? You have to feed it something it can digest, like formula. Well, these people (potential converts) are spiritual babies. Don't sell them more than they can handle, or they will die.' If a recruit started getting angry because he was learning too much about us, the person working on him would back off and let another member move in to spoon feed some pablum."[6] The magician and persuasion artist Gregory Wilson calls this reach and withdrawal: "When I reach, you withdraw. I withdraw, you reach."[7]

Another shortcoming of excessive force is that it's usually temporary. If someone exercises enough force, of course, most of us have the good sense to keep our rebelliousness to ourselves. Point a gun at someone's head, or offer them enough money, and you can get most people to do about anything. But if it's hearts and minds you're after, this won't carry you far. People will obey, but only as long as the gun is at their head. Overt force elicits short-term, public compliance, but it's not very effective at changing internal beliefs. "Sheer, naked force has many disadvantages as a means of social control, not the least of which is that, when it's applied, people are aware of being oppressed and therefore may seek freedom," observed former marketing director David Edwards. "It's much more effective to get people to want to obey, to believe that disobedience is sin and obedience is virtue."

The CIA's "non-coercive counter-intelligence interrogation" procedures, which I referred to earlier, are founded on the least necessary force principle.[8] The CIA has certainly, in the past, showed a willingness to use direct, physical coercion to obtain its goals. It's well documented how it has experimented with techniques like forced confessions, drugs, and hypnosis. But even the CIA has learned that the best way to get information from an interrogatee is to avoid the appearance of pressure. The training manual observes that "the non-coercive interrogation is not conducted without pressure. On the contrary, the goal is to generate maximum pressure, or at least as much as is needed to induce compliance. The difference is that the pressure is generated inside the interrogatee. His resistance is sapped, his urge to yield is fortified, until in the end he defeats himself." The training manual adds that "manipulating the subject psychologically until he becomes compliant, without applying external methods of forcing him to submit, sounds harder than it is."[9] Unfortunately, it's right.

The key, always, is to apply the least necessary force every step of the way—just enough to kindle the conversion process without dousing it with external justification. The Hollywood superproducer Peter

Guber, when asked the secret of his success, put it well: "What I learned was that power is all perception, that its nonuse is its most powerful use. The trick is to use the least amount of power to create the maximum amount of change. Someone who has elegance can apply power selectively, like a laser, and carefully, almost unobtrusively, so that you don't feel that you're being overpowered. You feel like you're being motivated."[10]

Beware the Illusion of Choice

Persuasion that is exercised invisibly and with minimal force creates an illusion of choice. Consider the case of Patty Hearst, believed by many people (not the least of whom her lawyers) to be another textbook case of brainwashing. How else to explain why this wealthy, well-liked, attractive, and by all appearances emotionally stable young woman would leave her privileged way of life to become a soldier in the gritty Symbionese Liberation Army, an organization that violently opposed virtually everything and everyone from Patty's past?

On one level, of course, Patty was clearly coerced, even terrorized, by her SLA captors. She was kidnapped from her university apartment under a barrage of gunfire and then made to endure an incessant ordeal of revolutionary rhetoric and psychological and physical abuse, including a period of fifty days she spent blindfolded in a closet. When Patty emerged from her ordeal, she announced that she'd joined the SLA, taken on the name Tania, and denounced her parents. Most famously, she appeared on the nightly news carrying a carbine during an SLA holdup of a San Francisco bank—the robbery for which she eventually was tried, convicted, and sent to prison. Patty's legal team argued that Patty's persona of Tania represented nothing more than robotic obedience created by an ordeal of torture.

But what her lawyers couldn't explain was why Patty was so passionate about her new identity. Tania looked and sounded very much like a woman acting under her own volition and not at all like the stereotype of the zombielike puppet associated with brainwashing. Why, for example, did she pass up chances to escape before the bank robbery? Why, when Tania jilted her fiancé, did she so fervently plea for nothing more than that he, too, "could become a comrade." When Tania addressed the world, it was a heartfelt plea to accept her new way of life. "All I expect," she said, "is that you try to understand the changes I've gone through."

The fact is that Tania truly believed in her new identity. This didn't mean she wasn't victimized. What her lawyers and the jury overlooked, however, was that Patty's conversion wasn't produced by the brute force of the SLA as much as their psychology. During the course of Patty's confinement, her captors gradually reduced their overt pressure and, at the same time, engaged in progressively more rational dialogue. They slowly returned her freedom. Finally, they left her with the illusion of choice. "At the last second before Tania took off her blindfold Cinq [SLA leader Cinque] reminded her that she could walk freely out the door and that we would help her return to her family and friends," one of her captors, William Harris, testified later. "We all wanted Tania to stay, but we wanted to make sure that she saw all her options and was making a strong choice with no regrets or indecision."[11] When, at this juncture, Tania chose to remain, she crossed a psychological line. She'd become one of them—a true believer.

Or consider Marshall Applewhite, a.k.a. Do, the father of the Heaven's Gate cult. If you think all cult leaders spew fire and brimstone, you never heard this man speak. He looked and sounded less like Hitler in Berlin than Leslie Nielsen in *The Naked Gun*. But Do knew psychology. He bound his vulnerable following together with promises of magical fixes: savior spacecrafts, "graduating to the next level," a utopian life with ultimate meaning if they followed his lead. (Applewhite also lied a lot. For example, he added time pressure to their suicide decision by spreading false rumors that his body was "disintegrating" and that he'd be dead within six months.)

But Applewhite's greatest sales talent was communicating the perception of choice. Not only were members free to come and go but, at one point, Applewhite offered a thousand dollars to anyone who'd leave the group. No one took up the offer. If you stayed on at camp (called Central), however, it required sacrifices. Members were to check in with leaders every twelve minutes. You were assigned a "check partner" to protect against backsliding and individualistic thinking. Anyone who wavered from the cause was sent to a decontamination zone. Your family was a thing of the past. Men were encouraged to get castrated; many did. How do you explain these commitments to yourself after you just turned down a cash reward to leave? In fact, Applewhite's very lack of charisma added to the illusion of choice, because they certainly couldn't attribute staying on to his oratory skills. I'm here because I choose to be.[12]

Rewards: Less Is More

The least-force rules also hold true when it comes to positive rewards. Too much is not only ineffective at winning hearts and minds; it can also undo enthusiasm that already exists.

Imagine a little girl who loves to draw. Give her a box of Magic Markers and she plays for hours on end. Her teacher wants to encourage the girl's passion. The teacher has just taken a course in behavior modification where she learned—correctly—that the best way to increase an overt response is to reward it. One afternoon, when the girl looks tired and frustrated, the teacher offers her a prize if she'll do a few drawings. The next day, the girl has her award prominently displayed. Has the teacher's strategy worked?

Social psychologists Mark Lepper, David Greene, and Richard Nisbett designed an experiment to test this question. They went into a nursery school and identified a group of students who, left on their own, enjoyed spending lots of time drawing. Some of these students were told that a visitor was coming to class to observe their work and they'd win a special "Good Player Award" if they drew pictures for him. "See? It's got a big gold star and a bright red ribbon, and there's a place here for your name and your school," the students were informed. Other students were also asked to draw pictures for the visitor but were told nothing about a reward. After the visitor left and the first group got their awards, the teachers monitored the amount of time students now chose to spend drawing. The teachers found that over the next two weeks, students who'd been given an award were now only half as likely to spend their free time drawing as were the students who'd received no award. Further, according to ratings by outside observers, the quality of the award students' pictures was considerably inferior to those drawn by the no-award students. Once you're a pro, the students seemed to say, it's hard to get excited about what you used to do as an amateur.[13]

As a university professor, I'm all too well acquainted with the scenario. By the time students get to the college level, their intrinsic interest has long since been undermined by a lifetime of overly controlling extrinsic motivators. They've been pushed and pulled by so many exams and grades that only the most extraordinary among them take my class because of a passion for learning. It's humbling to realize that every student's favorite lecture seems to be no lecture at all: if I tell students I'm canceling the next lecture, they greet the news with cheers and outright handclapping, none of which I've heard after even my best lectures. (And the applauders include students who like me.) It's not that they're necessarily bored by what I have to say. It's just that all the papers, exams, and other assignments take priority, so any intrinsic interest the students once had is relegated to a back burner. I can prepare and perform the best lecture in the world, I can yell and holler until I'm exhausted, and when I ask for questions the only one I'm liable to get is "Will this be on the exam?"

This is very strange if you think about it. The precursors to the first universities, in the Middle Ages, consisted of groups of learners who would hire outside experts to assist them with problems they couldn't master on their own. The professor was employed by the students, and if he didn't produce, he was fired. This arrangement still exists in nondegree learning contexts. When, for example, I'm hired to speak to community groups—often giving the same lecture I might give to my regular classes—the audience is there simply because it wants to be, and we all know the one who's expected to produce is me. If I don't, I won't be hired back. In many nondegree programs—for example, lifelong learning and extended-education classes—there's a report card at the end of the class. But it's filled out by the students, not the instructor.

In traditional university settings, however, the arrow of evaluation has been reversed. Students pay my salary, yet I decide whether they're doing a good job. The average cost of an education in private universities is, conservatively, about $750 per credit. This works out to about $50 per lecture hour. I've often thought that we should make students buy tickets for each lecture rather than having them pay tuition by the semester. If people coughed up that kind of money for a rock concert, I wonder how many of them would cheer if the group announced the performance was canceled. But, alas, that's what happens when you overstuff students with extrinsic rewards. The passion for learning gets pretty much lost in the process.

Extrinsic reinforcers don't always undermine intrinsic interest. That occurs mostly when the reinforcers are too obviously coercive:

when you offer to buy your son a car if he raises his grades or threaten to take the car away if his grades go back down; or when an athlete is paid to play or a musician is paid to perform. Take away the money and the recipient now asks, "Why bother?" When extrinsic reinforcers are offered in a less-controlling manner, they may actually enhance intrinsic interest. This happens when the rewards seem to simply provide information about your performance rather than coerce you to perform. In the Good Players Award study, for example, a third group of students heard nothing about an award initially but, after they turned in their drawings, were informed they'd done such a good job that they deserved something special. These student spent more of their subsequent free time drawing than even the no-reward group did. After all, we take pleasure doing what we do well.

Winning hearts and minds means propelling people from the inside. If we receive too much reward, we may do what's asked, but only as long as the goods are coming. To be captured for the long haul, we need to convince ourselves we're doing it because we want to.

Guilt and Shame Are More Powerful Than Rules and Laws

The most direct route to internalization is through that formidable regulating agency we refer to as our conscience. The conscience, our inner voice of oughts and should nots, is an enigmatic animal. It's an agent of self-control over which we seem to have no control. It's the storehouse of our very innermost beliefs about morality, yet its contents seem to have been planted by everyone but ourselves—by our parents, teachers, society, and collective cultural heritage. The voice comes from inside of us, yet it mostly seems to operate against us. Is it us or them speaking? As scientists are best able to tell, the conscience is not localized in a single structure of the brain. But there's nothing ambiguous about its effects. What makes the conscience so powerful is that it's not only judge and jury but also has the means—guilt and shame—for enforcing its decisions.

Guilt and shame enforce society's expected standards of behavior—what we call social norms. These norms are generally unwritten. But don't let their invisibility fool you. We understand implicitly what constitutes appropriate social behavior and that when we misbehave the consequences are painful. There is ostracism or humiliation from other people that in turn lead to self-punishment.

We often think of legal authorities—the police, the courts, prisons—as the most formidable enforcers of our society's rules. But because social norms are so powerful, there's still a gaping flaw in this system. Laws simply threaten you with formal penalties. They work through fear of external threats. Once the enforcers are gone, you're safe. With social disapproval, however, the punishment persists inside the transgressor. Shame and guilt are like having little policemen living in your mind. They never go away.

Consider, for example, highway speed laws. Anyone who's watched a pack of speeders suddenly slow down when a police car makes its appearance, then shoot back up to their original speeds when the patrolman is safely out of sight, knows what I'm talking about. Many speeders treat beating the law as a game. They invest in devices like radar detectors or communicate by radio to learn whether it's safe to speed up ahead. But what would happen if, instead, we could tap into speeders' sense of social responsibility? Say you're speeding along and come upon a car with a vulnerable-looking, motherly type inside. On her window you see a photo of a cute little boy and girl and below that a sign that says, "My eight-year-old son Mikey and my six-year-old daughter Emily were killed in an accident with a speeder. Please don't speed." I bet that would keep you under the legal limit well after the woman's car was out of sight.

When social norms operate effectively there's no need for rules or laws. I don't have to write into my class syllabus that any students caught not wearing clothes to class will have their grades lowered. Their own aversion to shame takes care of that. Formal rules are only needed when norms break down. For example, because there's sometimes a student or two in my classes who suffers no shame when they're caught plagiarizing, I have to establish formal punishments—an F in the class, filing a disciplinary report—for transgressors. Laws put teeth into failing norms.

Laws and norms aren't inherently incompatible. One of the most provocative new movements in law enforcement, in fact, appeals to shame and ostracism rather than simple fear of getting caught. One target, for example, is the so-called victimless crime of prostitution. The traditional procedure for enforcing prostitution laws entails a policeman who poses as a customer and then arrests the hooker. The problem with this approach, as the police are the first to tell you, is that the same woman will be back the next night, or she will move to a new location. In response, law enforcement in many cities are now reversing the sting operation by having a female officer pose as a prostitute and then arrest the customer. The assumption is that the customer is more likely to be connected to his family and community by norms of traditional moral behavior and so must face the more formidable punishment of public humiliation and ostracism. Similarly, many communities are reversing drug sting operations from traditional "buy busts"—whereby an undercover officer posing as a drug buyer arrests the dealer—to "sell busts"—in which the officer poses as a dealer and then arrests the buyer.[14]

Sometimes, in fact, purely law-based punishments send the opposite of the intended message. Meting out fines to people who can afford them, for example, may proclaim nothing more than money really counts. If you give fines to a landlord who repeatedly disobeys housing violations, they may simply become a license fee to run slums. When you fine a wealthy tax evader instead of sending him to prison, doesn't it say that he can buy his way out of anything?

Instead of fining or sending low-level felons to prison, some judges are experimenting with shame-based sentences. Drunk drivers in New York have been sentenced to display brightly colored DUI bumper stickers on their cars; in Texas, they've been given stickers like this one: "The owner of this vehicle is on probation in the County Court of Law of Fort Bend County, Texas, for driving while intoxicated. Report unsafe driving to Adult Probation Department." Nonviolent sex offenders in Florida and Oregon are being required to post warning signs on their property. In California, a shoplifter was ordered to wear a T-shirt proclaiming "I am a thief." In Seattle, a woman was made to wear a sign that read "I am a convicted child molester." A South Carolina man was sentenced to sit outside the courthouse for ten days with a sign that read "I am a Drunk Driver." People convicted of public urination in Hoboken, New Jersey—even millionaire executives—are required to sweep city streets. Minors convicted of misdemeanors in Maryland are in some cases being required to get on their knees and apologize to their victims. They're released only if the victim is convinced of the sincerity of the apology.

Some strategies are designed to provoke empathy with the victim. Burglars in Tennessee have been sentenced to open their houses to their victims and allow the victims to take anything they want. A man convicted of assaulting his ex-wife was required to "let the ex-wife spit in his face." The judge explained, "It's my way to express upon him the humiliation of his act." A New York slumlord was sentenced to house arrest in one of his rat-infested apartments.[15] A national organization called the Victim Offender Reconciliation Program (VORP) has victims and their offenders meet together in a voluntary, unofficial environment where the victim describes, face-to-face, how he was damaged—monetarily, emotionally, socially—by the criminal act.

Some of the most radical norm scholars advocate the systematic transformation of norms themselves. Law professor Cass Sunstein, a leader of this movement, offers the example of the changes in public attitudes toward smoking that took place in the late eighties and early nineties. They had less to do with health concerns, he observes, than with the effects of normative social pressure. There was little progress in antismoking regulations after the surgeon general's initial 1964 declaration that smoking was dangerous. It wasn't until 1986, when the surgeon general issued his report on the dangers of secondhand smoke, that the public began treating smokers as inconsiderate, immoral pariahs who were dangerous to others as well as themselves. Smoking rates steeply declined.[16] I, personally, was a smoker during those transition years, and I'll never forget the impact on me the first time I saw a no-smoking sign in a restaurant that was also labeled "ENFORCED BY CUSTOMERS." The reason recent draconian no-smoking laws (in states like my own, it's against the law to smoke in bars) have encountered such little resistance is they reflect the dominant cultural attitude that smoking is a violation of the norm of social responsibility.

Or consider the striking success of the juvenile gun-control program in Charleston, South Carolina. The public schools in Charleston, like those in many big cities, have had a long-standing problem with students carrying guns. The city had experimented with several traditional policies—zero tolerance, severe punishment, education programs, weapons buybacks—with the usual lack of success. The problem, as law professor Dan Kahan explains, is that "juveniles carry weapons less to protect themselves from violence than to acquire status among their peers. Against the background of social norms, possessing a weapon expresses confidence and a willingness to defy authority, dispositions that juveniles believe their peers respect." The conventional punishments for carrying weapons, in fact, can activate a counterproductive norm. "What makes guns appealing to juveniles is their connotation of defiance," Kahan observes. "By showing just how much authorities resent guns, buy-backs, sanctions, and education campaigns all accentuate the message of defiance that possessing one projects."

To counter this effect, Charleston offered a cash reward to anyone who simply reported a fellow student carrying a weapon. One's peers now became the agents of control. Once students began turning their colleagues in—which they did—it dispelled the perception that possessors were universally admired by their peers. "Showing off your gun under these circumstances doesn't mark you as tough and cool," Kahan points out. "It marks you out as a chump." With this new set of norms now dominant, the incidence of juvenile gun possession dropped to virtually zero.[17]

As with all profound persuasion, however, the key to effectively challenging a norm is avoiding the appearance of too much force. "If the law condemns too severely—if it tries to break the grip of the contested norm (and the will of supporters) with a 'hard shove'—it will likely prove a dead letter and could even backfire," Kahan observes. "If it condemns more mildly—if it 'gently nudges' citizens toward the desired behavior and attitudes—it might well initiate a process that culminates in the near eradication of the contested norm and the associated types of behavior."[18]

There is considerable controversy in the legal academy as to whether policy makers should act as "norm entrepreneurs." Opponents argue, for good reason, that it raises enormous ethical questions. Empowering policy makers to control social values is, after all, a rather Orwellian notion. As pure social psychology, however, the approach is pitch perfect. With laws based solely on fear, you merely obey because you have to. When laws are driven by accepted norms, you obey because you're too embarrassed not to.[19]

Self-Justification: The Road to Perpetual Persuasion

Westerners strive for personal consistency—to do what we say, say what we do, and convince ourselves that our present actions are compatible with those we performed in the past.[20] We disapprove of people who think one thing and do another. It smells of hypocrisy and phoniness. As a result, when our beliefs are inconsistent with our actions, it creates an unpleasant state of mind—one that we feel compelled to reduce, in the same way we want to eat when we're hungry or get warm when we're cold. Psychologists refer to this tension as cognitive dissonance.

Say, for example, you smoke cigarettes but also know cigarette smoking is hazardous to your health. The behavior and the attitude are in a state of dissonance, which you're driven to reduce. There are a number of ways you can do this. The most sensible strategy is to quit smoking. But as anyone who's been a smoker knows, quitting is no easy task. Instead, you rationalize.

You could, for example, add information that minimizes the health risk: "No one in my family has ever had lung cancer." "My brand is low in tar and nicotine." Or you could focus on exceptions: "My Uncle Harry smoked two packs a day his whole life and lived until ninety." "My Cousin Benny died of lung cancer at fifty and he never touched a cigarette." You might trivialize the importance of the inconsistency: "I need to smoke to relax and to keep my weight down, both of which are more important to me than worrying about getting cancer thirty years from now." "Everyone has to die of something." Any smoker you ask can probably add his own justifications to this list. What's important is all of these examples reduce your dissonance, but none result in the one change that can save your life—quitting smoking. And here's the crux of the problem: the less you change your behavior, the more you rationalize; and the more you rationalize, the less likely you'll quit smoking.

Dissonance will only be aroused, however, if the other rules in this chapter are followed. If I comply because you've forced me to, the force is all the justification I need. Dissonance thrives on the illusion of choice. To arouse my dissonance, you need to be subtle, to stay in the background, so I'll see no one to blame but myself.

In a classic experiment, Leon Festinger and J. Merrill Carlsmith had subjects work for an hour on an extremely boring task: turning pegs a quarter of a turn to the right and then a quarter of a turn to the left. The subjects were then told the actual purpose of the study was to investigate the effect of expectations on performance. Another subject was sitting in the waiting room, and it was important he be convinced that this was going to be an interesting experiment. The research assistant who usually did the job of convincing the other subject, the subjects were told, couldn't make it today. "Could you fill in and do this?" the anxious experimenter pleaded.

Subjects were assigned to one of two groups. Half of them (the insufficient justification group) were offered a small sum—about $5 by today's standards—to lie to the next subject about how interesting the experiment was. The other half (the sufficient justification group) were paid handsomely—about $100 by today's standards—to lie.[21] Assume you go along with the request. After you've deceived the poor soul in the waiting room and ruined his next hour, another research assistant asks you to fill out a questionnaire asking how interesting you actually found the experiment.

The question is which of the two groups is more likely to believe its own lie? Common sense says the more you pay someone to tell a lie, the more they'll believe it. Cognitive dissonance theory, however, predicts the opposite: if someone is paid a lot of money he has sufficient justification for lying; there's little dissonance and, so, no need to rationalize. But if someone is paid only $5—the minimal pressure group—he needs to come up with a reason for lying. The most convenient rationalization is to persuade oneself that it wasn't really a lie, after all. This is exactly what Festinger and Carlsmith found. Subjects paid only $5 to lie rated the task more than twice as interesting as did those who were paid $100.[22]

Cognitive dissonance is the mind controller's best friend. If dissonance can be created between what you think and what you do, you'll try your best to change one or the other. And changing your thoughts is usually the easier way out. Once the wheels of self-justification begin turning, the persuader sits back and watches you do his work for him.

When Behavior Is Controlled, the Mind Follows

It is common sense that people's inner beliefs may drive their external behavior. If you're attracted to a certain person, you should be more likely to socialize with that person. If you favor a brand of toothpaste, you're more prone to buy it. Of course, our internal thoughts don't *always* predict our public behavior, but, overall, what we do obviously reflects what we think.

But beliefs and behaviors are also related in a more remarkable way. It turns out that the arrow is as likely to point in the reverse direction.

As social psychologist David Myers observes, "If social psychology has taught us anything during the last 25 years, it is that we are likely not only to think ourselves into a way of acting but also to act ourselves into a way of thinking."[23] In other words, the saying "I'll believe it when I see it" is as valid the other way around: "I'll see it when I believe it."

In a famous study, social psychologist Philip Zimbardo turned the basement of the Stanford University psychology building into a mock prison. Subjects were a group of psychologically normal young men who happened to be in Palo Alto for the summer. They were divided into prisoners and guards based on flips of a coin. The experiment was scheduled to last for two weeks.

To Zimbardo's astonishment, the two groups quickly came to act like their real prison counterparts. The prisoners became despondent. Some broke down. In less than thirty-six hours, one had to be discharged because of "extreme depression, disorganized thinking, uncontrollable crying and fits of rage." Over the next three days, three other prisoners had to be released with similar anxiety symptoms. A fifth prisoner was released when he developed a psychosomatic rash over his entire body, an apparent reaction to his parole appeal being rejected by the mock parole board.

The behavior of the guards was even more disturbing. All, to one degree or another, flexed their power. They made the prisoners obey trivial and often inconsistent rules. Prisoners were forced to perform tedious, pointless work, such as moving cartons from one closet to another or continuously picking thorns out of blankets (an unpleasant task created by the guards having dragged the blankets through thorny bushes). They were made to sing songs or laugh or stop smiling on command; to curse and malign each other publicly; to clean out toilets with their bare hands. They were required to continuously sound off their numbers and do push-ups, occasionally while guards stepped on their backs or made another prisoner sit on them. The situation got so out of hand that the planned two-week experiment had to be aborted after six days and nights.[24]

The Stanford prison experiment shows how seamlessly playing a role may turn to becoming the role. Act the part of prisoner and you soon feel like a prisoner; play a guard and you'll start thinking like a guard. Doing turns to believing.

Cults thrive on this effect. Most of them rigidly control every waking moment of a member's behavior—what he eats, the clothes he wears, when he sleeps, incessant rituals, his every task. Leaders know a crammed schedule not only restricts a recruit's mind from dangerous wandering but leads to internalizing thoughts and feelings that are conducive to the group. Some cults go further. Like British acting coaches, they require members to practice detailed mannerisms—speech, posture, facial expressions—that are unique to the group. But they insist that members believe in what they're doing. When a member appears to be just mechanically obeying, he may be accused of not caring or not trying enough, of being selfish and impure. In the Moonies, poor performers might be told to imitate an older group member, even to mimic the tone of his voice. "The leaders cannot command someone else's thoughts," ex-Moonie Steven Hassan observed, "but they know that if they command behavior, hearts and minds will follow."[25]

For an insight into how saying turns to believing, consider another study. E. Tory Higgins and his colleagues asked college students to read a personality description of a person and then to summarize the description for someone they were told either liked or disliked the person. Not surprisingly, the subjects described the target in more glowing terms to admirers. But then, having said positive things, they actually believed what they said: asked to recall what they'd originally read, the positive-oriented subjects recollected the original description as more positive than it actually was. In other words, you adjust your presentation to please the listener and, in so doing, convince yourself in the process.[26]

When you play a part, it becomes that much likelier you'll play it again, and with greater intensity. "He who permits himself to tell a lie once," wrote Thomas Jefferson, "finds it much easier to do it a second and third time, till at length it becomes habitual; he tells lies without attending to it, and truths without the world's believing him. This falsehood of the tongue leads to that of the heart, and in time depraves all its good dispositions." As Jefferson understood, the act of taking a stance galvanizes the belief behind the stance.

Public displays are especially self-persuasive. Before many Middle Eastern suicide bombing missions, a ritual videotape is recorded by the terrorist's recruiters. The video, filmed hours before the attack, shows the bomber giving a last testament of his commitment to the cause. The bomber knows that whenever possible, scenes of his approaching attack and news stories showing the results of the attack will be added to the tape and given over to his family as a souvenir for posterity. Journalist Joseph Lelyveld, who interviewed both terrorists and the families of suicide bombers, observes how this ritual is a "key stage in the psychological prepping that deepens the candidate's conviction that he is about to perform a great deed for his family, his people and his faith, that he has reached the point of no return."[27]

Failure May Persuade You More Than Success

Another consequence of cognitive dissonance is that a belief may actually get stronger when it's proven wrong. The more you stand to lose, and the more foolish you look, the greater the dissonance and, so, the greater the pressure to prove you were right in the first place. In other words, if you're in the business of mind control, sometimes nothing succeeds like failure.

Say, for example, you've been a dedicated member of a group and are now confronted with evidence that your group's cause is just plain wrong. Would you admit that you made a mistake and leave? If you'd already committed enough, probably not.

Consider the classic case of Marian Keech, a charismatic, self-proclaimed clairvoyant from Wisconsin who prophesied that much of the Americas would be destroyed by a massive flood just before dawn on the coming December 21. Keech had been receiving messages through "automatic writing" from the Guardians, a group of superior beings who lived on the planet Clarion. Fortunately for us doomed earthlings, the Guardians said that they'd be dropping by in their flying saucers on the dreaded date to pick up Keech and any disciples who took the trouble to join her. A group of individuals, many from considerable distances around the country, believed the story and traveled to join Keech and make preparations for the Guardians' visit. The disciples staked a great deal on their decision. They were ridiculed by friends, and in some cases quit their jobs or dropped out of college. A few abandoned their spouses.

Leon Festinger and his fellow researchers joined the group under false pretenses to chronicle its development, in particular to observe changes in the intensity of members' beliefs and commitment to the cause. In the weeks before the predicted flood, the researchers found, converts showed virtually no desire to promote their cause. They shunned opportunities to publicize their beliefs and recruit converts and invariably turned away reporters.

On the morning of December 20, Keech received a message that her group would be picked up at precisely midnight. Members were instructed to remove all metal from their clothing. Everyone obediently complied, carefully removing zippers and clasps from their skirts, pants, and shirts. After an all-night vigil, they waited for the Guardians. Cynical reporters surrounded the event. When spacemen failed to appear at midnight, four and a half hours of tremendous tension ensued. The disciples sat in stunned silence; by 4:30 Keech was crying. But at 4:45 she became elated. She said she'd just received a telepathic message from the Guardians saying that her group of believers had spread so much light with their unflagging faith that God had spared the world from the cataclysm.

After this lame explanation, you might expect followers to become disillusioned and make a quick retreat for home. A few—mostly fringe members who hadn't invested much energy or time—did split off. But here's the important part. Most disciples not only stayed but, having made that decision, were now even more convinced than before that Keech had been right all along. Even more notable was what they did to convince themselves they were right: they set out to convince others. In a far cry from their previous secrecy, members immediately contacted all newspapers and national wire services to herald their message. In the days that followed, they held numerous press conferences, held open houses, and explained their beliefs in great detail to as many newcomers who would listen. Being wrong had turned them into true believers.[28]

Marian Keech's story has been reenacted in many variations. Psychology professor Ray Hyman, who at the time was investigating the claims by the disciples of Maharishi Mahesh Yogi and transcendental meditation that they could perform miracles such as levitation and invisibility, summed it up nicely in his report: "It is all too easy to view Dr. Rabinoff [a physics Ph.D. who was lecturing nationally about TMers' miracles] as some self-deluded misfit. But, I suspect, he typifies most of us in the way we cope with the stresses of life and the search for the Answer to Big Questions about the Meaning of It All. Once an individual, especially a fairly bright one, latches onto a belief system that offers comfort and universal answers, then nature has provided him with innumerable mechanisms to avoid facing up to discomforting challenges to that belief."[29]

The more one endures, the greater the need to self-justify. Nansook Hong was raised by her parents in the Moonie church. At age fifteen, she was handpicked to marry Reverend Sun Myung Moon's oldest son, Youngjin Moon. Hong lived fourteen years among the royal Moon family before leaving her emotionally troubled and abusive husband. In her subsequent book, *In the Shadow of the Moons*,[30] Hong detailed the pathologies she endured. She then struggled to explain what kept her from leaving for so long:

> Much has been written about the coercion and brainwashing that takes place in the Unification Church. What I experienced was conditioning. You are isolated among like-minded people. You are bombarded with messages elevating obedience above critical thinking. Your belief system is reinforced at every turn. You become invested in those beliefs the longer you are associated with the church. After ten years, after twenty years, who would want to admit, even to herself, that her beliefs were built on sand?
>
> I didn't, surely. I was part of the inner circle. I had seen enough kindness in the Reverend Moon to excuse his blatant lapses—his toleration of his son's behavior, his hitting his children, his verbal abuse of me. Not to excuse him was to open my whole life up to question. Not just my life. My parents had spent thirty years pushing aside their own doubts.[31]

We're compelled to justify our commitments. If there's no justification in sight—that invisible umpire, again—you'll look to your own motives for an explanation. There lies the biggest problem of all: once the process begins, it becomes self-perpetuating. If I did it, I must believe it. And if believe it, I'm more likely to do it again, and more so.

NINE

Jonestown

Or, the Dark End of the Dark Side of Persuasion

Nobody joins a cult. They just postpone the decision to leave.
—Anonymous cult member

The most frightening recording I've ever heard is the tape of the last hour at Jonestown, those final minutes of that unfathomable early evening of November 18, 1978, when 918 members of the People's Temple lined up for their cup of cyanide-laced Kool-Aid and then lay down in orderly rows to die.[1] Hearing the final sounds of so many decent lives coming to an end is horrible enough. But what I find more chilling is how many victims continued to the end to believe in Jones and his insane message. Some people did, in fact, resist drinking the poison (they were forcibly injected with hypodermic needles) and a few escaped. But they were only a handful. The vast majority not only willingly obeyed Jones's orders but, as one hears on the final tape, did so with enthusiasm.

At first, as the poison is being prepared, you hear Jones preaching to his followers. They're behind him all the way, applauding and shouting encouragement after each phrase. It sounds eerily like any inspirational Sunday service.

"It was said by the greatest of prophets from time immemorial: No man takes my life from me. I lay down my life. . . . If we can't live in peace than let's die in peace," says Jones. The crowd cheers.

"So my opinion is that you be kind to children, and be kind to seniors and take the potion like they used to take it in ancient Greece, and step over quietly, because we are not committing suicide. It's a revolutionary act. We can't go back. They won't leave us alone. . . . And there's no way, no way, we can survive," he continues. More cheers.

"If we can't live in peace then let's die in peace." A loud cheer.

"If this [Jonestown] only worked one day it was worthwhile." Another loud cheer.

As the final tape progresses, we hear children and babies crying in the background while the poison takes hold (neither as quickly nor as painlessly as Jones's medical assistant had forecast). At the same time, however, Jones now begins conducting a bizarrely civilized, open, rational meeting with his followers—each of whom is by now well aware that it will soon be his turn to take the poison.

"Anyone that has any dissenting opinion, please speak," Jones says in a kind voice.

A few members step up to the microphone to protest. "Is it too late for Russia?" a woman asks. (Jones had previously talked about moving the temple to Russia if their problems in Guyana got out of hand.) Jones explains why Russia is no longer an alternative. Then he returns to working up the crowd.

"I've lived for all and I'm going to die for all." Big cheers.

"To me death is not a fearful thing. It's living that's treacherous." More cheers.

Perhaps the most telling exchange comes when an amiable, long-term follower named Christine Miller speaks out. Miller becomes a convenient foil for Jones.

"I feel like as long as there's life there's hope," she pleads.

"But sometime everybody dies," Jones responds. "That hope runs out because everybody dies. I haven't seen anybody yet who didn't die. I'd like to choose my own death for a change. Being tormented to hell, that's what I'm tired of." The crowd applauds and shouts in approval.

"I'm going to tell you . . . that, without me, life has no meaning," Jones continues. "I'm the best friends you'll ever have. . . . I've always taken your troubles on my shoulder and I'm not going to change now. . . . This is a revolutionary suicide council. I'm not talking about self-destruction," Jones responds. The crowd applauds him.

"I think that there were too few who left for twelve hundred people to give up their lives. . . . I look at all the babies and I think they deserve to live," Miller pleads.

"I agree, but don't they deserve much more? They deserve peace," Jones responds. "The best testimony we can give is to leave this god-damn world." The crowd applauds.

"We all came here for peace," Miller answers.

"Have we had it?" Jones asks.

"No," Miller answers. The crowd cheers Jones.

As Miller persists, the crowd begins to shout her down.

"Look sister, it's over," one man calls out. "We made . . . a beautiful day." The crowd cheers him.

When Miller desperately continues, the crowd now angrily turns on her.

"You're afraid to die."

"You're no fucking good, goddamn it."

"You're only standing here because of him."

"Sit down. Sit down. Sit down."

After a while Miller tearfully turns to Jones for protection from the belligerent crowd. "People get hostile when you try to [state your opinion]," Miller desperately says to Jones. He graciously accepts her gesture. "I have no quarrel with you coming up. I like you. I personally like you very much. . . . Your life is precious to me," he soothes her. The crowd watches all-loving Father at his compassionate best.

We hear Jones urging everyone to hasten with the process. As the suicides continue, members now voluntarily come to the podium to offer gratitude to Jones before stepping away to line up for their dose of poison.

"Folks, there is nothing to cry about," a woman gleefully pronounces. "We should be happy about this. We should cry when we come into this world. But when we leave it, we leave it peacefully. I was just thinking about Jim Jones. He has suffered and suffered and suffered. I'm looking at so many people crying. I wish you could not cry . . . but just thank Father."

"I appreciate you for everything. You're the only, you're the only," another follower announces to Jones.

"I wouldn't be alive today [without Jones]. I just want to thank Dad because he was the only one who stood up for me when I needed it. Thank you, Dad," from another woman.

"I'd like to thank Dad for giving us life and also death. And I appreciate the way our children are going because, like Dad said, when they [the enemy Fascists] come in they're going to massacre our children and those they capture are going to [be made to] grow up to be dummies like they want them to be, not to be officials like the one and only Jim Jones. Thank you, Dad."

"This is the most loving thing [Dad] could have done, the most loving thing all of us could have done," a man says. "It's been a pleasure walking with all of you in this revolutionary struggle. There's no other way I'd rather go than to give my life for socialism . . . and I thank Dad very, very much."

The crowd, diminishing by the minute, applauds and cheers after each testimonial. Even after the suicides, testimonials continued to appear. The body of one woman was found with a message she'd written on her arm during the suicides: "Jim Jones is the only one." Another woman left a long letter praising Jones just before she killed herself, which read in part: "I want you who read this to know Jim was the most honest, loving, caring, concerned person who I have ever met and knew." A survivor who happened to be away at the dentist during the suicides told an interviewer a year later: "If I had been there, I would have been the first one to stand in that line and take that poison and I would have been proud to take it. The thing I'm sad about is this: that I missed the ending."[2]

There's no question that freedom of choice was severely limited during the final hour of Jonestown. In fact, most people believed—rightly so—that escape was nearly impossible. The compound was surrounded by armed guards who were trusted enforcers for Jones. And even if a person did escape, Jonestown was so isolated in the jungle that it was extremely unlikely they'd find their way to safety. With no way out, it's not surprising that so many acquiesced to Jones's final order.

But what the tape of the final hour makes clear is that Jones had extracted something much more than passive obedience from his followers.[3] What we hear at the end are the voices of true believers. The effects of coercion are easy to explain. But the more difficult question is how such a by-then obviously monstrous man so thoroughly captured all those hearts and minds.

The behavior of people in Jonestown was, unquestionably, often pathological. But there is no better example than Jonestown of how even the most abnormal behavior can be explained by the "normal" principles of social psychology. Look beyond the paranoia and the guns and you see a supersalesman who exerted most every rule of persuasion in this book.[4]

To begin with, Jones masterfully induced trust. We saw in an earlier chapter that three characteristics of a source lead to trustworthiness: authority, honesty, and likability. When the target is extreme mind control, the persuasion expert wants to convey these features to the extreme. The leader seeks the image that he and only he (no sexism intended here; cult leaders are rarely a she) has the characteristics needed to direct the group, that only he merits the authority to dictate members' every movement. Sometimes leaders simply puff up their biographies to make themselves look special. In Jones's case, the deception was more creative.[5]

Jones carefully crafted his image as a miracle worker. He would attract new members in a city by running advertisements and distributing leaflets heralding his supposed powers:

Pastor Jim W. Jones, the greatest healing ministry through Christ on Earth today!

The Blind See! The Deaf Hear! Cripples Walk! See the SIGNS, MIRACLES and WONDERS that God is MANIFESTING through PASTOR JONES![6]

Incredible! . . . Miraculous! . . . Amazing! . . . the Most Unique Prophetic Healing Service You've Ever Witnessed! Behold the Word Made Incarnate in Your Midst![7]

At church on Sunday, Jones delivered on his promises. The needy lined up on stage to receive Jones's healing powers. People walked up blind and left with sight. Elderly people would struggle up in walkers and wheelchairs, receive Jones's blessings, and briskly walk away on their own volition. Jonestown survivor Deborah Layton recalls watching, at her first service, an extremely aged, hunchbacked woman hobble toward the pastor: "She talked of extreme pain in her lower back and as she spoke, Jim held out his left hand and touched her gently around her neck and forehead. . . . I watched in awe as he placed both his hands firmly on the old woman's lower spine. The next moment the bent grandma straightened her torso and screamed and shouted 'Thank you, Jesus. Thank you, Jesus. The pain is gone. You healed my body. Thank you, God. Thank you, Jim.'"[8]

Most dramatic of all were the cancer cures. With the choir singing in the background and the audience on its feet chanting, Jones or one of his assistants would reach into the throat of the afflicted and pull out a vile-smelling mass of tissue. The patient, cured, was left gagging. "Stay away, that's a cancer," Jones might shout out. "If you keep trusting in me," Jones once declared, "I'm going to free you of cancer, I'm going to lower your blood pressure, you're going to have the best health you ever had." [9]

The definitive demonstration of Jones's paranormal healing abilities—in retrospect, one with horrible consequences—was his supposed power over death. On various occasions Jones claimed to have resurrected himself from the effects of poison that would have killed ten horses, from bullet wounds that were large enough for nurses to put their fingers in, and from a litany of usually fatal diseases he'd caught from members of the congregation. He also claimed he could protect his followers from death. No member had died since 1959, he liked to say many years after that date. And if they did die, Jones said, he had the power to resurrect them. "You've seen three people drop dead and you saw them resurrected," he announced, for example, at one service. "Their attitudes were prejudiced and they would drop dead, but I resurrected them. And I've done it sixty-three times in eleven months this year in a public meeting." A few weeks before he'd said it was fifty-two times, but never mind.[10]

Jones also appeared to be psychic. He made predictions and offered revelations that hit the mark with uncanny accuracy. Deborah Layton, for example, recalls her first meeting with Jones. She had anonymously come up to meet him after attending her first People's Temple service. "Wait," Jones stopped her, "I feel something." He then closed his eyes and seemed to be getting a message from somewhere outside of himself. "Why, you must be Larry's sister. I have been concentrating on your coming soon."[11] Jones was correct: her brother was temple member Larry Layton.

The revelations could be remarkably specific. Former member Phyllis Chaiken was startled when Jones correctly told her, "Phyllis, I know that you at one time considered making a reservation at the Sheraton Hotel, and that you have had communications with Planned Parenthood, and that you have been eating donuts."[12] Jones told people he didn't understand what was responsible for his psychic powers. He just knew he had them. "I have a high level of energy, of universal faculty, that can know thoughts, that can even transmit myself. Don't even understand it myself."[13]

Occasionally Jones's miracles took eerily biblical proportions. Jonestown survivor Jeannie Mills recalled one such occasion:

> There were more people than usual at the Sunday service, and for some reason the church members hadn't brought enough food to feed everyone. It became apparent that the last fifty people in line weren't going to get any meat. Jim announced, "Even though there isn't enough food to feed this multitude, I am blessing the food that we have and multiplying it—just as Jesus did in biblical times."
>
> Sure enough, a few minutes after he made this startling announcement, Eva Pugh came out of the kitchen beaming, carrying two platters filled with fried chicken. A big cheer came from the people assembled in the room, especially from the people who were at the end of the line.
>
> The "blessed chicken" was extraordinarily delicious, and several of the people mentioned that Jim had produced the best-tasting chicken they had ever seen.[14]

These displays were extremely impressive. What most followers didn't know, however, was they were stage-managed, theatrical performances. The cancers were actually rancid chicken gizzards planted by sleight of hand in the sufferer's throat. The resurrections were prepared performances. It was so theatrical that trusted temple members would sometimes be disguised with heavy makeup and wigs in order to act out parts from the audience or stage.

The psychic powers? Jones's revelations were prepared by sending people to sift through a person's garbage for letters, foods, and any other items that would give him information to use later. When this wasn't enough, temple intelligence teams developed ploys to get into the target's home for material. They used ruses such as having a broken-down car, needing to use a phone, offering a baby-sitter service, or—what was often their most successful strategy—posing as poll takers. Jones's revelation to Phyllis Chaiken, for example, becomes less startling knowing that he'd received a report from one of his spies beforehand that listed the following items in Chaiken's garbage:

> box Hostess Old Fashioned Donuts .59 (has sugar, shortening with fat preservative added)

envelope addressed to Phyllis from Planned Parenthood

ad in newspaper clipped out for Sheratin [*sic*] Hotels and Motor Inns[15]

Once inside the home, spies would note pictures on the wall, information about children, the names of relatives in different cities—any particulars that could be used for dramatic impact later. The most important target in the home was the bathroom. Intelligence gatherers would ask to use the bathroom and then scan the medicine cabinet to learn the potential recruit's physical ailments, which Jones would later divine at Sunday service.

The blessed chicken? Jeannie Mills later recalled that "one of the members, Chuck Beikman, a man who had come with Jim from Indianapolis, jokingly mentioned to a few people standing next to him that he had seen Eva drive up a few minutes earlier with buckets from the Kentucky Fried Chicken stand. He smiled as he said, 'The person that blessed that chicken was Colonel Sanders.'"[16]

Not all of Jones's followers were fooled by his miracles. Some of the long-term and higher-ranking members were well aware of the trickery and deception.[17] But even these people often swore that once Jones established a "metaphysical bond" with someone, his powers were truly amazing. "Real miracles," they insisted, "followed fake ones."[18] Jones himself said that he was convinced that authentic healings grew out of the trickery: "There are people with me right now got healed fifteen, twenty years ago, and are still O.K. So, I can't explain it. I can heal, I know that. But how it works, I don't know."[19]

Those who were aware that Jones faked his psychic and healing powers justified the trickery as necessary means to greater ends. They were vehicles allowing Jones to actualize what they believed were even higher powers: his wisdom, revolutionary vision, energy, charisma, and extraordinary understanding of human nature that held the potential to erase the problems of the world. This reputation was reinforced by the many prominent figures who surrounded Jones. During the years the temple was located in Ukiah, in northern California, there were visits from such notables as President Carter's wife Rosalynn, Indian rights activist Dennis Banks, and civil rights activist Angela Davis, and frequent visits from California governor Jerry Brown, San Francisco mayor Willie Moscone, and California State Assembly speaker Willie Brown. During a dinner honoring Jones, Willie Brown introduced the influential church leader by proclaiming, "Let me present to you a combination of Martin Luther King, Angela Davis, Albert Einstein, and Chairman Mao."[20] In 1976, Democratic vice presidential candidate Walter Mondale had written Jones, a contributor to his campaign, a letter of thanks: "Knowing of your congregation's deep involvement in the major social and constitutional issues of our country is a great inspiration to me." (Jones used this letter to help persuade the Guyanese authorities to allow him to set up the Jonestown commune.)[21]

Jonestown survivors—like former members of every other destructive cult—are often asked what kept them there. Living conditions were extremely harsh, day-to-day life was filled with fear, and members underwent increasing physical, sexual, and psychological abuse as time went by. They stayed for many reasons. One of the most important, however, was their awe of the great Jim Jones. What greater authority existed than this man who was so respected by so many people? As Deborah Layton said, "Who was I to criticize him?"[22]

Escalating the Commitments

Jones was a master salesman at getting his foot in the door with potential members. He was not only a charismatic speaker; he also honed his presentation to fit the needs of the audience. Some recruits—typically white, middle or upper class, and educated—were drawn by the humanitarian spirit of the temple. These former members recall how Jones seemed to embody the Peace Corps and the civil rights movement rolled into one. Other recruits, many of whom came from the lower rungs of society—the unemployed, the urban poor, minorities, the elderly, a few ex-addicts—were attracted by Jones's promises of magical cures for their disease and suffering. Whatever you were searching for, the People's Temple promised answers.

Little was asked from a new member. You came to services voluntarily and might give a few hours of your time each week working for the church. The commitments escalated slowly, in small increments. More and more of your time was required. Services and meetings became longer, increasing to whole weekends and several evenings each week. Even children had to learn to sit through ordeals as long as eight and nine hours at a time. You were expected to attend out-of-town services held to recruit new members. When the temple was housed in Ukiah, the entire core family of four hundred took a ten-hour bus ride to Los Angeles for recruiting work every other weekend.

You were gradually asked to hand over more of your possessions. One week Jones introduced the "church commitment": members in good standing were to begin giving 25 percent of their income to the temple. The next week he asked, "Who in this room still has a checking or savings account?" The week after that: "Who still has a life insurance policy?" Eventually, members were required to sign over all personal property, their houses, social security checks—everything. After a while you were made to live in the temple in order to save money and help the temple work more efficiently. Children were often cared for by other families. Contact with outsiders was strongly discouraged.[23]

Each commitment increased the temple's hold in two ways. First, on a practical level, members' lives became increasingly entwined in the temple web. They not only became dependent on the temple for their everyday survival needs but, even more critically, for their social needs. Losing the support and approval of their fellow members became unthinkable. Jones enhanced this thinking by preaching that the outside world was such an unfriendly place that there was no way they could survive without the group.[24] Once this message took hold, peer pressure ensured that it spread to become the norm. Second, on a psychological level, members felt pressured to rationalize their behaviors. As in Milgram's obedience experiment, each time you obey a request it becomes less likely you'll disobey the next one. At some point you accept that you're part of the program. Now the dissonance cycle sets in, driving you to believe that you've made the right choice. The greater the level of the commitment, the more likely you'll acquiesce to the next commitment, and so the greater the pressure to rationalize.[25] As ex-member Jeannie Mills later observed:

> We had to face painful reality. Our life savings were gone. Jim had demanded that we sell the life insurance policy and turn the equity over to the church, so that was gone. Our property had all been taken from us. Our dream of going to an overseas mission was gone. We thought that we had alienated our parents when we told them we were leaving the country. Even the children whom we had left in the care of Carol and Bill were openly hostile toward us. Jim had accomplished all this in such a short time! All we had left now was Jim and the Cause, so we decided to buckle under and give our energies to these two.[26]

The requests became more pathological. During their weekly meetings, members would be asked to admit the worst things they'd ever done. Before each service, they were required to stop at a table and write self-incriminating letters or sign blank documents that were given over to Jones. They were asked to sign documents admitting they'd molested a child or contemplated killing the president. Jones asked them to do this to "prove your loyalty to Socialism." If they objected, it denoted a "lack of faith" in Jones and the cause. Jonestown survivor Deborah Layton, a seven-year temple member who served on the prestigious Planning Commission, recalls: "To prove my loyalty, I wrote detailed plans on how I was going to torture and murder the governor, my congressman, and the President; I lied about having stolen items from a store in town, anything to show I was not afraid. Having to make up these stories didn't seem that troublesome at first because Father explained that they were only supposed to prove our faith in him."[27]

Then came the physical punishments and humiliations. Even those started off relatively mildly. Members might be asked if they were willing to be physically punished after they'd done something very wrong. Later, transgressors might be punished with two or three whacks. Only later yet did the beatings escalate to sadistic levels.

Winning Hearts and Minds

Critically, Jones disguised brute force as normative pressure. Survivors have recounted many instances of physical beatings, druggings, public chastisements, and sexual and other humiliations. Jones almost always orchestrated these punishments. Twisted psychologist that he was, however, Jones kept himself in the background as much as possible. Instead, he forced members to testify against each other. Children condemned their parents; parents consented to and assisted in beating their children; spouses and lovers were made to sexually humiliate their partners. Members were photographed holding rubber hoses over beating victims after the victim had been beaten by someone else. Jones had attorneys write up a release form that victims had to sign before they were beaten. In the case of a child under eighteen, a parent was required to sign that he or she had asked Jones to discipline their child and to specify the number of whacks.

Deborah Layton recalls the deviousness of Jones's pressure. Once when the group was still in northern California, for example, Jones became upset because Deborah seemed to be getting overly involved in activities outside the temple. He said nothing directly to Deborah but, instead, arranged a setup to rein her in. Jones called an emergency meeting of the Planning Commission, many of whom were Deborah's close companions. Soon after the meeting began, a member stood up and charged Deborah with acting treasonably. Then another rose and accused Deborah of taking advantage of special privileges, citing a specific example Deborah later realized could only have been supplied by Jones. Another told Deborah that she was too close to her parents and a spoiled brat. "From 7 P.M. until the next morning," Deborah recalls, "I was yelled at, spit on, and humiliated."

After the ordeal had ended, Jones came to Deborah's room and apologized for the harsh treatment. "I would have stepped in, darling," Deborah recalls Jones saying, "but it would have looked as though I was playing favorites. You know how much I care about you. You are one of my most committed followers, but this will be good for your inner strength."

Deborah responded precisely as Jones anticipated. "'Thank you, Father,' I whispered, so appreciative of his taking the time to speak with me. At least I could hold on to the fact that Father still loved and understood me; he was only trying to make me strong."[28] Only years later did Deborah realize how she'd been manipulated.

Stephen Jones, who is Jim and his ex-wife Marcie's only natural son, survived the suicides because he was in Georgetown, the Guyanese capital, playing in a basketball tournament for the Jonestown team. Stephen, who was a teenager during the Guyana period, had an extremely contentious relationship with his father. Stephen's defiance posed a serious threat to Father's public image. But how to discipline his own son—a rebellious teenager, no less—without it leading to inevitably greater behavior problems and further loss of face posed a thorny challenge to the elder Jones. Stephen, who now lives in northern California, explained to me how Jim dealt with the problem by deviously manipulating others to confront him in public.

One night, for example, as Stephen was accusing his father during a public meeting, Jim gave a surreptitious hand signal to Marcie to step forward. Marcie was a sympathetic figure in Jonestown. It was common knowledge that she had her own problems with Jim and was trying in her own way to reverse his excesses. She realized, however, that publicly defying her husband in this situation would invite major repercussions for everyone. So she obeyed Jim's command and confronted Stephen, acting as if she was the one upset with Stephen for his insubordination. Stephen now felt cornered: in part because he was being attacked; in part because he knew that if he didn't confront his mother it would appear the two of them were in an alliance, which would put his mother in serious trouble with Jim. Seeing no alternative, he now began shouting at Marcie. At this point, everyone turned against Stephen. "I thought I was going to be lynched," he recalled. "Every person in there wanted to take me on." By channeling his control through normative peer pressure, Jim disciplined both Stephen and Marcie, just as he had Deborah Layton.

Jonestown members were racked with dissonance over their actions. But Jones fed them justifications to perpetuate their behaviors. Even in the best of situations, when you let something go on too long, when your sunk costs become too deep, it becomes very difficult to admit that you've made a mistake. It's that much worse when a charismatic individual like Jim Jones controls your every input and exploits this power to convince you that the only truly disastrous decision you could make would be to turn your back on him. With the flair of a supersalesman, Jones threw his followers off kilter by manipulating their actions. Then, to win their hearts and minds, he fed them rationalizations, disguised as social philosophy, that swallowed them to a deeper level.

Jones stressed, for example, that the cause demanded adherence to strict rules. "Sacrifice is the robe of the chosen few," he told them again and again. Doubts, he preached, were counterproductive. Ex-members recall how after a while they lost perspective and no longer knew what to think. Deborah Layton says she eventually just made a decision to persevere at any cost: "I had to prove to myself and my parents that I could stay committed to a project and see it to the end."[29] Then, to mentally survive, she justified the pathology:

> It's hard to explain why I didn't realize something was seriously wrong; why I stayed deaf to the warning calls ringing in my ears. I ignored my doubts and my conscience because I believed that I could not be wrong, not that wrong. A healer, socialist, and important civic leader could not possibly be an immoral abuser, a blackmailer, a liar. It did not occur to me that Jim could be all those things. I thought

that it must be extremely painful for Father to sacrifice his own good-
ness for the larger cause, as he did when he committed—or ordered
us to commit—reprehensible or illegal acts. I saw his moral trans-
gressions as purely altruistic—something like the means justify the
end. And who was I to criticize him? My own development, I was told
(and believed), was not advanced enough to allow me to understand
Father's motives and actions. I could only hope to be enlightened by
imitating his example and striving to become wiser, more principled,
and closer to him.[30]

Other Jonestown survivors tell similar stories of confusion and subsequent self-justification. Jeannie Mills recalled a particularly painful
occasion when she and her husband had consented to having their
sixteen-year-old daughter, Linda, beaten for committing a relatively
minor offense (being caught hugging a girlfriend whom Jones decided
was a traitor). To teach her a lesson in good judgment, Jones ordered
seventy-five whacks with the board. Mills recalled how, afterward, their
situation prevented rational thought:

> As we drove home, everyone in the car was silent. We were all afraid
> that our words would be considered treasonous. The only sounds
> came from Linda, sobbing quietly in the back seat. When we got into
> our house, Al and I sat down to talk with Linda. She was in too much
> pain to sit. She stood quietly while we talked with her. "How do you
> feel about what happened tonight?" Al asked her.
>
> "Father was right to have me whipped," Linda answered. "I've
> been so rebellious lately, and I've done a lot of things that were
> wrong. . . . I'm sure Father knew about those things, and that's why
> he had me hit so many times."
>
> As we kissed our daughter goodnight, our heads were spinning. It
> was hard to think clearly when things were so confusing. Linda had
> been the victim, and yet we were the only people angry about it. She
> should have been hostile and angry. Instead, she said that Jim had actu-
> ally helped her. We knew Jim had done a cruel thing, and yet everyone
> acted as if he were doing a loving thing in whipping our disobedient
> child. Unlike a cruel person hurting a child, Jim had seemed calm,
> almost loving, as he observed the beating and counted off the whacks.
> Our minds were not able to comprehend the atrocity of the situation
> because none of the feedback we were receiving was accurate.[31]

Then, in the final months before the suicides, Jones escalated his
demands a last incredible notch. He began conducting fake suicide

drills—what became known as "white nights." The initial drills were limited to the elite Planning Commission; soon they involved the entire populace of Jonestown. They occurred about once a month at first, then every couple of weeks, and grew longer and longer over time. Each would begin with loud sirens awakening exhausted followers in the middle of the night. Then Jones's voice came screaming over the loudspeaker: "Danger! Security alert! Hurry everyone. Danger is near! . . . White Night!"[32] Everyone would hear gunfire booming from the jungle. "Hurry to the pavilion," Jones would yell. "The mercenaries are out there and they're coming in!"[33] Terrified followers would then be handed a drink supposedly laced with poison. "Do you want to let the mercenaries slit your wrists or do you want to drink this poison yourself?" Jones would ask. Everyone would sit there until the sun came up, waiting to die while they listened to Jones rant about the mercenaries and the CIA coming in to slit their wrists and kill their children.

The fake suicides—like so many of Jones's demands—were framed as loyalty tests. Jones told his followers that they proved whether they were committed enough to follow the cause to the end. An ex-member recalled how after a while on one white night, "Jones smiled and said, 'Well, it was a good lesson. I see you're not dead.' He made it sound like we needed the 30 minutes to do very strong, introspective type of thinking. We all felt strongly dedicated, proud of ourselves . . . [Jones] taught that it was a privilege to die for what you believed in, which is exactly what I would have been doing."[34]

Followers didn't know that the gunshots came from people Jones, himself, had planted in the jungle. So each time the sirens sounded, the frightened populace would drink the potion and wait to die. Why not take poison and commit revolutionary suicide when the only alternative was giving their enemies, who were rapidly closing in on them, the satisfaction of torturing and murdering them and their families? And then, after a few hours, they'd realize it was just another one of Dad's loyalty tests. (People have questioned whether members may have thought the final suicides were just another loyalty test. All evidence indicates otherwise. To begin with, everyone understood the enormity of Congressman Leo Ryan's visit and how devastated Jones was when several members defected with the congressional party. And, if any doubt about the authenticity of the poison remained, it was certainly erased by the sight of the first babies dying.)

The people of Jonestown were no strangers to force. Guns were sometimes literally pointed at their heads. But Jones always made it seem that the real dangers were at the hands of outsiders. The true enemies were the fascists, the racists, the mercenaries, and the CIA, all of whom were trying to destroy them. Since Jones was by nature paranoid to begin with, he made this argument with compelling sincerity. And since paranoia is so often a self-fulfilling prophecy, it didn't take long before his fears were confirmed by real enemies. The punishments Jones and his henchmen doled out, he said, weren't meant to hurt his flock, just to keep them strong and disciplined enough to fight the real enemies. And so the wheels of self-justification persisted, eventually raging out of control, each commitment paving the way for the next.

Richard Clark, who escaped from Jonestown by walking into the jungle just hours before the suicides, understands why so many people fell for Jones's deceptions. After all, he points out, Jones had also fooled most of the important politicians and opinion makers in California. What bothers him is the self-deception. "Seems like people would never face the problem," Clark observed. "They would say the reason things were wrong was the CIA or something. You could never get a person to say, 'Jim Jones has got me out here in the jungle and he's starving me and he's trying to kill me.'"[35] What Clark didn't understand—and Jones undoubtedly did—was that self-justification was the most normal reaction to their pathological predicament. For most people, it was the only escape the situation permitted.

These are the people Jones was addressing that last hour in the jungle. His final command was layered upon years of lesser ones and an incessant process of normative pressure and self-justification. "I think what's most important for people to understand is nobody joins up with somebody they think is going to hurt them or kill them," Deborah Layton now teaches. "It can happen in any abusive relationship. A woman thinks a guy is good-looking, he's so nice, you go out on a few dates, he buys you a few presents. Then, one time, he hits you. But then he apologizes. You think, he's usually so good to me, and he bought me that present. Then maybe you have a child together. Then he hits you and the child. It's often so far down the road that you realize, 'Oh my God. There's something definitely wrong here.' But by that time you're in so many ways entrapped. And that's how I think it happened at Jonestown. It was so gradual."[36]

It's often been asked whether Jones actually believed in what he was doing. On one level, certainly, Jones can be written off as little more than an egotistical, power-driven, sadistic manipulator. But another part of Jones—the Jones people were drawn to in the first place—was a religious man and a committed freedom fighter with an established history of dedicated work for worthy social causes.

When I play the tape of the last hour for people, their first question often is how such a document exists. They assume Jim Jones would have destroyed every record of his hideous crimes in the same way the Nazis tried to eliminate theirs before abandoning the concentration camps at the end of World War II. What they don't realize is that Jones truly believed his life and deeds were the stuff of greatness. He believed that the People's Temple had been the greatest social movement of our time, that the Jonestown community was the precursor of heaven on earth, and that he, himself, was God's chosen messenger. As a result, Jones wanted Jonestown recorded for posterity. This final hour, he preached to his unfortunate followers, wasn't suicide but "a revolutionary act." So, naturally, that was recorded, too.

This benevolent image was no doubt the one Jones preferred of himself. Retaining it, however, required him to justify his pathological behaviors not just to his followers but to himself. By most evidence, he was successful in this self-deception. "My father believed his own bullshit better than anyone else," his son Stephen observed to me. This is precisely what the theory of cognitive dissonance would have predicted. After all, Jones had more to justify than all of them.

From the Pathological to the Normal

Jackie Speier, now a California state senator, was a member of Congressman Leo Ryan's entourage during the ill-fated visit to Jonestown that set off the suicides. She survived the murders at the airstrip—in which Ryan, three newsmen, and a defector were killed by a group from Jones's security force—by playing dead. Looking back on the insanities of Jonestown, Jackie Speier today offers these words: "No one should ever be so arrogant as to think it can't happen to them. We're all susceptible on one level or another."[37]

Jonestown dramatically illustrates the psychological principles that win hearts and minds. Groups like this are perilous minefields of exploitative social psychology. The best way to level the playing field against the Jim Joneses, or any people or organizations that don't have our best interests at heart, is to understand their weapons of persuasion. They are also vivid reminders of the illusion of invulnerability. If there's a single common statement I've heard from former cult members, it's the admonition that it can happen to anyone.

But it's important to recognize that the principles for winning hearts and minds pertain as much to the normal as to the pathological. Even when the goals of long-term conversion are admirable—being a good teacher, an effective parent, a well-intentioned friend—the psychology is disturbingly similar to that used by malintentioned manipulators. The content of the message may be different, but the form remains basically the same. Psychologist Margaret Singer has spent nearly three decades counseling former cult members and trying to decipher the persuasive power these groups hold. "I concluded," Singer observes, "that cultic groups were not using mysterious, esoteric methods" but had simply "refined the folk art of human manipulation and influence."[38]

It's really rather simple: move gradually, apply the least necessary force, remain invisible, and create the illusion of choice. The mind of the subject will take over from there. As the sign over the rostrum in Jonestown warned, "Those who do not remember the past are condemned to repeat it."

TEN

The Art of Resistance

Or, Some Unsolicited Advice for Using and Defending against Persuasion

Fool me once, shame on you. Fool me twice, shame on me. Fool me three times, shame on both of us.
—Stephen King, *On Writing*

To be forewarned is to be forearmed. If you can recognize the psychology of persuasion, and learn to spot the danger signs, you've taken the first steps toward defending against uninvited manipulators. Awareness alone, however, doesn't guarantee successful resistance. As the hippie radical Abbie Hoffman once observed about the then-fashionable warnings about drug abuse: "The simplistic 'Just Say No' to drugs campaign is a little bit like telling a manic-depressive to 'Just Cheer Up.'" The psychology of persuasion plays on fundamental human responses. It's difficult enough to rise above a habit we may have developed over months or years. But these patterns have been refined and passed down over many generations. As a result, they have enormous power. This is why the warning to never underestimate your vulnerability is so crucial.

But the illusion of invulnerability is a difficult loop to break. After all, if the illusion is a defense against reality, an infusion of reality could actually stimulate the illusion. This is, in fact, what research often demonstrates: When you challenge a deeply entrenched illusion too directly, your message—like any other overly forceful attempt at persuasion—can boomerang. In a study by social psychologist Rick Snyder, for example, students were asked to estimate their age of death.

Not surprisingly, average estimates far exceeded—by an average of about nine years—the actuarial norms for longevity. Then, in a follow-up study, a group of students were given a lecture about the illusion of invulnerability and were specifically forewarned that it leads most people to overestimate their own age of death. Some students accepted this information and, upon later questioning, adjusted their personal death estimates to accurate levels. On the whole, however, forewarning had virtually no effect on the newly educated subjects' estimates. They, too, overestimated their likely age of death by an average of nine years. Being forewarned did, however, have one consequence: it stimulated many subjects to generate reasons why they, personally, truly were uniquely invulnerable. In other words, like the followers of Marian Keech, they responded to being challenged not by abandoning their original beliefs but by actively justifying them and, in the end, clinging to them more staunchly than ever.[1]

Beyond Forewarning

Simple forewarning is least effective when it's restricted to armchair intellectualizing. Sometimes people need more aggressive and specific intervention. Here are some techniques that have proved effective.

Stinging

Sometimes people need a good sting to push them out of their self-deluding comfort zone. They need a little of their susceptibility rubbed in their face.

If you recall, one firmly established invulnerability illusion is the common belief that advertising works on everyone but ourselves. Social psychologists Brad Sagarin, Robert Cialdini, William Rice, and Sherman Serna decided to challenge this illusion and see if, in the process, they could help people become more resistant to devious advertising. Their studies focused on the popular advertising tactic whereby well-known authority figures are employed to sell products they know nothing about—ads, for example, showing Chuck Yeager pontificating on Rolex watches.

The first experiment tested the effectiveness of simple verbal forewarning. Subjects were given a minilesson on the devious ways illegitimate authorities are used in advertisements. They were taught exactly what tricks to watch out for. Afterward, subjects rated a series of ads, some of which used illegitimate authorities. At first glance, it seemed, these forewarned subjects learned their lesson well: they were more likely to rate ads that used illegitimate authorities as manipulative than were a control group of subjects. But there was a more important question: were the forewarned subjects any more resistant to the ads? Apparently not. When asked whether they were now more likely to use the product, the forewarned group proved themselves no less persuaded than the control group.

Next, Sagarin and his colleagues tried stinging. Subjects in this experiment heard the same tutorial on the devious use of authority figures in advertising and were again asked to rate various ads. This time, however, they were immediately confronted with their gullibility. "Take a look at your answer to the first question. Did you find the ad to be even somewhat convincing? If so, then you got fooled. . . . Take a look at your answer to the second question. Did you notice that this 'stockbroker' was a fake?" In effect, subjects were forced to acknowledge their own personal susceptibility. They were then asked to evaluate a new set of ads. The sting worked. These subjects were not only more likely to recognize the manipulativeness of deceptive ads; they were also less likely to be persuaded by them.[2]

My students and I have used stinging to ward off gullibility in other problem situations. In certainly the most impressive of these studies, Kennard Nears, who is now a doctoral student in school psychology, targeted gullibility in an extremely perilous realm—the abduction of children by strangers. With most abductions, children are lured by gentle persuasion rather than forceful kidnapping. The most commonly used tactics involve offers of affection, gifts, and assistance or appealing to the child for help for an emergency. Kennard, who has an adolescent daughter, was in the midst of a situation in which he was frightened something like this might happen to her. In response, he'd given his daughter the usual lecture about not going off with strangers and explaining whom to watch out for. But when he put his daughter to a real-life test, by having a strange woman (actually, Kennard's friend) gently entice her to leave a store, the gregarious young girl was off in a flash.

Kennard's daughter is, unfortunately, representative of most American children. When asked how they'd respond to a stranger's invitation, nearly all children swear they'd never accept. But research shows otherwise. In one typical study, 75 percent of children with no training in child abduction prevention agreed to go off with a stranger (who was actually an accomplice of the experimenter). More discouraging yet, among children who were given prevention training, an identical 75 percent later agreed to go off with the stranger.[3]

Kennard wanted to convert this self-deceptive gullibility to preventative advantage. The program, which he made available to parents on a volunteer basis, consists of a controlled, attempted abduction that, for most children, becomes a light sting. Parents bring their children to a food court or other manageable public area (at our university, in his original study), buy them a drink, then leave them at a table while they supposedly go off to the bathroom. Immediately afterward, a well-dressed "abductor" approaches the child and asks for help finding a nearby building or, in the case of younger children, finding a lost puppy. If the child gets up to follow the stranger, the abduction is terminated. The child's parent, who has observed everything from nearby, immediately returns to the table and explains to the child what occurred. Later, both the experimenter and the abductor join the pair. To give immediate feedback, the experimenter plays a videotape of the encounter that just took place. The child is then asked to explain and then rehearse ways he or she might have handled the situation more effectively. All this is done in a supportive and nonaccusatory manner. To cushion the impact of the lesson, the experimenter explains to the child that most children are gullible in this situation. The parent and child are later encouraged to continue their discussion elsewhere over lunch or snacks. They're also given the videotape for later review. By stinging the children in this controlled, nonhysterical, educational manner, they're given the opportunity to develop safe responses to specific, potentially dangerous situations rather than simply acquiring a generalized fear of strangers.[4]

Stinging can be effective for at least two reasons. First, it breaks through the illusion of invulnerability which, in turn, motivates us to take preventative measures. Second, the poison serves as an inoculation, a technique that we turn to next.

The Inoculation Method

Research shows that if you subject people to weak versions of a persuasive message, they're less vulnerable to stronger versions later on, in much the same way that being exposed to small doses of a virus immunizes you against full-blown attacks. In a classic study by William McGuire, people were asked to state their opinion on an issue. They were then mildly attacked for their position and given an opportunity to refute the attack. When later confronted by a powerful argument against their initial opinion, these subjects were more resistant than were a control group. In effect, they developed defenses that rendered them immune.[5]

It's informative to consider cultures in which people have little experience challenging opposing opinions. The practice of adversarial debate has a long history in the West, going back to classical Greece. But in some Far Eastern cultures—China and Japan, most prominently—the idea of contentiously challenging someone in public is considered rude and unacceptable. In these cultures, where the predominant goal of social behavior is to maintain the appearance of harmony, to scrutinize another person's idea is to criticize the character of the person voicing it. One way traditional Chinese and Japanese cultures have preserved harmony is by encouraging the belief that there's truth to any argument, even opposing arguments.[6]

"If you present Westerners an argument that is contrary to their prior belief," observes cross-cultural psychologist Ara Norenzayan, "they'll apply a naive form of logic and ask themselves which one is 'true,' the new belief or their own? Unless the new argument is very strong, they'll be likely to generate reasons why their prior belief is right and the new one wrong, and not be susceptible to the new argument." In other words, they become inoculated. "East Asians on the other hand," Norenzayan continues, "will use a completely different reasoning strategy. Faced with the same argument that is contrary to their prior belief, they will immediately 'see' that there is some truth to the opposing view, and move their opinion in the direction of the new argument."[7]

In inoculation theory terms, this means that people in China and Japan have little opportunity to build up antibodies to persuasive messages. There are, of course, numerous upsides to the Far Eastern way of thinking. It's promoted a tradition of moderation and tolerance in daily life; and, certainly, we can't underestimate the long, relatively peaceful domestic histories many of these cultures have enjoyed without the benefit of Western methods of discussion and rhetoric. But confronted by undesirable persuasion, the East Asian aversion to argument and counterargument leaves these cultures at a disturbingly dangerous disadvantage. Without a history of inoculation, they're susceptible to even small doses.

Since 1984, I've been teaching a course on the psychology of persuasion and mind control. Probably the most effective component of the course is an exercise that requires students to experience the impact of a persuasive professional firsthand. The students have disturbingly little difficulty finding situations for the assignment. Over the years, they've put themselves at the mercy of everything from car salesmen, time-share seminars, and Tupperware-style hostesses to street hustlers and 900 numbers selling communication time with the dead, to name a few. The students analyze the tactics used against them, observe how they reacted to the tactics, and then consider what they would have liked to have said if they had it to do over again. The exercise serves to strengthen their resistance—their antibodies, if you like—to the hucksters they encounter the next time around.

The inoculation procedure has been used effectively in public education programs. The psychologist Richard McAlister and his colleagues, for example, applied it to the formidable task of helping junior high school students resist peer pressure to smoke cigarettes. With high school students serving as the teachers, seventh graders were shown commercials appealing to the attractiveness of the smoker image—for example, how women who smoke are liberated. They were encouraged to respond with counterarguments, such as "She's not really liberated if she's hooked on tobacco." The students also participated in role-plays in which, for example, they were called a chicken for turning down a cigarette and then practiced how they might respond; for example, "I'd be a real chicken if I smoked just to impress you." Participants underwent a series of these sessions throughout the seventh and eighth grades. The inoculations were successful. Compared with a group of junior high school students from similar backgrounds who hadn't received the training, the inoculated students were only half as likely to begin smoking.[8]

Scripts

Writing and rehearsing scripts can be a particularly valuable outcome of the inoculation process. When we're coerced with time pressure, for example, most of us find it difficult to step away. At the point of impact, it requires what seems like an act of heroic rebellion to demand a pause in the negotiations. Since most of us are averse to conflict and certainly don't want to appear—God forbid!—rude, the path of least resistance is usually to drift along with the current. This is where scripts are useful. When a voice inside you warns that something here doesn't feel right, you might, for example, train yourself to say: "I'm sorry, but my (husband/wife/boyfriend/girlfriend/mother/father) and I have an agreement that we never make a significant (purchase/decision/commitment) before discussing it together at home." When my old friend Lenny feels cornered, he likes to say: "I have what my therapist calls an impulsive disorder which keeps me from saying no to people. He made me promise I'd never make an important decision on the spot." It's not a very good line for making new friends, Lenny tells me, but it's helped him escape a number of high-pressure situations.

You can also rehearse different roles. Write down your most vulnerable situations. Then consider your knee-jerk response in these situations and draw up a list of alternative responses you'd like to have at your disposal. Practice them. Then practice the even more difficult task of rising above your knee-jerk response and, instead, reaching into your cast of actors for the performance that best suits the situation. Try, for example, to experiment with social disapproval. Put yourself in situations in which you experience rejection. Practice being a deviant in some situations. Practice saying no. The fact that many selves reside inside you presents dangers, but it also offers opportunities. The *right* responses are inside you waiting to happen, too. With work, you can cultivate whom you want to be at this time, in this place. The more selves in your arsenal, the better your chances of trotting out the right player for the given problem.

Practice Critical Thinking

You can also hone more general, fundamental skills to increase your resistance. This line of defense falls into the broad category of becoming a better thinker or—to use the currently fashionable term—a good critical thinker. Here are a few faculties you might work on.

Think Like a Scientist

Practice arriving at decisions through a logical, systematic, objective process. The scientific method consists of generating a hypothesis, gathering data that bears on your hypothesis, and then reconsidering your hypothesis in light of your data. It may sound bleakly computer-like to make choices about your life as if you were a scientist handling chemicals in a laboratory. But, at the least, the answers that emerge through this process will give you a sensible starting point. There'll be plenty of room to add a more human touch later on.

You might try an eight-step decision-making strategy developed by cognitive psychologists known by the acronym of PROACT (*p*roblem, *o*bjectives, *a*lternatives, *c*onsequences, and *t*rade-offs).[9]

- Clearly define your problem. What is it you're trying to decide? Be sure you're addressing what's actually the significant problem.
- Specify your objectives. Think through where you want this decision to take you.
- Force yourself to consider alternative courses of action. If there weren't alternatives, you wouldn't be making a decision. Be imaginative here.
- Evaluate the consequences of all possible decisions. How effectively will each alternative satisfy your objectives?
- What are the trade-offs of each course of action? List the pros and cons of potential choices. Articulate your priorities and see which choice strikes the best balance.
- Address uncertainties. What could happen in the future, how likely is it to occur, and how will it effect your decision?
- What is your risk tolerance? Which alternative offers the right level of risk *for you*?
- Plan ahead. How may this decision affect other decisions you make in the future? Recognize that any important decision is going to alter the nature of other decisions you make later. Try to predict the long-term sequence that any choice will set in motion.

There are no guarantees these eight steps will keep you from being duped. After all, there's a certain degree of risk in any decision. But if you follow this approach, or perhaps develop a systematic alternative that is more suited to your temperament and needs, there's less chance you'll make a serious error. With apologies for bringing up the topic again, I think sensible decision making is a little like handicapping racehorses. I agree with the novelist Richard Russo who wrote, in *The Risk Pool:*

> I have often thought, and occasionally argued with people who consider themselves educators, that courses in handicapping should be required, like composition and Western civilization, in our universities. For sheer complexity, there's nothing like a horse race, excepting life itself, and keeping the myriad factors in balanced consideration is fine mental training, provided the student understands that even if he does this perfectly there is no guarantee of success. The scientific handicapper will never beat the horses . . . but he *will* learn to be alert for subtleties that escape the well trained eye. To weigh and evaluate a vast grid of information, much of it meaningless, and to arrive at sensible, if erroneous, conclusions, is a skill not to be sneezed at.[10]

Thinking systematically requires not just figuring out the best horse but applying good betting strategy. Are you sure enough about your choice, considering the potential payoff, to make it worth making a bet, or should you sit this race out and wait for the next one? And, most important of all, you should always decide *before* you get to the track how much you're willing to lose. My image of good critical thinking in the world of persuasion experts? I think of a computer scientist handicapping the Kentucky Derby. He's likely to be wrong about any given race but, in the long run, will end up with more money than someone who reacts from the gut.

Learn to Reframe Your Problem in Different Lights

There's an old joke about a young priest who asks his bishop, "May I smoke while praying?" The bishop answers emphatically that he may not. Later, the young priest encounters an older priest puffing on a cigarette while praying. The young priest scolds him: "You shouldn't be smoking while praying! I asked the bishop and he said I couldn't." "That's strange," the older priest answers. "I asked the bishop if I could pray while I'm smoking and he told me it was okay to pray any time."[11]

Beware of exploitive professionals who frame their requests in misleading ways. Be especially on guard when they play to your fear of danger and loss. The easiest way to assess the effects of a frame is to remove it. If you place a dark frame around a picture, all the colors appear lighter. But if you take the frame away, the colors return to their initial appearance.

It's best if you can physically remove yourself from the context. When this isn't possible, try to remove yourself psychologically. Learn to watch yourself as an outsider would, from as detached a distance as you can. Without objectivity, you're a sitting duck. "The secret of propaganda," observed Joseph Goebbels, Adolf Hitler's chief of propaganda, is that "those who are to be persuaded by it should be completely immersed in the ideas of the propaganda, without ever noticing that they are immersed in it."[12]

We're especially vulnerable to manipulations in unfamiliar situations, even more so when we have no clear measure of value. It's that anchor point problem. When faced with novelty and uncertainty we scan for anything to get our bearings. Unfortunately, this provides an easy handle for manipulators. Learn to recognize when people try to trap you with faulty comparisons. A misleading anchor point—letting you know, perhaps, how unhappy you are compared to your peers or how terrible or expensive other alternatives you're considering are—frames the subsequent pitch so it appears better than it is.

Learn to reframe as innovatively as you can. Imagine yourself in a picture frame store experimenting with a stack of different frames. View your situation from different perspectives and watch how each alters your perception of the situation. Look for distortions. Find neutral frames that avoid extreme points of view.

Learn to Ask Disconfirming Questions

Invite information that will prove your initial judgment wrong. We're very good at finding support for what we want to believe, but it's all too easy to fall into the myopic trap of assuming the only thing to see is what we happen to be looking at. As the famous psychologist Abraham Maslow observed, "To the man who only has a hammer in the toolkit, every problem looks like a nail."[13]

When you've arrived at an important decision, force yourself to postpone it. During your time out:

Search for conflicting information. Recognize that a lazy voice inside you will want to trivialize or find fault with counterarguments. But force yourself to consider them with an open mind. Weigh all evidence with equal rigor.

Find a person to play devil's advocate. Ask him or her to argue against your decision. Consult with the person to make a list of the reasons you *shouldn't* continue with your tentative choice.

When seeking advice from others, be careful not to lead them on. If your friends know you want them to confirm your choice, they probably will. Emphasize that you need honest input. And be careful whom you select for feedback. If you look for yes-men, you'll no doubt find them.

Groupthink

Asking disconfirming questions is especially important when it comes to group decisions. If you're sitting around a table with other intelligent people, it's easy to assume the majority decision must be a good one. But the conjoint intelligence of groups tends to be less than the sum of its parts; too often, in fact, it regresses to the lowest common denominator.

Group decisions are prone to special conformity pressures—what psychologist Irving Janis called "groupthink." Groupthink may be caused by implicit self-censorship, whereby you're hesitant to challenge the group majority either because you're afraid of ridicule or reluctant to waste the group's time. This creates a self-perpetuating cycle, in which private dissenters become convinced they're the only deviants, which leads to an apparent consensus, which further increases the pressure for self-censorship. There also may be overt pressure not to buck the majority opinion. During the decision-making process of the Kennedy administration's Bay of Pigs fiasco—a prime example of groupthink—Attorney General Robert Kennedy took aside Arthur Schlesinger, who'd disagreed with the decision to invade, and told him: "You may be right or you may be wrong, but the President has made his mind up. Don't push any further."[14] This is fine for collegiality but leads to bad decisions.

Making matters worse, once an apparent consensus is achieved the group focuses almost solely on information that confirms the majority opinion. In the end, groupthink leads to hasty decisions, often supporting the leader's initial suggestion. Paradoxically, the more capable the individuals in a group, the more likely they are to trust each other

and, so, the more prone the group is to the illusion of invulnerability—
and eventual groupthink.

When you're involved in group decisions, have the discipline to
speak your mind. Choose leaders who encourage criticism. Suggest
that someone be assigned the role of devil's advocate. Finally, once a
decision is reached, insist on a cooling-off period. Consider using the
words of Alfred Sloan Jr.: "Gentlemen, I take it we are all in complete
agreement on the decision here. . . . Then I propose we postpone further discussion of this matter until our next meeting to give ourselves
time to develop disagreement and perhaps gain some understanding of
what the decision is all about."[15]

Do You Really Need a Biscuit?

Ask marketers their job and you're liable to hear something along
the lines of J. Paul Getty's axiom: "Find a need and fill it." This is an
admirable goal, one that fits squarely in the grand American tradition
of necessity being the mother of invention. But what does constitute
a need or necessity in today's "developed" society? For most of us,
consumerism has less to do with trying to put food on the table than
deciding what new gadget or automobile or home improvement to
buy. It's become the salesperson's task to convince you that you need
his or her product. Invention has been turned into the mother of
necessity.[16] "It is our job to make women unhappy with what they
have," observed supersalesman B. Earl Puckett.[17] Or men, he might
have added.

There was considerable fanfare not long ago when the corporate
giant Unilever bought out Ben & Jerry's ice cream. But perhaps a more
disturbing event passed more quietly when, just a week later, Unilever
bought another company: Slimfast. This means the same people who
make Cherry Garcia and Chunky Monkey are also pushing the
nation's most popular diet drink. Talk about corporate diversity. A
company now creates a need for one product and that product creates
a need for the other.[18]

Be careful when the same people who want to fill your expectations
are also in the business of creating them. Never forget that the most
popular of marketing axioms is that "Perception is more important than
reality" and that the guiding principle of the hard sell, as an early critic

of advertising put it, "is first to create the fear, and then offer a branded antidote."[19]

There is a long American tradition of trying to persuade people that they need things. In 1898, when the National Biscuit Association (Nabisco) introduced its first line of biscuits, the company came up with the catchy name Uneeda Biscuit. Uneeda was marketed with the very first million-dollar advertising campaign behind the slogan: "Lest you forget, we say it yet, Uneeda Biscuit." (The product was so successful it was soon followed by imitators like Uwanta beer and *Ureada Magazine*.)[20]

Beware, I say, of strangers who tell you what you need. Watch out for people who offer to plug holes you never saw before. Distrust those who shout, "Buy me and you will overcome the anxieties I have just reminded you of."[21] If you didn't realize you needed a new car until a salesman told you so; or if you thought your carpet looked clean enough until a vacuum cleaner peddler gave a free demonstration to show you otherwise; or if you weren't aware your psyche needed fixing until a religious group recruiter gave you a free personality test that showed you're in bad need of help—then it's time to sound the warning alarm. Never ask a barber if you need a haircut.

Be Skeptical, Yet Open

Say you've learned all the lessons in this book and now fully recognize your vulnerability to persuasion. This brings us to yet another problem. And it's a slippery one. Once you accept your vulnerability, how do you stay cautiously on alert without becoming a gloomy, untrusting cynic? Where do you the draw the line between healthy skepticism and doomsday paranoia?

There was recently a front-page newspaper article about a forty-three-year-old Los Angeles lawyer named Robert Hirsh who was being investigated for an unusually prolific history of personal litigation. Hirsh has filed eighty-two lawsuits in the last eighteen years, against a range of individuals that include his home contractors, his clients, his brokers, the hotels and restaurants he frequents, the airlines he flies, his former employers, his wife's former employers, and his insurance company. He even sued the religious elders at his synagogue for botching his wedding. While his targets portray Hirsh as an opportunistic exploiter of the legal system, Hirsh sees himself as a vulnerable consumer trying to see to it people don't take advantage of him. His bottom-line explanation for all the lawsuits: "I'm not going to be a patsy."[22]

I experienced something of this attitude when I was selling cars. One experienced colleague, for example, took me aside and told me: "All you need to know in this business is this: All customers are liars. And all salesmen are crooks." (I won't repeat what he had to say about managers.) This viewpoint was echoed by many other salesmen I met.

In a way, the cynicism expressed by Hirsh and my sales colleagues demonstrates an extreme acceptance of what this book is about. To their credit, these individuals aren't likely to be caught off guard or victimized by overgullibility. Their wariness has undoubtedly protected them from many an exploitative person. But what a miserable way to live your life.

Fortunately, the world most of us inhabit isn't as filled with conniving and lying as a used-car lot or Robert Hirsh's mind. It's only the occasional manipulator you usually need to watch out for. The challenge is to find a balance between openness and skepticism, to approach the world as a critical thinker but without always assuming the worst. As the philosopher Jacob Needleman observed, it's good to keep an open mind, but not so open that your brains fall out.

Practitioners of mindfulness distinguish between two levels of awareness. There's first-order mindfulness, in which you practice attending directly to the details at hand. Since attending to every detail of every moment is, however, beyond our capacities, there's an even more important skill—learning to decide what information most warrants mindfulness, or what's known as second-order mindfulness. "The most important function task for any CEO, and for the rest of us, is choosing what to be mindful about," observes social psychologist Ellen Langer. "Rather than spending all day inspecting every expense account or widget in the factory, the mindfully mindful executive chooses where to pay attention."[23]

Healthy resistance to persuasion requires a similar executive activity. There are really two problems here: the how and the when. It's one thing to be capable of resisting persuasion and another to learn when to put these skills into action.

The first charge of second-order mindfulness is to recognize which types of exploitation are most dangerous. There's a substantial difference, for example, between the obvious lie ("This beer tastes great") and the insidious lie ("This beer makes you great").[24] It's often the covert ones, the nonobvious manipulations, that should summon our full attention.

Another second-order task is to distinguish between persuasion and exploitation. Most all social interaction is, in a sense, persuasion; and all persuasion is, by its very definition, manipulative. But whereas some persuasion is meant to exploit, other forms aim to educate. We need to learn which persuasion to resist, which to embrace, and which can be safely ignored.

One of the best ways to cue second-order mindfulness is to become sensitive to contexts and your environment. This brings us back to the grand lesson of social psychology: the power of the situation. You can learn to monitor how situations affect you. Keep a record of how you feel in different situations over the course of the day. It could be a journal or a simple list. If you want to take a high-tech approach to this task, there are (free)[25] software packages that allow you to program a palmtop computer to beep at random intervals throughout the day and ask you questions about where you are, what you are doing, and how you feel. After a week or more of this, you'll have a systematic record of the "you" that comes out in different situations. You'll have a better idea what situations to seek in order to bring out your best, and what situations should make you put your guard up. Be especially on alert for triggers that cause you to respond automatically and mindlessly, particularly those situations in which the intensity of your reaction exceeds the seeming importance of the situation.

Practice Persuasion with Integrity

To be known as a persuasion expert in today's world is to arouse suspicion. It's a label that reeks of manipulation and exploitation. There was a less cynical time not long ago, however, when the art of persuasion had a very different connotation. In his pioneering 1937 psychology textbook, Floyd Ruch wrote that "the whole destiny of human society depends upon the influencing of human behavior."[26] Persuasion was seen as an essential skill in living—the art of "winning friends and influencing people," as the famous Dale Carnegie tag line put it.

Professions that rely on persuasion have developed bad reputations. Advertising is a good example. It's hard to believe that just a couple of generations ago no less a man than Franklin Delano Roosevelt made this comment about advertisers:

> If I were starting life over again, I am inclined to think that I would go into the advertising business in preference to almost any other. . . . It is essentially a form of education; and the progress of civilization depends on education. . . . The general raising of the standards of modern civilization among all groups of people during the past half century would have been impossible without the spreading of the knowledge of higher standards by means of advertising.[27]

Today, of course, people rarely associate advertising with ethical principles. The purpose of the endeavor, it's widely assumed, is little more than selling as much as you can, however you can, with little regard for what it is you're selling or its consequences for the consumer. "Don't tell my mother I'm in advertising," one Madison Avenue executive commented. "She thinks I play piano in a whorehouse."[28] And advertising is hardly the only persuasion-centered profession that has suffered a loss of public trust. I'll resist lawyer and politician jokes.

It can be argued that a book like this, which spells out techniques for persuasion and mind control, is a manual for malintentioned manipulators. This is, of course, a legitimate fear. In response, I could regress to an "if guns are outlawed then only outlaws will have guns" defense (which, face it, isn't completely without merit). But I prefer the sensibility of yet another advertising legend. I feel much the same way about studying the principles of persuasion and mind control as the J. Walter Thompson Agency, in a 1925 sales pitch, did about their services: "Advertising is a non-moral force, like electricity, which not only illuminates but electrocutes. Its worth to civilization depends on how it is used."[29]

The fact is that the art of persuasion remains as essential a skill today as ever before. Its reach stretches well beyond the domain of hucksters and con artists. Persuasion is the essence of successful parenting, teaching, and psychotherapy; making friends; achieving intimacy; motivating performance; fighting for what you believe in; and achieving your goals. Persuasion is, in a sense, nothing less than the fabric of social communication. What's the point of communicating if not to have an impact on the listener? It's important to understand the psychology of persuasion not only so we can ward off undesirable intruders but, just as critically, to become practitioners of the art ourselves. Whether you're out to improve yourself or to make the world a better place, how else to succeed than through good psychology? The ability to persuade—both others and ourselves—may be the most indispensable of social skills.

It's a principle I appreciate well in my vocations of teaching and writing. After all, am I not in the business of trying to change people's beliefs? To achieve my goal, I must convince and persuade; and to do this, I use the same psychology as does any good salesman or leader. I want my consumers to believe I'm a trustworthy authority with their best interests in mind. I want them to like me. I lay out my case patiently, in small increments, involving their active participation whenever possible, and do my best to have them arrive at conclusions they claim as their own.[30] And why should teaching be different from any other salesmanship? As the advertiser-turned-critic Earl Shorris observed, "From the age of Solomon to the age of Gallo, there has been no essential change in the method of selling. Like philosophy, selling does not become outdated. If dogs or turtles participated in these activities, the methods of . . . persuasion might be different, but the human mind determines how one can speak to it, then and now, here and there, without exception."[31]

Still, there's an irony here—a rather sticky ethical problem, to be sure. If education is basically a matter of persuasion, and the psychology of effective persuasion is fairly similar no matter what you're selling, then teaching people to ward off undesirable persuasion must employ pretty much the same psychological techniques you're preparing the student to be on guard against. An extreme example are the cult deprogrammers of the 1970s. They would "rescue" the minds of cult members by first isolating them in an apartment or motel room for two or three days. All incoming information was filtered while the cult member was be flooded with anti-cult teachings. The deprogrammers might use threats in the early stages to get their target's attention and then shift to softer, even spiritual appeals to complete the reconversion. In other words, they fought the cult's brainwashing with their own brainwashing.[32]

How, then, to distinguish between ethical persuasion and unethical manipulation? Although both engage similar psychology, there are important differences. A caring teacher isn't out to exploit his students for personal gain, certainly not in the direct way that an exploitative salesman or cult leaders are. When Apple Computer advises you to "think different," the company actually wants you to buy its computer. When, on the other hand, an ethical teacher advises you to "question authority," he hopefully includes himself in his admonition. And he earns no commission whether you do or don't. Most important, ethical persuasion doesn't have a deceptive agenda. Pupils understand what they're getting in to. They know their bottom-line commitment and what will be expected of them.

The best teachers produce students who can think for themselves. They cultivate a climate that favors respect for dissent. "The true teacher," Bronson Alcott observed, "defends his pupils against his own personal influence."[33] Teaching critical thinking, I'd like to believe, is not an inherent contradiction in terms.

The fact is that persuasion and psychology are essential human activities. They define our social being, never more so than today. As our singular and collective attention become increasingly prone to the beck and call of the mass media, sophisticated marketing research, and advancing technology, the art of persuasion is in its boom years. It's up to each of us to use the psychology wisely and ethically, to see that it illuminates rather than electrocutes.

NOTES

Preface

1. Hovland, C., Lumsdaine, A., and Sheffield, F. (1949). *Experiments on Mass Communication: Studies in Social Psychology in World War II*, vol. 3 (Princeton, N.J.: Princeton University Press).

2. Quoted in Clark, Eric (1988), *The Want Makers: Inside the World of Advertising* (New York: Penguin Books), p. 291.

Chapter One: The Illusion of Invulnerability

1. Orwell, George (1949), *1984* (New York: Harcourt Brace Jovanovich), p. 5.

2. See, for example, Weinstein, N. D. (1987), "Unrealistic Optimism about Susceptibility to Health Problems: Conclusions from a Community-Wide Sample," *Journal of Behavioral Medicine* 10, pp. 481–500; and Weinstein, N. D. (1989), "Optimistic Biases about Personal Risks," *Science* 246, pp. 1232–1233.

3. Smoking data are taken from the following studies: Lee, C. (1989), "Perceptions of Immunity to Disease in Adult Smokers," *Journal of Behavioral Medicine* 12, pp. 267–277; Gibbons, F. X., McGovern, P. G., and Land, H. A. (1991), "Relapse and Risk Perception among Members of a Smoking Cessation Clinic," *Health Psychology* 10, pp. 42–45; and Segerstrom, S., McCarthy, W., Caskey, N., Gross, T., and Jarvik, M. (1993), "Optimistic Bias among Cigarette Smokers," *Journal of Applied Social Psychology* 23, pp. 1606–1618.

4. Snyder, C. R. (1997), "Unique Invulnerability: A Classroom Demonstration in Estimating Personal Mortality," *Teaching of Psychology* 24, pp. 197–199.

5. Baker, L., and Emery, R. (1993), "When Every Relationship Is above Average: Perceptions and Expectations of Divorce at the Time of Marriage," *Law and Human Behavior* 17, pp. 439–450.

6. Burger, J. M., and Burns, L. (1988), "The Illusion of Unique Invulnerability and the Use of Effective Contraception," *Personality and Social Psychology Bulletin* 14, pp. 264–270.

7. Weinstein, N. D. (1980), "Unrealistic Optimism about Future Life Events," *Journal of Personality and Social Psychology* 39, pp. 806–820.

8. Lehman, D., and Taylor, S. (1987), "Date with an Earthquake: Coping

with a Probable, Unpredictable Disaster," *Personality and Social Psychology Bulletin* 13, pp. 546–555.

9. Burger, J. M., and Palmer, M. L. (1992), "Changes in and Generalization of Unrealistic Optimism Following Experiences with Stressful Events: Reactions to the 1989 California Earthquake," *Personality and Social Psychology Bulletin* 18, pp. 39–43.

10. Young, Edward (1989), *The Complaint: Night Thoughts* (orig. publ. 1797) (Cambridge, U.K.: Cambridge University Press).

11. See, for example, Lewinsohn, P. M., Mischel, W., Chaplin, W., and Barton, R. (1980), "Social Competence and Depression: The Role of Illusory Self-Perceptions," *Journal of Abnormal Psychology* 89, pp. 203–212.

12. Heine, S. J., and Lehman, D. R. (1995), "Cultural Variation in Unrealistic Optimism: Does the West Feel More Vulnerable Than the East?" *Journal of Personality and Social Psychology* 68, pp. 595–607.

13. Survey data concerning beliefs about the future in Japan and the United States are reported in Levine, Robert (1992), "Why Isn't Japan Happy?" *American Demographics*, June, pp. 58–60. This article is based on results from 1989–1990 public opinion polls taken in Japan by the Japanese Cabinet Public Information Office and in the United States by the Gallup organization.

14. Newport, F. (1998), "Americans' Satisfaction and Well-Being at All-Time High Levels," Gallup News Service, October 23, Princeton, N.J.: Gallup Organization.

15. Surveys reported on the web site of the Pew Research Center, available at http://people-press.org/commentary/display.php3?AnalysisID=44.

16. Gallup poll taken March 8–9, 2002, reported at http://www.gallup.com/poll/releases/pr020319.asp.

17. See, for example, Alicke, M. (1985), "Global Evaluation as Determined by the Desirability and Controllability of Trait Adjectives," *Journal of Personality and Social Psychology* 49, pp. 1621–1630; and Dunning, D. (1993), "Words to Live By: The Self and Definitions of Social Concepts and Categories," in Suls, J., ed., *Psychological Perspectives on the Self*, vol. 4 (Hillsdale, N.J.: Lawrence Erlbaum Associates).

For an excellent description of differences between Eastern and Western cultures regarding the effect, see Markus, H., and Kitayama, S. (1991), "Culture and the Self: Implications for Cognition, Emotion and Motivation," *Psychological Review* 98, pp. 224–253.

18. Levine, R., Fast, N., and Gerber, J. (2002), "Teaching about Vulnerability to Persuasion." Manuscript submitted for publication.

19. Subjects were 77 percent female and 23 percent male with an average age of twenty-five years. Results were relatively consistent across gender.

20. Kruger, J., and Dunning, D. (1999). "Unskilled and Unaware of It: How Difficulties in Recognizing One's Own Incompetence Lead to Inflated Self-Assessments," *Journal of Personality and Social Psychology* 77, pp. 1121–1134. See also Goode, E. (2000), "Among the Inept, Researchers Discover, Ignorance Is Bliss," *New York Times*, January 18, p. D7.

21. These findings are reviewed in Kruger and Dunning (1999).

22. Damasio, Antonio R. (1994), *Descartes' Error: Emotion, Reason, and the Human Brain* (New York: Putnam), p. 62.

23. Ibid., p. 64.

24. Darwin, Charles (1871), *The Descent of Man, and Selection in Relation to Sex* (Princeton, N.J.: Princeton University Press).

25. See Kulik, J. A., and Mahler, H. I. M. (1987), "Health Status, Perceptions of Risk, and Prevention Interest for Health and Nonhealth Problems," *Health Psychology* 6, pp. 15–27; Lee, C. (1989); Burger and Burns (1988); and Lehman and Taylor (1987).

26. Actually, the use of psychological tests to predict behavior has a considerably longer history. Some four thousand years ago the Chinese were requiring their civil service officials to demonstrate their competence through a sophisticated battery of oral exams every three years.

27. The question of just how stable traits remain over time and across situations is a matter of considerable controversy in psychology. For two good reviews of the evidence, see Kenrick, D. Y., and Funder, D. C. (1988), "Profiting from Controversy: Lessons from the Person-Situation Debate," *American Psychologist* 43, pp. 23–24; and Mischel, W. (1990), "Personality Dispositions Revisited and Revised: A View after Three Decades," in Pervin, A., ed., *Handbook of Personality: Theory and Research* (pp. 111–134) (New York: Guilford Press).

28. Kilbourne, Jean (1999), *Deadly Persuasion* (New York: Free Press), p. 27.

29. Coen, R. J. (1999), "Spending Spree," *The Advertising Century* (*Advertising Age* special issue), pp. 126, 136.

30. *The Nader Page* (January 28, 2005), "Super Bowl Advertising." Available at http://www.nader.org/intercst/012805.html.

31. Ryan, S. C. (1999), "Victoria's Secret Success at Super Bowl Has Ad World Abuzz," *Boston Globe*, February 3, pp. D1, D7.

32. Kilbourne (1999).

33. Ibid., p. 34.

34. Kaiser Family Foundation (October 2004), "Prescription Drug Trends." Available at http://www.kff.org/rxdrugs/upload/Prescription-Drug-Trends-October-2004-UPDATE.pdf.

35. Pear, R. (2000), "Marketing Tied to Increase in Prescription Drug Sales," *New York Times*, September 20, p. A16.

36. Abraham, M., and Lodish, L. (1990), "Getting the Most out of Advertising and Promotion," *Harvard Business Review* (May–June), pp. 50–60.

37. Schlosser, E. (2001), *Fast Food Nation* (Boston: Houghton-Mifflin).

38. PBS *Frontline* (1998), "Obesity," November 11.

39. Huston, A., Donnerstein, E., Fairchild, H., Feschbach, N., Katz, P., Murray, J., Rubinstein, E., Wilcox, B., and Zuckerman, D. (1992), *Big World, Small Screen: The Role of Television in American Society* (Lincoln: University of Nebraska Press).

40. Center for Science in the Public Interest (1988), "Kids Are as Aware of Booze as Presidents, Survey Finds," September 4, CSPI press release, Washington, D.C.

41. Dagnoli, J. (1991), "JAMA Lights New Fire under Camel's Ads," *Advertising Age* (December 16).

42. Schlosser (2001), p. 43.

43. McNeal, J. U. (1992), *Kids as Customers: A Handbook of Marketing to Children* (New York: Lexington Books).

44. Liebert, R. M., and Sprafkin, J. (1992), *The Early Window*, 3rd ed. (New York: Pergamon Press).

45. Gerber, J., Burgos, K., Rodriguez, A., Massey, M., and Levine, R. (2001), "Self-Other Differences in the Effect of Technical Information on Ad Credibility," paper presented at the annual convention of the Western Psychological Association, Maui, Hawaii, 3–6 May.

Other surveys conducted over the years have replicated our results across a wide variety of people and products. See Wilson, T. D., and Brekke, N. C. (1994), "Mental Contamination and Mental Correction," *Psychological Bulletin* 116, pp. 117–142.

46. Marriott, Michell (2001), "Playing with Consumers," *New York Times*, August 30, pp. D1, D6.

47. Farhi, P. (1998), "AOL Gets Its Message out in 'Mail,'" *Washington Post*, December 17, available at http://www.washingtonpost.com/wp-srv/style/movies/features/aolinmail.htm.

48. Lipman, J. (1989), "Outcry over Product Placement Worries Movie, Ad Executives," *Wall Street Journal*, April 7, p. B6.

49. Bovee, C., Thill, J., Dovel, G., and Wood, M. (1995), *Advertising Excellence* (New York: McGraw-Hill).

50. Bader, Jenny L. (2001), "Brand-Name Lit: Call Me Tiffany," *New York Times*, September 9, p. 2 WK.

51. Kilbourne (1999), p. 65.

52. Savan, Leslie (1994), *The Sponsored Life: Ads, TV, and American Culture* (Philadelphia: Temple University Press), pp. 6–7.

53. *Morning Edition* (2002), National Public Radio, April 5.

54. Schlosser (2001).

55. Frank, Thomas (1999), "Brand You: Better Selling through Anthropology," *Harper's Magazine* (July), pp. 74–79.

56. *Frontline* (2001), "The Merchants of Cool: An Interview with Dee Dee Gordon and Sharon Lee," February 27 Transcribed on PBS web site at: http://www.pbs.org/wgbh/pages/frontline/shows/cool/interviews/gordonandlee.html.

57. Kilbourne (1999).

58. From Underhill, Paco (1999), *Why We Buy: The Science of Shopping* (New York: Simon & Schuster). See also Gladwell, M. (1996), "The Science of Shopping," *New Yorker*, November 4, pp. 66–75.

59. Underhill (1999), p. 47.

60. Ibid., pp. 77–78.

61. Ibid., pp. 102, 119.

62. Ibid., pp. 33, 44.

Chapter Two: Whom Do We Trust? Experts, Honesty, and Likability

1. An excellent discussion of symbols of authority as a source of influence can be found in Cialdini, Robert (2000), *Influence: Science and Practice*, 4th ed. (Boston: Allyn & Bacon).

2. This was well before his unfortunate problems with Internet ethics in 1999.

3. Erickson, B., Lind, E. A., Johnson, B. C., and O'Barr, W. M. (1978), "Speech Style and Impression Formation in a Court Setting: The Effects of Powerful and Powerless Speech," *Journal of Experimental Social Psychology* 14, pp. 266–279.

4. MacLachlan, J., and Siegel, M. H. (1980), "Reducing the Costs of TV Commercials by Use of Time Compressions," *Journal of Marketing Research* 17, pp. 52–57.

5. Brown, D., Scheflin, A. W., and Hammond, D. C. (1998), *Memory, Trauma Treatment, and the Law* (New York: W. W. Norton).

6. Gerber, J., Burgos, K., Rodriguez, A., Massey, M., and Levine, R. (2001), "Self-Other Differences in the Effect of Technical Information on Ad Credibility," paper presented at the annual convention of the Western Psychological Association, Maui, Hawaii, 3–6 May.

7. Dr. Charles Edwards, quoted in Safir, L., and Safire, W. (1982), *Good Advice* (New York: Times Books), p. 6.

8. Cooper, J., Bennett, E., and Sukel, H. (1996), "Complex Scientific Testimony: How Do Jurors Make Decisions?" *Law and Human Behavior* 20, pp. 379–394.

9. Two of twelve graduate nurses said they would have given the medication.

10. Hofling, C. K., Brotzman, E., Dalrymple, S., Graves, N., and Pierce, C. M. (1966), "An Experimental Study in Nurse-Physician Relationships," *Journal of Nervous and Mental Disease* 143, pp. 171–180.

11. Davis, N., and Cohen, M. (1981), *Medication Errors: Causes and Prevention* (Philadelphia: George F. Stickley). See also Cialdini (2000).

12. Randi, J. (2001), "The Art of 'Cold Reading,'" James Randi Educational Foundation, available at http://www.randi.org/library/coldreading/index.html.

13. Randi, James (1982), *Flim-Flam: Psychics, ESP, Unicorns and Other Delusions* (Amherst, N.Y.: Prometheus Books), pp. 270–271.

14. Ibid., p. 263.

15. Quoted in Fellows, Bob (2000), *Easily Fooled* (Minneapolis: Mind Matters).

16. Randi (1982), p. 61.

17. Wilson, Gregory (2002), "How to Influence Anyone with Five Magic Words," lecture at California State University, Fresno, April 24.

18. Fellows (2000), pp. 20–22.

19. Quoted in Lederer, R. (2000), "Political Bloopers," *Funny Times*, (November), p. 8.

20. Hartshorne, H., and May, M. A. (1928), *Studies in the Nature of Character*, vol. 1: *Studies in Deceit* (New York: Macmillan).

21. Baumeister, R., Bratslavsky, E., Finkenauer, C., and Vohs, K., "Bad Is Stronger Than Good," *Journal of General Psychology*, in press.

22. Martin, D. (2000), "What's in a Name: The Allure of Labels," *New York Times*, January 9, p. 2 WCK.

23. Fox, Stephen (1997), *The Mirror Makers: A History of American Advertising and Its Creators* (Urbana: University of Illinois Press), p. 71.

24. *Printers' Ink* poll (1945), *Printers' Ink*, September 28.

25. Martin (2000).

26. In a 1927 advertisement.

27. Fox (1997), p. 89.

28. Lavington, Camille (1997), *You've Only Got Three Seconds: How to Make the Right Impression in Your Business and Social Life* (New York: Doubleday).

29. Tripp, C., Jensen, T. D., and Carlson, L. (1994), "The Effects of Multiple Products Endorsements by Celebrities on Consumers' Attitudes and Intentions," *Journal of Consumer Research* 20, pp. 535–547.

30. Petersen, Melody (2002), "Heartfeld Advice, Hefty Fees: Companies Pay Stars to Mention Prescription Drugs," *New York Times*, August 11, sec. 3, pp. 1, 14.

31. Ross, R. P., Campbell, T., Wright, J. C., Huston, A. C., Rice, M. L., and Turk, P. (1984), "When Celebrities Talk, Children Listen: An Experimental Analysis of Children's Responses to TV Ads with Celebrity Endorsement," *Journal of Applied Developmental Psychology* 5, pp. 185–202.

32. Quoted in Savan, Leslie (1994), *The Sponsored Life: Ads, TV, and American Culture* (Philadelphia: Temple University Press), pp. 8–9.

33. United Colors of Benetton, "Customer Service and Sales Training," in Rushkoff, D. (1999), *Coercion: Why We Listen to What "They" Say* (New York: Riverhead Books), p. 13.

34. This discussion of infomercials is largely based on a fine essay by Leslie Savan, "TV in Its Underwear," in Savan (2000), pp. 305–307.

35. Kunkel, D. (1986), "Children and Host-Selling Television Commercials," unpublished manuscript, Department of Human Development, University of Kansas, Lawrence.

36. Askari, Emilia (2002), "Marketing to Younger Tastes: Kids Eat Up Fast-Food Ad Blitz," *Detroit Free Press*, April 8, p. A1.

37. Many industrialized nations have concluded that advertising directed at children should not be allowed. Children's advertising on radio and television is illegal, for example, in Belgium, Norway, Denmark, and the Canadian province of Quebec. Greece and Sweden have argued for a ban against children's advertising throughout the European Union. An attempt to pass similar laws in the United States in the 1970s was defeated by a coalition of advertising agencies, television stations, and food and toy companies. See Kilbourne, Jean (1999), *Deadly Persuasion* (New York: Free Press).

38. The magician-persuasion expert Gregory Wilson calls this OTOBIA: overcoming the obection before it arises.

39. Hemsley, G. D., and Doob, A. N. (1978), "The Effect of Looking Behavior on Perceptions of a Communicator's Credibility," *Journal of Applied Social Psychology* 8, pp. 136–144.

40. Reported in Rosen, Emanuel (2000), *The Anatomy of Buzz* (New York: Doubleday), pp. 5–6.

41. Price, L. L. and Feick, L. F. (1984), "The Role of Interpersonal Sources

in External Search: An Informational Perspective," in Kinnear, Thomas C., ed., *Advances in Consumer Research*, vol. 11 (Ann Arbor, Mich.: Association for Consumer Research), pp. 250–253.

42. *Frontline* (2001), "The Merchants of Cool: Landscape." Reported on PBS web site at http://www.pbs.org/wgbh/pages/frontline/shows/cool/tour (February 27).

43. Rosen (2000), p. 212.

44. Saturn ad from Sivulka, Juliann (1998), *Soap, Sex and Cigarettes* (Belmont, Calif.: Wadsworth), p. 393.

45. Voight, J. (2000), "Hal Riney & Partners Saturn," *Adweek Online*, available at http://www.adweek.com/creative/top20/index.asp.

46. Quoted in Gladwell, Malcolm (2000), *The Tipping Point* (New York: Little, Brown, p. 20. Linda Price has written many articles on mavens. See, for example, Price, L. L., Feick, L. F., and Guskey, A. (1995), "Everyday Market Helping Behavior," *Journal of Public Policy and Marketing* 14, pp. 255–267.

47. For a personality measure of mavenism, see Feick, L., and Price, L. (1987), "The Market Maven: A Diffuser of Marketplace Information," *Journal of Marketing* 51, pp. 83–97.

48. See, for example, Dion, K., Berscheid, E., and Walster, E. (1972), "What Is Beautiful Is Good," *Journal of Personality and Social Psychology* 24, pp. 285–290; and Aronson, E., Wilson, T. D., and Akert, R. M. (1997), *Social Psychology*, 2nd ed. (Reading, Mass.: Addison-Wesley).

49. Survey reported in Simmons, Annette (2001), *The Story Factor* (Cambridge, Mass: Perseus).

50. Burger, J., Messian, N., Patel, S., del Prado, A., and Anderson, C. (2002), "Incidental similarity and compliance," manuscript submitted for publication.

51. Schlosser, E. (2001), *Fast Food Nation* (Boston: Houghton Mifflin), pp. 50–51.

52. I completed the entire training with Cutco but, given the obvious ethical concerns, quit before going out on any actual sales calls. (Quotes are from handouts distributed during training.)

53. Joseph Gerber, conversation with author, Fresno, Calif., 3 December 1999.

54. Detailed descriptions of the pyramid arrangement and questions about cultlike techniques in Amway are found at a number of web sites. See, for example, http://www.freedomofmind.com/groups/amway/amway.htm.

55. Rushkoff (1999).

56. Ridley, Matt (1996), *The Origins of Virtue* (New York: Penguin).

57. Walker, Rob (2005), "A Seller's Edge," *New York Times Magazine*, January 16, p. 26.

Chapter Three: Killing You with Kindness

1. Gouldner, A. W. (1960), "The Norm of Reciprocity: A Preliminary Statement," *American Sociological Review* 25, pp. 161–178.

2. Ridley, Matt (1996), *The Origins of Virtue* (New York: Penguin).

3. Regan, D. T. (1971), "Effects of a Favor and Liking on Compliance," *Journal of Experimental Social Psychology* 7, pp. 627–639.

4. Christopher, Robert C. (1983), *The Japanese Mind* (Tokyo: Charles E. Tuttle).

5. Japan was sealed off from foreigners until the arrival of Commodore Perry in 1853.

6. Melton, J. G. (1993), *Encyclopedic Handbook of Cults in America*, rev. and updated ed. (New York: Garland Publishing).

7. Greene, R., and Ellfers, J. (1998), *The 48 Laws of Power* (New York: Viking).

8. For further discussion of the topic of time and control, see my book: Levine, Robert (1997), *A Geography of Time* (New York: Basic Books).

9. Central Intelligence Agency (1963), *KUBARK Counterintelligence Interrogation*, CIA classified publication, obtained through the Freedom of Information Act in 1997 and distributed on the Internet at http://www.parascope.com.

10. There's good reason that the KUBARK manual reads more like the writing of social scientists than Ian Fleming or Tom Clancy. It was largely based on a previous CIA report, "Brainwashing: A Guide to the Literature," which was prepared by the decidedly social scientific–sounding group called the Society for the Investigation of Human Ecology.

11. Central Intelligence Agency (1963), pp. 72–73.

12. The membership of the Unification Church has suffered from several embarrassing incidents over the past few years. Most damaging were the revelations about the psychological pathologies of Moon and his family revealed by Moon's former daughter-in-law Nansook Hong in her 1998 book *In the Shadow of the Moons: My Life in the Reverend Sun Myung Moon's Family* (Boston: Little, Brown).

13. Lofland, J. (1978), "'Becoming a World-Saver' Revisited," in Richardson, J. T., ed., *Conversion Careers* (Beverly Hills, Calif.: Sage).

14. Barker, Eileen (1984), *The Making of a Moonie: Choice or Brainwashing?* (Oxford, U.K.: Basil Blackwell), p. 95.

15. Neufield, K. Gordon (1999), "Moon Madness Remembered," available at http://meltingpot.fortunecity.com/namibia/538/x-2a.html. Also, email interview with author, 30 September 1999.

16. Lofland (1978), p. 225.

17. Martin, H. V. (1999), "The Truth about the Moonies, Neds and Aetna," *Napa Sentinel*, December 21.

18. If Reverend Moon offered the promised land, why were recruiters so deceptive about their identity? Craig Maxim, a former member who is now an active critic of the organization, observed to me how "secrecy and deception are almost moral imperatives of the Moonies." It's what's known in the church as "heavenly deception." Members were conditioned to believe people were unfairly prejudiced against Moon's name. Newcomers, they were told, wouldn't be open to True Father's teachings if they knew it was him too soon. Moon himself preached the importance of heavenly deception: "Telling a lie," he explained, "becomes a sin if you tell it to

take advantage of a person, but if you tell a lie to do a good thing for him that is not a sin. Even God tells lies very often; you can see this throughout history."

19. Lofland (1978), p. 226.

20. "Moonies" (1997), KRON-TV documentary, San Francisco, May 5.

21. Galanti, Geri-Ann (1994), "Reflections on 'Brainwashing,'" in Langone, M., ed., *Recovery from Cults: Help for Victims of Psychological and Spiritual Abuse* (pp. 85–103) (New York: W.W. Norton).

22. Barker (1984), pp. 173–174.

23. Lofland (1978), p. 229.

24. Ibid.

25. Yamamoto, J. I. (1977), *The Puppet Master: An Inquiry into Sun Myung Moon and the Unification Church* (Downers Grove, Ill.: Intervarsity Press).

26. Craig Maxim, email interview with author, 30 September 1999.

27. Galanti (1994), p. 100.

28. Shah, Idries (1970), *The Dermis Probe* (London: Cape).

29. Greenberg, M. S., and Westcott, D. R. (1983), "Indebtedness as a Mediator of Reactions to Aid," in Fisher, J. D., Nadler, A., and DePaulo, B. M., eds., *New Directions in Helping*, vol. 1 (pp. 85–112) (New York: Academic Press); and Eisenberger, R., Cotterell, N., and Marvel, J. (1987), "Reciprocation Ideology," *Journal of Personality and Social Psychology* 53, pp. 743–750.

30. Reischauer, E. O. (1981), *The Japanese* (Cambridge, Mass.: Harvard University Press).

31. Yang, M. M. (1994), *Gifts, Favors, and Banquets: The Art of Social Relationships in China* (Ithaca, N.Y.: Cornell University Press).

32. Ridley (1996), p. 119.

Chapter Four: The Contrast Principle

1. For the classic work on how colors influence one another, see Albers, Josef (1975), *Interaction of Color* (text of the orig. ed.) (New Haven, Conn.: Yale University Press).

2. Heinz Kusel, telephone conversation with author, 26 November 1997.

3. Fox, Stephen (1997), *The Mirror Makers: A History of American Advertising and Its Creators* (Urbana: University of Illinois Press), p. 70.

4. Although details about the car were omitted from mass advertising ads, they were made available in specialized automobile publications.

5. In Minsky, L., and Calvo, E. (1994), *How to Succeed in Advertising When All You Have Is Talent* (Lincolnwood, Ill.: NTC Business Books), p. 70.

6. Quotes from Fiona Jack are from (1) Keever, Hilary (1999), "The Product Is Nothing," *Adbusters*, no. 24; and (2) by personal communication. For information about the related "Buy Nothing" campaign, see http://shell.ihug.co.nz/~stu/buynothing/.

7. Brown, D. (1953), "Stimulus-Similarity and the Anchoring of Subjective Scales," *American Journal of Psychology* 66, pp. 199–214.

8. For a thorough description of lateral inhibition, see, for example, Coren,

S., Ward, L., and Enns, J. (1994), *Sensation and Perception*, 4th ed. (New York: Harcourt Brace).

9. Ibid.

10. From an interview with Amil Gargano in Minsky and Calvo (1994), p. 172.

11. Quoted in Friedman, Thomas (1989), *From Beirut to Jerusalem* (New York: Doubleday).

12. The actual population of Turkey was estimated at 66,493,970 as of July 2001.

13. Hammond, J., Keeney, R., and Raiffa, H. (1999), *Smart Choices: A Practical Guide to Making Better Decisions* (Boston: Harvard Business School Press).

14. Russo, J. E., and Schoemaker, P. J. H. (1989), *Decision Traps* (New York: Simon & Schuster), p. 27.

15. From Hammond, Keeney, and Raiffa (1999), p. 208.

16. Aspirin was essentially the only nonprescription pain reliever at the time. The ibuprofen derivatives were not yet on the market.

17. Fox (1997), p. 160.

18. Bem, Daryl J. (1970), *Beliefs, Attitudes, and Human Affairs* (Belmont, Calif.: Brooks/Cole). See also Bem, Daryl, personal communication, January 30, 2001.

19. Simonson, I., and Tversky, A. (1992), "Choice in Context: Tradeoff Contrast and Extremeness Aversion," *Journal of Marketing Research* 29, pp. 281–295.

20. These ratios, initially discovered by Weber, are described in Rathus, S. A. (1990), *Psychology*, 4th ed. (Fort Worth: Holt, Rinehart & Winston).

21. Uhl, J. (1971), "Consumer Perception of Experimental Retail Food Price Changes," *The Journal of Consumer Affairs* 5, pp. 174–185.

22. See, for example, Monroe, K. (1971), "Measuring Price Thresholds by Psychophysics and Latitudes of Acceptance," *Journal of Marketing Research* 8, pp. 460–464.

23. See Monroe, K. (1973), "Buyers' Subjective Perceptions of Price," *Journal of Marketing Research* 10, pp. 70–80.

24. Gupta, S., and Cooper, L. G. (1992), "The Discounting of Discounts and Promotion Thresholds," *Journal of Consumer Research* 18, pp. 401–411.

25. Lambert, Z. (1975), "Perceived Prices as Related to Odd and Even Price Endings," *Journal of Retailing* 51, pp. 13–22.

26. Wright, John, Unpublished data, personal communication, March 29, 1999.

27. Stiving, M., and Winer, R. (1997), "An Empirical Analysis of Price Endings with Scanner Data," *Journal of Consumer Research* 23, pp. 57–67.

28. Schwarzwalk, J., Raz, M., and Zvibel, M. (1979), "The Applicability of the Door-in-the-Face Technique When Established Behavioral Customs Exist," *Journal of Applied Social Psychology* 9, pp. 576–586.

Chapter Five: $2 + $2 = $5

1. Thaler, Richard (1985), "Mental Accounting and Consumer Choice," *Marketing Science* 4 (3), pp. 199–214.

2. Ibid., p. 202.

3. Ibid.

4. Smith, E., and Nagle, T. (1995), "Frames of Reference and Buyers' Perception of Price and Value," *California Management Review* 38, pp. 98–116.

5. For two excellent reviews of research on this topic, see Taylor, Shelley (1991), "Asymmetrical Effects of Positive and Negative Events: The Mobilization-Minimization Hypothesis," *Psychological Bulletin* 110 (1), pp. 67–85; and Baumeister, R. F., Bratslavsky, E., Finkenauer, C., and Vohs, K, *Review of General Psychology* (in press).

6. Schopenhauer, Arthur (1970), *Essays and Aphorisms*, ed. and trans. R. J. Hollingdale (London: Penguin), pp. 42–43.

7. Hansen, C., and Hansen, R. (1988), "Finding the Face in the Crowd: An Anger Superiority Effect," *Journal of Personality and Social Psychology* 54 (6), pp. 917–924.

8. Kahneman, D., and Tversky, A. (1984), "Choices, Values, and Frames," *American Psychologist* 39, pp. 341–350.

9. Tversky, A., and Kahneman, D. (1981), "The Framing of Decisions and the Psychology of Choice," *Science* 211, pp. 453–458.

10. Adapted from Thaler (1985), p. 54.

11. Tversky and Kahneman (1981).

12. Odean, T. (1998), "Are Investors Reluctant to Realize Their Losses?" *Journal of Finance* 53, pp. 1775–1799.

13. Hulbert, Mark (1999), "The Psychology of Selling Losers," *New York Times*, February 21, p. Bu-8.

14. Hammond, J., Keeney, R., and Raiffa, H. (1999), *Smart Choices: A Practical Guide to Decision Making* (Boston: Harvard Business School Press), pp. 197–198.

15. Urbany, H., Bearden, W., and Weilbaker, D. (1988), "The Effect of Plausible and Exaggerated Reference Prices on Consumer Perceptions and Price Search," *Journal of Consumer Research* 15, pp. 95–110.

16. Garabino, E., and Slonim, R. (1995), "Effects of Price History and Change Awareness on Sales and Perceptions," paper presented at the Behavioral Perspectives on Pricing Conference, Marketing Science Institute, Cambridge, Mass., April.

17. Surowiecki, J. (2000), "The Priceline Paradox," *New Yorker*, May 22, p. 34.

18. This example, and several other concepts in this subsection, are adapted from an excellent review of research on the influence of frames of reference on buyers' behavior: Smith, E., and Nagle, T. (1995), "Frames of Reference and Buyers' Perception of Price and Value," *California Management Review* 38, pp. 98–116.

19. From "Bill Gates's Wealth Index," web site maintained by Brad Templeton, reported in *Harper's Magazine*, January 1998, p. 22.

20. As of January 21, 2002, Gates's net worth was estimated to be $72.934 billion. For hourly updates on Gates's worth, see Phillip Greenspun's web site, "Bill Gates Personal Wealth Clock" (http://www.webho.com/WealthClock).

21. Russo, J. E., and Schoemaker, P. J. H. (1989), *Decision Traps* (New York: Simon & Schuster).

Chapter Six: The Hot Button

1. Milgram, S. (1970), "The Experience of Living in Cities," *Science* 167, pp. 1461–1468.

2. Probably the best application of the notion of system overload—an engineering term—to social behavior is social psychologist Stanley Milgram's model of urban behavior. Milgram argues that the rapid pace of life in modern cities confronts people with more sensory inputs than they are able to process, creating what he calls psychological overload. The larger the city, the greater the overload. The overloaded urbanite adapts by screening out everything nonessential to his goals. See ibid.

3. As discussed by Lawrence Shainberg, in "Sunbeams" (2000), *Sun* 295, p. 48.

4. Kelly, George A. (1955), *A Theory of Personality: The Psychology of Personal Constructs* (New York: W. W. Norton), p. 8.

5. Iyengar, S., and Lepper, M. (2000), "When Choice Is Demotivating: Can One Desire Too Much of a Good Thing?" *Journal of Personality and Social Psychology* 79, pp. 995–1006. See also Goode, E. (2001), "In Weird Math of Choices, 6 Choices Can Beat 600," *New York Times*, Januay 9, p. D7.

6. Mills, Jeannie (1979), *Six Years with God* (New York: A & W Publishers), p. 136.

7. Moon held a mass marriage in August 1995 of about 35,000 couples in a stadium in Korea. His public relations people claimed instead that 360,000 couples were married around the world via videolink. Ex-member Steven Hassan, who was told by officials to lie about numbers like these on many occasions, points out, "Of course, they can't prove this impossible number."

8. Not infrequently, Jones assigned the most attractive followers—men and women—to himself.

9. Survivors told me about having to put a pillow over their heads to sleep until they got used to the noise.

10. Al and Jeannie Mills defected from Jonestown in 1975, three years before the mass suicides, taking with them many of the most important temple documents. Throughout 1976, 1977, and 1978 they were among the most vocal temple critics, pleading with the press, public officials, and the federal government to have Jim Jones exposed. During this time, the Mills were repeatedly terrorized and were placed on top of an alleged "death list" of temple enemies. On the final tape at Jonestown, recorded as the suicides were taking place, Jones blamed Jeannie Mills by name and vowed that his followers in California "will not take our death in vain." More than one year after the suicides, Al and Jeannie Mills and their daughter were murdered in their Berkeley home. The murders have never been solved.

11. Mills (1979), p. 147.

12. Orwell, George (1949), *1984* (New York: Signet), p. 254.

13. Hassan, Steven (1988), *Combatting Mind Control* (Rochester, Vt.: Park St. Press), p. 62.

14. These situations are adapted, in part, from Pratkanis, A., and Aronson, E. (1991), *Age of Propaganda: The Everyday Use and Abuse of Persuasion* (New York: W. H. Freeman).

15. Cialdini, R. B., and Schroeder, D. (1976), "Increasing Compliance by Legitimizing Paltry Contributions: When even a Penny Helps," *Journal of Personality and Social Psychology* 34, pp. 599–604.

16. Cialdini, Robert (2000), *Influence: Science and Practice*, 4th ed. (Boston: Allyn & Bacon).

17. Worchel, S., Lee, J., and Adewole, A. (1975), "Effects of Supply and Demand on Ratings of Object Value," *Journal of Personality and Social Psychology* 32, pp. 906–914.

18. Petty, R. E., and Cacioppo, J. T. (1984), "The Effects of Involvement on Responses to Argument Quantity and Quality: Central and Peripheral Routes to Persuasion," *Journal of Personality and Social Psychology* 46, pp. 69–81.

19. Ogilvy, David (1971), *Confessions of an Adversiting Man* (New York: Ballantine Books), p. 92.

20. Fuller, R. G., and Sheehy-Skeffington, A. (1974), "Effects of Group Laughter on Responses to Humorous Materials: A Replication and Extension," *Psychological Reports* 35, pp. 531–534.

21. Nosanchuk, T. A., and Lightstone, J. (1974), "Canned Laughter and Public and Private Conformity," *Journal of Personality and Social Psychology* 29, pp. 153–156.

22. From Steven Booth-Butterfield's lectures on the topic of persuasion and influence, available at http://www.noctrl.edu/~ajomuel/crow/lecture.html (March 2000).

23. Singer, Margaret (1996), *Cults in Our Midst* (San Francisco: Jossey-Bass).

24. Schein, Edgar (1961), *Coercive Persuasion: A Socio-psychological Analysis of the "Brainwashing" of American Civilian Prisoners by the Chinese Communists* (New York: W. W. Norton).

25. Quotes about Diesel jeans stores are from St. John, Warren (2002), "A Store Lures Guys Who Are Graduating from Chinos," *New York Times*, July 14, sec. 9, pp. 1, 8.

26. Gitomer, Jeffrey (1994), *The Sales Bible* (New York: Morrow).

27. Cialdini (2000).

28. Lorenz, K., and Tinbergen, N. (1938), "Zeit," *Tierpsychologie*, 2, pp. 1–29.

29. Tinbergen, N. (1951), *The Study of Instinct* (Oxford, U.K.: Oxford University Press).

30. Described in Hickman, C. P., and Roberts, L. S. (1994), *Biology of Animals*, 6th ed. (Daybook, Iowa: William C. Brown Publishers).

31. Described in Audesirk, T., and Audesirk, G. (1996), *Biology: Life on Earth*, 4th ed. (Englewood Cliffs, N.J.: Prentice-Hall).

32. In a survey of 460 men and women at a local shopping mall, 81 percent of respondents said they'd heard of Poverello House. Ninety-two percent of them had positive or very positive impressions of the organization, and only one person

had a negative impression. Unpublished data obtained through Poverello House, Fresno, Calif.

33. The importance of the "good cause" phrase became even clearer another condition in which we tried using the name Poverello House alone. In this condition, subjects were asked: "Would you like to buy a cookie? It's for the Poverello House." It was a disaster: only three of thirty of those customers bought cookies.

34. Approximately equal numbers of men and women were approached in each condition. Overall, there were no gender differences in purchasing. However, males who didn't buy cookies were more likely than female nonpurchasers to offer an excuse. For a more complete description of the study, see Burgos, K., Rodriguez, A., and Levine, R. (2000), "Gaining Charity Donations when 'It's for a Good Cause,'" paper presented at the annual meetings of the Western Psychological Association, Portland, Oreg., April.

35. Burgos, K., and Levine, R. (2000), "The Effects of Solicitor Credibility and Stating 'It's for a Good Cause' on Gaining Charitable Purchases," unpublished honor's thesis, California State University, Fresno.

36. Pratkanis and Aronson (1991).

37. Langer, E., Blank, A., and Chanowitz, B. (1978), "The Mindlessness of Ostensibly Thoughtful Actions: The Role of 'Placebic' Information in Interpersonal Interaction," *Journal of Personality and Social Psychology* 36, pp. 635–642.

38. Cohen, D., Nisbett, R., Bowdle, B. F., and Schwarz, N. (1996), "Insult, Aggression, and the Southern Culture of Honor: An 'Experimental Ethnography,'" *Journal of Personality and Social Psychology* 70, pp. 945–960.

39. Cohen, Dov (1997), "*Ifs* and *Thens* in Cultural Psychology," in Wyer, R., ed., *The Automaticity of Everyday Life: Advances in Social Cognition*, vol. 10 (Mahwah, N.J.: Lawrence Erlbaum Associates), p. 124.

40. Reed, John (1981), "Below the Smith and Wesson Line: Reflections on Southern Violence," in Black, M., and Reed, J. S., eds., *Perspectives on the American South: An Annual Review of Society, Politics, and Culture* (pp. 9–27) (New York: Gordon & Breach), p. 13.

41. For a description of these and other manifestations of the culture of honor in the South, see, for example, Cohen, D., Vandello, J., and Rantilla, A. (1998), "The Sacred and the Social: Cultures of Honor and Violence," in Gilbert, P., and Andrews, B., eds., *Shame: Interpersonal Behavior, Psychopathology, and Culture* (New York: Oxford University Press), pp. 261–282.

42. Settle, R., and Alreck, P. (1986), *Why They Buy: American Consumers Inside and Out* (New York: Wiley), p. 129.

43. From Savan, Leslie (1994), *The Sponsored Life: Ads, TV, and American Culture* (Philadelphia: Temple University Press), pp. 71, 143.

44. Thank you to Professor Roberta Asahina for the blue jeans examples.

45. William Feather, quoted in Murphy, Edward F. (1978), *The Crown Treasury of Relevant Quotations* (New York: Crown), p. 15.

46. Dao, J. (2001), "Ads Now Seek Recruitment for 'An Army of One,'" *New*

York Times, January 10, pp. A1, A16. See also Truscott IV, L. (2001), "Marketing an Army of Individuals," *New York Times*, January 12, p. A23.

47. Han, S., and Shavritt, S. (1994), "Persuasion and Culture: Advertising Appeals in Individualistic and Collectivistic Societies," *Journal of Experimental Social Psychology* 30, pp. 326–350.

48. Mitchell, R., and Oneal, M. (1994), "Managing by Values," *Business Week*, September 12, pp. 38–43.

49. Kilbourne, Jean (1999), *Deadly Persuasion* (New York: Free Press).

50. You can check your VALS classification by filling out a questionnaire on the Internet at http://future.sri.com/vals/valshome.html.

Chapter Seven: Gradually Escalating the Commitments

1. Schlosser, E. (2001), *Fast Food Nation* (Boston: Houghton Mifflin).

2. From Steven Booth-Butterfield's lectures on the topic of persuasion and influence, available at http://www.noctrl.edu/~ajomuel/crow/lecture.html (March 2000).

3. Apologies for the sexist term *salesman* in this discussion. In fact, however, I encountered very few auto saleswomen in my research.

4. The company and managers for whom I personally sold cars were honest and professional. The present discussion is in no way intended to imply otherwise.

5. From McMahon, Ed (1989), *Ed McMahon's Superselling* (New York: Prentice-Hall).

6. This person asked to remain anonymous.

7. LeDuff, C. (2001), "If the Hard Sell Is an Art, This Man Is Michelangelo," *New York Times*, November 3, p. A8.

8. Mowen, J. C., and Cialdini, R. B. (1980), "On Implementing the Door-in-the-Face Compliance Technique in a Business Context," *Journal of Marketing Research* 17, pp. 253–258.

9. Hall, E. T. (1959), *The Silent Language* (New York: Doubleday), p. 119.

10. Cialdini, R. B., Vincent, J. E., Lewis, S. K., Catalan, J., Wheeler, D., and Darby, B. L. (1975), "Reciprocal Concessions Procedure for Inducing Compliance: The Door-in-the-Face Technique," *Journal of Personality and Social Psychology* 31, pp. 206–215.

11. Burger, J. M. (1986), "Increasing Compliance by Improving the Deal: The That's-Not-All Technique," *Journal of Personality and Social Psychology* 51, pp. 277–283.

12. This scenario is adapted from the original experiments by Stanley Milgram. Subjects in his experiments, conducted in the early 1960s, were paid $4.50. Correcting roughly for inflation, this translates to about $25.00 today. For a complete description of Milgram's experiments, see Milgram, S. (1974), *Obedience to Authority: An Experimental View* (New York: Harper & Row).

13. Stanley Milgram interview on CBS's *60 Minutes*, 1979.

14. Milgram (1974).

15. Milgram found virtually identical levels of obedience in women as in men.

The main difference was that women exhibited greater anxiety as they administered the shock.

Chapter Eight: Winning Hearts and Minds

1. Quotes from Steven Hassan are taken from Hassan, Steven (1988), *Combatting Cult Mind Control* (Rochester, Vt.: Park Street Press), p. 535.

2. Personal communication from ex-member Gordon Neufeld, October 22, 1999.

3. Brehm, J. W. (1966), *A Theory of Psychological Reactance* (New York: Academic Press).

4. Masling, J. (1966), "Role-Related Behavior of the Subject and Psychologist and Its Effect upon Psychological Data," *Nebraska Symposium on Motivation* 14, pp. 67–103.

5. Brehm, S. S., and Weinraub, M. (1977), "Physical Barriers and Psychological Reactance: Two-Year-Olds' Responses to Threats to Freedom," *Journal of Personality and Social Psychology* 35, pp. 830–836.

6. Hassan (1988), p. 69.

7. Wilson, Gregory (2002), "How to Influence Anyone with Five Magic Words," lecture at California State University, Fresno, April 24.

8. Jensen, Derrick (2000), "An Interview with David Edwards," *The Sun*, June 5–13, p. 9.

9. Central Intelligence Agency (1963), *KUBARK Counterintelligence Interrogation*, CIA classified publication, obtained through the Freedom of Information Act in 1997 and distributed on the Internet at http://www.parascope.com., p. 52.

10. Shah, Diane K. (1989), "The Producers," *New York Times Magazine*, October 22, p. 27.

11. Quoted in Zimbardo, P., Ebbesen, E., and Maslach, C. (1977), *Influencing Attitudes and Changing Behavior* (Reading, Mass.: Addison-Wesley).

12. Thomas, Evan (1997), "The Next Level," *Newsweek*, April 7, pp. 28–35.

13. Lepper, M., Greene, D., and Nisbett, R. (1973), "Undermining Children's Intrinsic Interest with Extrinsic Reward: A Test of the Overjustification Hypothesis," *Journal of Personality and Social Psychology* 28, pp. 129–137.

14. Rosen, Jeffrey (1999), "The Social Police: Following the Law, Because You'd Be Too Embarrassed Not To," *New Yorker*, October 20–27, pp. 170–181.

15. Examples are from ibid. and Kahan, D. M. (1997), "It's a Shame We Have None," *Wall Street Journal*, January 15, p. A16.

16. Rosen (1999).

17. Kahan, D. M. (1999), "Privatizing Criminal Law: Strategies for Private Norm Enforcement in the Inner City," *UCLA Law Review* 46, pp. 1859–1872.

18. Kahan, D. M. (2000), "Gentle Nudges vs. Hard Shoves: Solving the Sticky Norms Problem," *University of Chicago Law Review* 67, pp. 607–645.

19. Ibid.

20. This need for consistency is not as strong in many other cultures. Con-

sider, for example, the distinction between *tatemai* and *honne* in Japan, or the Chinese proverb, "Cut toes, fit shoe."

21. In the actual experiment, which was carried out in the late 1950s, subjects were paid either $1 or $5 to lie. Adjusting for inflation, the payments translate to current values of roughly $5 versus $100.

22. Festinger, L., and Carlsmith, M. (1959), "Cognitive Consequences of Forced Compliance," *Journal of Abnormal and Social Psychology* 58, pp. 203–210.

23. Myers, David (1996), *Social Psychology*, 5th ed. (New York: McGraw-Hill), p. 131.

24. Zimbardo, Philip, et al. (1973), "The Mind Is a Formidable Jailer: A Pirandellian Prison," *New York Times Magazine*, April 8, pp. 38–57.

25. Hassan (1988), p. 59.

26. Higgins, E. T., and Rholes, W. S. (1978), "Saying Is Believing: Effects of Message Modification on Memory and Liking for the Person Described," *Journal of Experimental Social Psychology* 14, pp. 363–378.

27. Lelyveld, Joseph (2001), "All Suicide Bombers Are Not Alike," *New York Times Magazine*, October 28, p. 50.

28. Festinger, L., Riecken, H., and Schachter, S. (1956), *When Prophecy Fails: A Social and Psychological Study of a Modern Group That Predicted the Destruction of the World* (New York: Harper & Row).

29. Quoted in Randi, James (1982), *Flim-Flam! ESP, Unicorns and Other Delusions* (Amherst, N.Y.: Prometheus Books), p. 106.

30. Hong's book revealed the extent of corruption within the Moon family. This book, as well as the publicity surrounding her former husband's eventual suicide, is often cited as the primary cause of Moon's significantly reduced American following in recent years.

31. Hong, Nansook (1998), *In the Shadow of the Moons* (New York: Little, Brown).

Chapter Nine: Jonestown

1. *Jonestown Audiotape Primary Project: Transcripts*, tape no. Q 042 (Death tape), The Jonestown Institute, 18 November 1978. Transcribed by the author.

2. Osherow, N. (1995), "Making Sense of the Nonsensical: An Analysis of Jonestown." in Aronson, E., ed., *Readings about the Social Animal*, 7th ed. (San Francisco: W. H. Freeman).

3. The question of what constitutes free will is an extremely complicated one—it's certainly well beyond the scope of this book. Undoubtedly, had there been no physical threat or explicit coercion at Jonestown, few would have freely chosen to commit suicide.

4. A number of fine books describe Jonestown in considerably greater detail than the current discussion allows. My own favorite is Layton, Deborah (1998), *Seductive Poison* (New York: Anchor Books).

5. Hochman, J. (1990), "Miracle, Mystery, and Authority: The Triangle of Cult Indoctrination," *Psychiatric Annals* 20, pp. 179–187.

6. Reston, J. (1981), *Our Father Who Art in Hell* (New York: Times Books).

7. Kilduff, M., and Javers, R. (1978), *The Suicide Cult* (New York: Bantam). Also quoted in Osherow (1995) p. 74.

8. Layton (1998), p. 40.

9. Chidester, D. (1988), *Salvation and Suicide* (Bloomington: Indiana University Press), p. 58.

10. Ibid.

11. Layton (1998), p. 41.

12. Mills, J. (1979), *Six Years with God* (New York: A & W Publishers), p. 64.

13. Chidester (1988), p. 57.

14. Mills (1979), p. 151. Also quoted in Osherow (1995).

15. Mills (1979), p. 64.

16. Ibid., p. 151.

17. Members who became aware of the deceptions were strongly discouraged from revealing the information publicly. Jeannie Mills recalls what happened to Chuck Beikman after his Colonel Sanders comment: "During the evening meeting Jim mentioned the fact that Chuck had made fun of his gift. 'He lied to some of the members here, telling that the chicken had come from a local shop,' Jim stormed. 'But the Spirit of Justice has prevailed. Because of his lie Chuck is in the men's restroom right now, wishing that he was dead. He is vomiting and has diarrhea so bad he can't talk!'

"An hour later a pale and shaken Chuck Beikman walked out of the men's room and up to the front, being supported by one of the guards. Jim asked him, 'Do you have anything you'd like to say?'

"Chuck looked up weakly and answered, 'Jim, I apologize for what I said. Please forgive me.'

"As we looked at Chuck, we vowed in our hearts that we would never question any of Jim's 'miracles'—at least not out loud. Years later we learned that Jim had put a mild poison in a piece of cake and given it to Chuck."

18. Reston (1981), p. 47.

19. Chidester (1988), p. 74.

20. Layton (1998), p. 65.

21. Milsted, David (1999), *The Cassell Dictionary of Regrettable Quotations* (London: Cassell).

22. Layton (1998), p. 68.

23. Moonie recruits are sometimes asked to undergo an extended (e.g., forty-day) "condition," a penance exercise during which they cut off all communication with friends and family.

24. Former members of many cults recount being conditioned to have phobiclike reactions to even the thought of separating from the group. Ex-Moonie Steven Hassan, for example, describes how "people are made to have a panic reaction at the thought of leaving: sweating, rapid heartbeat, intense desire to avoid the possibility. They are told that if they leave they will be lost and defenseless in the face of dark horrors: they'll go insane, be killed, become drug addicts, or commit suicide. Actual tales of such cases are constantly told, both in lectures

and in hushed tones through informal gossip. It is nearly impossible for an indoctrinated cult member to feel he can have any security outside the group." Hassan, Steven (1988), *Combatting Mind Control* (Rochester, Vt.: Park Street Press), p. 64.

25. Osherow (1995).

26. Mills (1979), p. 230.

27. Layton (1998), p. 68.

28. Ibid., p. 64.

29. Ibid., p. 61.

30. Ibid., p. 69.

31. Mills (1979), pp. 268–269.

32. Layton (1998), p. 178.

33. Quoted by Deborah Layton in a guest lecture to Philip Zimbardo's Psychology 1 class, Stanford University, March 6, 2000.

34. Winfrey, C. (1979), "Why 900 Died in Guyana," *New York Times Magazine*, February 25, quoted in Osherow (1995), p. 81.

35. Quoted in Sullivan, D., and Zimbardo, P. G. (1979), "Jonestown Survivors Tell Their Story," *Los Angeles Times*, March 9, pt. 4, pp. 1, 10–12.

36. Layton (1998).

37. Quote is from an interview in the "Jonestown Revisited" special, *20/20*, ABC, October 1998. Facts about Speier are taken from *San Francisco Chronicle* (1998), "Surviving the Heart of Darkness," November 13, Peninsula sect., p. 1.

38. Singer, M. (1994), preface to Langone, M., ed., *Recovery from Cults: Help for Victims of Psychological and Spiritual Abuse* (New York: W. W. Norton), pp. xv–xix.

Chapter Ten: The Art of Resistance

1. Snyder, C. R. (1997), "Unique Invulnerability: A Classroom Demonstration in Estimating Personal Mortality," *Teaching of Psychology* 24, pp. 197–199.

2. Cialdini, R. B., Rice, W. E., and Serna, S. B., "Dispelling the Illusion of Invulnerability: The Motivations and Mechanisms of resistance to persuasion," *Journal of Personality and Social Psychology*, in press.

3. Poche, C., Yoder, P., and Miltenberger, R. (1988), "Teaching Self-Protection to Children Using Television Techniques," *Journal of Applied Behavior Analysis* 21, pp. 253–261.

4. Nears, K., and Levine, R. (1999), "Preventing Non-Parent Child Abduction," paper presented at the McNair Research Symposium, Fresno, Calif., May.

5. McGuire, W. (1964), "Inducing Resistance to Persuasion: Some Contemporary Approaches," in Berkowitz, L., ed., *Advances in Experimental Social Psychology*, vol. 1 (New York: Academic Press), p. 306.

6. Becker, C. (1986), "Reasons for the Lack of Argumentation and Debate in the Far East," *International Journal of Intercultural Relations* 10, pp. 75–92.

7. Ara Norenzayan, conversation with author, 1 December 2000.

8. McAlister, A., Perry, C., Killen, J., Slinkard, L., and Maccoby, N. (1980),

"Pilot Study of Smoking, Alcohol and Drug Abuse Prevention," *American Journal of Public Health* 70, pp. 719–721.

9. The PROACT method was developed by J. Hammond, R. Keeney, and H. Raiffa, and introduced in their 1999 book, *Smart Choices: A Practical Guide to Making Better Decisions* (Boston: Harvard Business School Press).

10. Russo, Richard (1988), *The Risk Pool* (New York: Random House), p. 121.

11. From Hammond et al. (1999), p. 200. I've modified their telling slightly.

12. Available at http://www.quoteland.com/topic.asp?CATEGORY_ID=165.

13. Abraham Maslow, quoted in Russo, J. E., and Schoemaker, P. J. (1989), *Decision Traps* (New York: Simon & Schuster), p. 149.

14. Robert Kennedy, quoted in Pratkanis, Anthony, and Aronson, Elliot (1991), *Age of Propaganda* (New York: W. H. Freeman), p. x.

15. Janis, Irving (1982), *Groupthink*, 2nd ed. (Boston: Houghton Mifflin). Also, for an excellent discussion of how to avoid faulty group decision making, see Russo, J. E., and Schoemaker, P. J. H. (1989), *Decision Traps* (New York: Simon & Schuster).

16. Boorstin, Daniel (1994), *Cleopatra's Nose: Essays on the Unexpected* (New York: Random House), p. 167.

17. B. Earl Puckett, quoted in Donadio, Stephen (1992), *The New York Public Library: Book of Twentieth-Century American Quotations* (New York: Stonesong Press), p. 71.

18. Pulfer, L. A. (2000), "Unilever Acquisition," *National Public Radio's Morning Edition*, April 21.

19. CBS radio journalist Dorothy Thompson commenting on the campaign methods during the 1940 presidential campaign, quoted in Fox, Stephen (1997), *The Mirror Makers: A History of American Advertising and Its Creators* (Urbana: University of Illinois Press), p. 308.

20. Ibid., p. 39.

21. Michael Schudson, quoted in Fitzhenry, Robert (1993), *The Fitzhenry & Whiteside Book of Quotations* (Markham, Ont.: Fitzhenry & Whiteside), p. 18.

22. Tyrrell, John (2000), "Lawsuits to Fit Any Occasion," *Los Angeles Times*, July 29, p. A-1. The apparent California record holder for the most personal lawsuits is Liang-Houh Shieh, a Yale law school graduate who filed dozens of suits against each of hundreds of former law partners and employers.

23. Langer, Ellen (1989), *Mindfulness* (Reading, Mass.: Addison-Wesley), p. 199.

24. Savan, Leslie (1994), *The Sponsored Life: Ads, TV, and American Culture* (Philadelphia: Temple University Press), p. 7.

25. A Palm Pilot program called ESP (Experience Sampling Program), developed at Boston College by Lisa Feldman Barrett and programmed by Daniel J. Barrett, is available free of cost at http://www2.bc.edu/~barretli/esp/

26. Ruch, Floyd L. (1937), *Psychology and Life* (Glenview, Ill.: Scott, Foresman).

27. Unattributed quotation from the Department of Advertising, University of Texas. Available at http://advertising.utexas.edu/research/quotes.

28. Fox (1997), p. 117. *Printer's Ink* (1931), June 18.

29. J. Walter Thompson Agency business pitch (1925) quoted in Lears, Jackson (1994), *Fables of Abundance: A Cultural History of Advertising in America* (New York: Basic Books), p. 224.

30. For an excellent discussion of teaching as a persuasive enterprise, see Friedrich, J., and Douglass, D. (1998), "Ethics and the Persuasive Enterprise of Teaching Psychology," *American Psychologist* 53, pp. 549–562.

31. Shorris, Earl (1994), *A Nation of Salesman* (New York: W. W. Norton), p. 141.

32. Forceful deprogramming, which became popular in the 1970s, is no longer the most frequent intervention of choice for getting people to leave cults. It's been replaced in recent years by noncoercive, voluntary exit-counseling procedures. For further information about available exit counseling, I recommend contacting the American Family Foundation (web site: http://www.csj.org; telephone: 239-514-3081; address: AFF, P.O. Box 2265, Bonita Springs, FL 34133).

33. Available at http://www.teacheruniverse.com/news/quotes.html.

INDEX